THE USE OF THE SEPTUAGINT
IN NEW TESTAMENT RESEARCH

D1572650

The Use of the Septuagint in New Testament Research

R. Timothy McLay

WILLIAM B. EERDMANS PUBLISHING COMPANY
GRAND RAPIDS, MICHIGAN / CAMBRIDGE, U.K.

12026346©©© 2003 Wm. B. Eerdmans Publishing Co.

Wm. B. Eerdmans Publishing Co.
255 Jefferson Ave. S.E., Grand Rapids, Michigan 49503 /
P.O. Box 163, Cambridge CB3 9PU U.K.

Printed in the United States of America

08 07 06 05 04 03   7 6 5 4 3 2 1

Library of Congress Cataloging-in-Publication Data

McLay, R. Timothy.
The use of the Septuagint in New Testament research / R. Timothy McLay.
p.   cm.
Includes bibliographical references and indexes.
ISBN 0-8028-6091-5 (pbk.: alk. paper)
1. Bible. O.T. Greek — Versions — Septuagint. 2. Bible. N.T. —
Criticism, Textual. 3. Bible. N.T. — Relation to the Old Testament. I. Title.
BS744.M35   2003
221.4′8 — dc21
2003052854

www.eerdmans.com

Dedicated to Luke

(1989-1996)

Contents

Contents

Preface

W hen I sat down in front of my computer to begin writing this book, I hardly felt the need to justify my reasons for doing so. In a virtual ocean of commentaries and texts probing the mysteries of the Hebrew and Christian Scriptures we might be able to siphon off a bucket that has been devoted to what we commonly refer to as the Septuagint. This puzzled me during my seminary days when I first became interested in this field of study. I asked myself, "Why do so many scholars explain away readings in the Septuagint that differ with the Masoretic Text?" "How can New Testament scholars discuss Paul's theology without taking account of the language and theology of the Septuagint?" There are some who argue that Paul did not read Hebrew, but everyone acknowledges that he knew Greek! He quotes the Septuagint everywhere! Surely there should be more study of the Greek Jewish Scriptures.

It has only been in recent years that the interest in the Septuagint has begun to grow. This is partly due to the influence of scholars such as Ilmari Soisalon-Soininen, Frank Cross, Emanuel Tov, Margarite Harl, and John Wevers on the world of scholarship through their writings and their students. Ironically, however, the most significant influence for the increasing interest in the Septuagint has been the discovery of Hebrew manuscripts in the desert. The Dead Sea Scrolls (DSS) have changed our understanding of the origins and development of the Hebrew Scriptures and have also opened a new window into life in Palestine at the beginning of the Common Era. The Septuagint has both benefited and suffered from this alliance with the DSS. The benefit has been that the profile of the Septuagint has been raised, particularly as a witness to reconstructing what might have been the original text of the Hebrew Scriptures. The drawback is that the Septuagint sometimes plays second fiddle for Qumran scholars who use it to support their particular theory about the Hebrew Scriptures based on the *DSS*.

A sober assessment of the current state of affairs suggests that we are in a period of transition. Qumran scholarship has reached only the toddler stage and will no doubt be influential in the years to come. Similarly, Septuagint scholarship is only in its early childhood, though some might prefer to think that it is in its preadolescent stage. New questions and paradigms will emerge in the years to come. The opportunity for significant work in the Septuagint remains for budding scholars. More importantly for the present work, Septuagint research has up until now played a relatively minor role in the world of New Testament scholarship. Therefore, it is my hope to make a small contribution to the field of Biblical Studies by demonstrating how an informed knowledge of the Greek Jewish Scriptures enhances our understanding of the New Testament.

My debt to the people who have contributed to the writing of this book is enormous. Former teachers, students, friends, and colleagues have all played a significant role and influenced my thinking in different ways. I want to acknowledge Leonard Greenspoon in particular because it was he who suggested that I begin with the quotation in Acts 15:16-18. My students (Jon, Will, Shelly, Jeremy, Shelly, and John) here at St. Stephen's University have acted as guinea pigs, and I thank them for their helpful suggestions. I should also like to thank Joel Marcus for reading a draft of the manuscript and offering numerous helpful suggestions. Thanks also to everyone at Eerdmans for bringing this project to completion. All of the above have contributed in various ways to the thought and argument of this book, but I alone am responsible for its content. I offer my sincerest apologies for any inadvertent errors and to those whose contributions deserved more recognition and treatment.

Without the constant support of my family, particularly of my wife, Martha, this book would never have come to fruition. I love you all more than can be expressed. Finally, I hope that in some way this book honors Him whose word is studied here.

TIM MCLAY

Abbreviations

AASF	Annales Academiæ Scientiarum Fennicæ
AB	Anchor Bible
ANRW	Aufstieg und Niedergang der römischen Welt
AOAT	Alter Orient und Altes Testament
Aq	Aquila
ASTI	Annual of the Swedish Theological Institute
AUSS	Andrews University Seminary Studies
BASOR	Bulletin of the American Schools for Oriental Research
BETL	Bibliotheca ephemeridum theologicarum loveniensium
BHS	Biblia Hebraica Stuttgartensia
Bib	Biblica
BIOSCS	Bulletin of the International Organization for Septuagint and Cognate Studies
BZ	Biblische Zeitschrift
CBQ	Catholic Biblical Quarterly
CBQMS	Catholic Biblical Quarterly, Monograph Series
ConBib.OT	Coniectanea Biblica, Old Testament Series
DHL	Dissertationes Humanarum Litterarum
DJD	Discoveries in the Judaean Desert
DSS	Dead Sea Scrolls
ETL	Ephemerides Theologicae Lovanienses
FN	Filologia Neotestamentaria
HB	Hebrew Bible
HE	Historia ecclesiastica
HR	E. Hatch and H. A. Redpath, *A Concordance to the*

Septuagint and Other Greek Versions of the Old Testament

HSM	Harvard Semitic Monographs
HTR	Harvard Theological Review
HUCA	Hebrew Union College Annual
IBS	Irish Biblical Studies
IEJ	Israel Exploration Journal
IOSCS	International Organization of Septuagint and Cognate Studies
JBL	Journal of Biblical Literature
JBLMS	Journal of Biblical Literature, Monograph Series
JJS	Journal of Jewish Studies
JNSL	Journal of Northwest Semitic Languages
JQR	Jewish Quarterly Review
JSOT	Journal for the Study of the Old Testament
JSOTSS	Journal for the Study of the Old Testament, Supplement Series
JSP	Journal for the Study of the Pseudepigrapha
JSPS	Journal for the Study of the Pseudepigrapha, Supplement Series
JSS	Journal of Semitic Studies
JSSM	Journal of Semitic Studies, Monographs
JTS	Journal of Theological Studies
KAT	Kommentar zum Alten Testament
LEH	*A Greek-English Lexicon of the Septuagint,* eds. J. Lust, E. Eynikel, K. Hauspie
LSJ	*A Greek-English Lexicon,* compiled by H. G. Liddell and R. Scott, rev. and aug. H. S. Jones
LXX	Septuagint, not necessarily in its oldest recoverable form (according to Rahlfs)
MIO	Mitteilungen des Instituts für Orientforschung
MSU	Mitteilungen des Septuaginta-Unternehmens der Akademie der Wissenschaften in Göttingen
MT	Masoretic Text
NA	Nestle-Aland
*NAWG,*I.phil.-hist. Kl.	Nachrichten der Akademie der Wissenschaften in Göttingen, I. philologisch-historische Klasse
NIV	New International Version
NRSV	New Revised Standard Version
NT	New Testament

NTS	New Testament Studies
OBO	Orbis Biblicus et Orientalis
OG	Old Greek
OT	Old Testament
OTE	Old Testament Essays
OTL	Old Testament Library
OTS	Oudtestamentische Studiën
PTA	Papyrologische Texte und Abhandlungen
RB	Revue Biblique
RevQ	Revue de Qumran
SBLDS	Society of Biblical Literature, Dissertation Series
SBS	Stuttgarter Bibel-Studien
SCS	Septuagint and Cognate Studies
SE	Stereotyped Equivalent
SEA	Svensk Exegetisk Arsbok
Sef	Sefarad, Madrid
Sem	Semitica
Septuaginta	Septuaginta, Vetus Testamentum Graecum Auctoritate Academiae Scientiarum Gottingensis editum
SJOT	Scandinavian Journal of the Old Testament
ST	Studia Theologica
Syh	The Syrohexaplaric translation of Paul of Tella
Sym	Symmachus
TH	Theodotion
TSK	Theologische Studien und Kritiken
TT	Translation Technique
TynBul	Tyndale Bulletin
UBS	United Bible Societies
VT	Vetus Testamentum
VTSupp	Supplements to Vetus Testamentum
WMANT	Wissenschaftliche Monographien zum Alten und Neuen Testament
WUNT	Wissenschaftliche Untersuchungen zum Neuen Testament
ZAW	Zeitschrift für die alttestamentliche Wissenschaft
ZNW	Zeitschrift für die neutestamentliche Wissenschaft

Introduction

Septuagint specialists might argue that this volume should be more appropriately entitled, The *Misuse* of the Septuagint in New Testament Research. Despite the fundamental importance of the Jewish Scriptures written in Greek[1] for understanding Judaism[2] and the origin and development of the Early Church and its Scripture, the study of the Septuagint continues to remain on the margins of New Testament research. The evidence for this is available in most every introductory text to the NT. While sections on mystery religions, Greek philosophies, the Essenes, and the Dead Sea Scrolls are plentiful, one looks in vain for a section on the LXX. A search of several NT introductions written since 1985 reveals that none has a section on the LXX.[3] In most cases the LXX receives only a passing reference in one or two sentences!

1. We will refer to these Greek Jewish Scriptures as the Septuagint (LXX) for sake of convenience. During the NT period there was no defined body of writings equivalent to what became the Jewish Scriptures such as are preserved in the canon of the Eastern Orthodox Church. These matters will be addressed in more detail below.

2. Despite the fact that there were many beliefs that were shared within Judaism, its expression was quite diverse, so that sometimes the plural Judaisms is employed. See J. Neusner, W. S. Green, and E. S. Frerichs, *Judaisms and Their Messiahs* (Cambridge: Cambridge University Press, 1987); E. P. Sanders, *Judaism: Practice and Belief, 63 BCE–66 CE* (Philadelphia: Trinity, 1992). For a concise overview of the development of Judaism see J. Trebolle Barrera, *The Jewish Bible and the Christian Bible: An Introduction to the History of the Bible* (Leiden and New York: Brill; Grand Rapids: Eerdmans, 1998), pp. 37-41.

3. Lee McDonald and Stanley E. Porter, *Early Christianity and Its Sacred Literature* (Peabody: Hendrickson, 2000); Bart Ehrman, *The New Testament: A Historical Introduction to the Early Christian Writings* (New York: Oxford University Press, 1997); E. Freed, *The New Testament: A Critical Introduction,* 2nd ed.(Belmont: Wadsworth, 1996); R. Pag-

It is not that the Septuagint is totally ignored in NT research. Individual articles and commentaries on the NT often exhibit judicious and provocative use of the Greek translations of the Hebrew Scriptures, but there is no volume available that provides a framework for understanding how the NT writings have been influenced because of their linguistic relationship with the Greek Jewish Scriptures. 2 Timothy 3:16 states, "All Scripture is inspired by God." We would all readily acknowledge that the referent for Scripture here is the authoritative writings of the Jews, but exactly which writings does it mean? Does 2 Timothy 3:16 refer to the Scriptures that were preserved in the Masoretic Text, which have come to be identified with the Hebrew Bible that later became the basis for the Protestant Old Testament, or does it refer to the Jewish Scriptures preserved in the Greek language that later became the basis for the Catholic Old Testament via their translation into the Old Latin and then the Latin Vulgate?[4] The number and content of the Jewish Scriptures that were later deemed as canonical are different in the two traditions. For example, the Protestant tradition is dependent upon the HB and counts the number of Old Testament books as thirty-nine, though the number of books in the HB is twenty-four: five of the Law, nine Prophets (1 and 2 Samuel and Kings count as one; Twelve Minor Prophets count as one), and eleven Writings (1 and 2 Chronicles count as one), while the LXX has fifty-three. We only have to compare the books that are contained in the Hebrew canon with the LXX to see that the LXX has a greater number and that there are also differences in the order of the books. Note, for example, that the book of Daniel is ordered with the Writings in the Hebrew Scriptures, while it appears with the Prophets in the LXX. The contents of the HB and the LXX are listed below, with the additional books that are found in the LXX underlined.[5]

---

eant, *Engaging the New Testament* (Minneapolis: Fortress, 1995); S. Harris, *The New Testament* (Mountain View: Mayfield, 1988); Luke T. Johnson, *The Writings of the New Testament* (Philadelphia: Fortress, 1986). Much better is the recent introduction by Paul Achtemeier, Joel Green, and Marianne M. Thompson, *Introducing the New Testament: Its Literature and Theology* (Grand Rapids: Eerdmans, 2001).

4. None of the Early Church councils ever determined a canon of Scripture for the Old Testament. Not until 1546 at the Council of Trent did the Roman Catholic Church officially adopt the Vulgate as its canon of Scripture. This was done mostly in response to Martin Luther's insistence that the Old Testament for Christians should be equivalent to the Hebrew canon recognized by Jews. Even though Jerome had insisted on using the Hebrew Scriptures as the basis for his translation (the Latin Vulgate), since the Vulgate was a revision of the Old Latin translation of the LXX, a number of books that Jerome did not translate were retained from the Old Latin in the Vulgate.

5. The books of the LXX are listed according to Rahlfs's *Septuaginta*. Note that the order of the Twelve Prophets is different in the HB and LXX as well.

Hebrew Bible	Septuagint
Law	Law
Genesis	Genesis
Exodus	Exodus
Leviticus	Leviticus
Numbers	Numbers
Deuteronomy	Deuteronomy
Prophets (Former)	History
Joshua	Joshua
Judges	Judges
	Ruth
Samuel (1 and 2)	1 Reigns = 1 Samuel
	2 Reigns = 2 Samuel
Kings (1 and 2)	3 Reigns = 1 Kings
Prophets (Latter)	4 Reigns = 2 Kings
Isaiah	1 Paralipomenon = 1 Chronicles
Jeremiah	2 Paralipomenon = 2 Chronicles
Ezekiel	<u>1 Esdras</u>
The Twelve	2 Esdras = Ezra-Nehemiah
Hosea	Esther
Joel	<u>Judith</u>
Amos	<u>Tobit</u>
Obadiah	<u>1 Maccabees</u>
Jonah	<u>2 Maccabees</u>
Micah	<u>3 Maccabees</u>
Nahum	<u>4 Maccabees</u>
Habakkuk	Poetry
Zephaniah	Psalms
Haggai	Proverbs
Zechariah	<u>Odes</u>
Malachi	Ecclesiastes
Writings	Song of Songs
Psalms	Job
Job	<u>Wisdom</u>
Proverbs	<u>Ecclesiasticus</u>
Ruth	<u>Psalms of Solomon</u>
Song of Songs	Prophecy
Ecclesiastes	The Twelve
Lamentations	Hosea
Esther	Amos

Daniel	Micah
Ezra-Nehemiah	Joel
Chronicles (1 and 2)	Obadiah
	Jonah
	Nahum
	Habakkuk
	Zephaniah
	Haggai
	Zechariah
	Malachi
	Isaiah
	Jeremiah
	<u>Baruch</u>
	Lamentations
	<u>Epistle of Jeremy</u>
	Ezekiel
	<u>Susanna</u>
	Daniel
	<u>Bel and the Dragon</u>

The differences that exist between the Hebrew and the Greek canons of Scripture, both of which were preserved by the Jewish community, indicate that it is potentially extremely important to decide what Scriptures were the intended subject of 2 Timothy 3:16. Given the fact that the NT, like the LXX, is written in Greek and that many of the citations of Scripture in the NT agree word for word with how the passage reads in Greek, it becomes all the more likely that the Greek Jewish Scriptures were a significant influence on the NT.

Obviously, there are NT scholars who are very responsible in their use of the LXX, and some may be more knowledgeable in the subject than myself. However, there are many scholars and students who might profit from a text devoted to *The Use of the Septuagint in New Testament Research*. Thus, this volume will attempt to address the needs of both of these audiences without neglecting either. The aim here is to introduce and address the fundamental issues of Septuagint study and the way in which they apply to NT research, and I am confident that this study will prove useful to many. In order to appreciate the Greek Jewish Scriptures, what we often refer to as the LXX, and their importance for understanding and interpreting the NT, our investigation will require that we provide the student with an understanding of the historical context in which the origin and transmission of the Scriptures occurred. This will help clarify the complex relationships between the Scriptures as we now know them in the NT, LXX, HB, and *DSS*. Knowledge of the original languages will be an asset because much of the discussion will be technical. However, concessions have also been made for students. English translations are provided, and there is a glossary of terms at the back of the book. It has also been my aim to write in a style that makes the technical nature of this subject more accessible to students.

One resource that will soon be available for students to help understand the LXX is a New English Translation of the Septuagint (NETS), which is being completed under the auspices of the International Organization for Septuagint and Cognate Studies.[6] A series of commentaries on the LXX for English speakers is also under way. This is being done for French readers in the series *La Bible grecque d'Alexandrie*.[7]

In this introductory chapter we will begin by defining some terminology and then introduce some issues as they relate to research in the LXX.

The Terminology: LXX and OG

An example of the unfamiliarity of some NT scholars with the more fundamental issues of the LXX is reflected in the misuse of the Septuagint texts and versions. For example, one often finds references in the footnotes of English translations of the Bible to a reading of the "LXX" without any explanation. To what does this mysterious "LXX" refer? Sometimes "LXX" refers to the reading in the Greek Jewish Scriptures that has been judged by the editor of a critical text to be most likely the original reading, that is, what is believed to be the closest approximation that we can make to what was probably written originally by the translator. In other cases "LXX" may refer to any reading that is found in any Greek manuscript of the Jewish Scriptures, which is not necessarily the original or even a very early reading. It could be any reading or word that appears in any Greek manuscript of a book in the LXX. In the same way, it is often stated that the NT writer quotes the "LXX" version of a biblical text, as opposed to the Hebrew version or the MT, without any clarification.[8]

---

6. The translation by Brenton is still quite readily available, but it is old and not based on the best available text for the LXX books. See L. C. L. Brenton, *The Septuagint Version of the Old Testament* (London: S. Bagster and Sons, 1844).

7. *La Bible grecque d'Alexandrie,* Traduction et annotation des livres de la Septante sous la direction de Marguerite Harl, Gilles Dorival et Olivier Munnich (Paris: Les editions du Cerf, 1986-).

8. Leonard Greenspoon has provided many examples of the above problems in two articles: "It's All Greek to Me: The Septuagint in Modern English Translations of the He-

Which Greek text is being quoted? Do we actually have a Greek witness with that reading or is it labeled a Septuagintal quote because it does not reflect what we have in the Hebrew? How is the use of a Greek text as opposed to the Hebrew reflected in the theology of the writer? Does it make any difference?

Part of the problem of the use of "LXX" is related to terminology. The name Septuagint derives from the tradition in the Letter of Aristeas that seventy-two (or seventy; hence the abbreviation LXX) elders translated the Pentateuch into Greek.[9] Strictly speaking then, LXX referred originally to the translation of the Pentateuch into Greek.[10] However, the term Septuagint is generally employed to refer to the Greek Jewish Scriptures, which consist primarily of translations of the books of the HB. These Greek Jewish Scriptures also contain additions to some of the books in the HB as well as independent works. Some of these additions and other works were translations from Hebrew or Aramaic, while other books were composed in Greek. A terminological difficulty is encountered when nonspecialists employ a reading from printed editions of the LXX (Rahlfs or Brooke-McLean) or a manuscript and refer to it as *the reading of the Septuagint* as though it represents the oldest recoverable form of the Greek text of that book. In such cases the text that is being used may represent a LXX reading, that is, it is part of the scriptural tradition that originated in the Greek Jewish community, but it does not necessarily represent the original reading for that book that can be critically reconstructed using textual criticism. For this reason, most specialists now reserve the term Old Greek (OG) to designate a text that in the judgment of the scholar represents the original translation of a book. Critical editions for many books of the Septuagint are now available and continue to be published in the Göttingen *Septuaginta* series.

---

brew Bible," in *VII Congress of the IOSCS*, ed. C. Cox, *SCS* 31 (Atlanta: Scholars Press, 1991), pp. 1-21; "The Use and Abuse of the Term 'LXX' and Related Terminology in Recent Scholarship," *BIOSCS* 20 (1987): 21-29.

9. The Letter of Aristeas may be read in H. B. Swete, *An Introduction to the Old Testament in Greek*, rev. R. R. Ottley (Cambridge: Cambridge University Press, 1914), pp. 532-606. An English translation is provided in R. Shutt, "Letter of Aristeas," in *The Old Testament Pseudepigrapha*, ed. James H. Charlesworth (Garden City, N.Y.: Doubleday, 1983), pp. 7-34.

10. For a new overview of the Septuagint in English see N. Fernández Marcos, *The Septuagint in Context* (Leiden: Brill, 2001). A less technical but broad-ranging survey is also provided by Karen Jobes and Moisés Silva, *Invitation to the Septuagint* (Grand Rapids: Baker, 2000). In French and German, see G. Dorival, M. Harl, and O. Munnich, *La Bible grecque des Septante* (Paris: Éditions du Cerf, 1988); and E. Tov, "Die griechischen Bibelübersetzungen," *ANRW* II.20.1 (1986): 121-89. Older English surveys include S. Jellicoe, *The Septuagint and Modern Study* (Oxford: Clarendon, 1968) and also *Studies in the Septuagint: Origins, Recensions, and Interpretations* (New York: Ktav, 1974).

In this volume we will follow conventional usage. Thus, OG will be employed to refer specifically to what is believed to be the oldest recoverable form of the Greek text of a particular book, and LXX will designate more generally that group of Greek Jewish Scriptures as they are commonly known. Occasionally, for the sake of convenience and stylistic variation, LXX will be used to designate the general body of Greek Scriptures that existed in the NT period, but normally we will refer to these writings more accurately as the Greek Jewish Scriptures. Further clarification about what we mean when we use the term LXX is given below.

The Terminology: MT and HB

Like LXX and OG, the relationship between the MT and the HB or Old Testament[11] is often misunderstood. The MT is traditionally associated with the HB because the notion of textual uniformity was encouraged by Judaism, and the printed edition of the Hebrew text is based on a complete codex from Ben Asher that is dated to 1008 c.e. However, this codex is merely one witness to the system of vocalizing the consonantal Hebrew text that was introduced by the Masoretes (hence the designation Masoretic Text). The fact that one particular codex is now the basis for the diplomatic edition of the HB that is published as *Biblia Hebraica Stuttgartensia*[12] does not make it equivalent to the Hebrew Bible. Thus, the MT is a witness to the HB just like the OG. Therefore, when we think of the Hebrew texts of the Scriptures that were used by the NT writers, it is more appropriate to use terminology like the Scriptures or the Jewish Scriptures rather than assume that they were using the MT.[13] Even terminology like Hebrew Scriptures is misleading given the fact that the books of Daniel and Esther have large portions in Aramaic as well as Hebrew. Consequently, in the cases where we refer more generally to the Hebrew text(s) of the Scriptures, the reader should be aware that we are including the Aramaic por-

---

11. We will use the term Hebrew Bible rather than Old Testament only because, as the discussion will demonstrate, there is already enough confusion about terminology in this particular area. Even though the term Old Testament is appropriate and valid for the Christian interpreter, the writers of the New Testament knew only Scripture.

12. K. Elliger and W. Rudolph, *Biblia Hebraica Stuttgartensia* (Stuttgart: Deutsche Bibelstiftung, 1977).

13. For an excellent discussion of these issues, see E. Tov, "The Status of the Masoretic Text in Modern Text Editions of the Hebrew Bible," in *The Canon Debate: On the Origins and Formation of the Bible,* ed. L. M. McDonald and J. A. Sanders (Peabody: Hendrickson, 2002), pp. 234-51.

tions as well. In some cases there was in all likelihood a Hebrew consonantal text of a particular book known to a NT writer that was very similar to what later became the MT, but it could not have been the MT. So, we will use MT to refer to the majority text that we have in Hebrew that witnesses to the HB. These concepts will become clearer in the course of this volume.

It should also be noted that the differences in content between the OG/ LXX and the HB of some books means that the chapter and verse divisions of Scripture are not always equivalent. In this volume all references to the Jewish Scriptures will refer in the first instance to the OG. If a reference is numbered differently in the HB, it will be noted in parentheses (e.g., Psa. 96(97):7). English translations basically follow the chapter and verse divisions of the HB, but sometimes there is a difference by one verse.

The Terminology: Scripture and Canon

In any discussion of what the NT writers were doing and what books were considered normative for the Early Church, it is crucial to understand the distinction between *Scripture(s)* and *canon. Scripture(s)* is a book that enjoys authoritative status for a faith community, while a *canon* is the official list of books that have been given official status as THE inspired Scriptures for a faith community.[14] It is crucial for our discussion to highlight this difference because the use of Scripture by the NT writers does not necessarily imply the notion that they recognized a canon of Scripture. In fact, we will argue that there was not a Hebrew or Greek canon of Scripture during the period of the Early Church. Thus, when we speak of how the Greek or Hebrew Scriptures were read by and/or influenced the NT writers, we are speaking of Scripture in the broadest possible terms. The NT community did not know the Greek Jewish Scriptures in the exact form that have been preserved for us in the LXX, even though we commonly use the designation Septuagint or LXX (as described in the preceding paragraphs) to refer to the Greek Jewish Scriptures. Likewise, the NT community did not know the Hebrew Jewish Scriptures in the form that has been preserved in the MT. Therefore, it is possible that some writings were regarded as authoritative or as Scripture to that community, writings that were not included within the Hebrew or Greek canons

---

14. See the thorough discussion and definition of the terms involved by E. Ulrich, "The Notion and Definition of Canon," in *The Canon Debate: On the Origins and Formation of the Bible,* ed. L. M. McDonald and J. A. Sanders (Peabody: Hendrickson, 2002), pp. 21-35.

of Scripture at the time when they were officially formed. To impart our notion of the HB or the LXX on the Early Church is an anachronism. Thus, HB will be employed here to refer specifically to those Scriptures written in Hebrew and Aramaic that are part of the Hebrew canon.

Issues in LXX Research

As we have already noted, there is a need for a more informed knowledge about the LXX in NT research. Part of the problem is that scholars in the field of biblical studies — and scholars in many other fields — are becoming more and more specialized in limited areas of research and are, thus, increasingly dependent upon the conclusions of scholars in adjacent fields to buttress their own findings. Unfortunately, this may not bode well for the scholar whose argument presupposes as an essential ingredient to its development conclusions that are beyond his or her expertise to assess. Obviously, there are many instances where this is unavoidable because scholars do have to rely upon the integrity of other researchers in order to advance their own disciplines. However, what is one to do when the experts in another field disagree? How does one establish a fulcrum in order to weigh the validity of various options? Do we even realize the foundations upon which our arguments are based and the implications to the same if the foundations prove to be sand?

An example at this juncture may be helpful. It was once commonplace in scholarly circles to refer to a recension of the LXX by "Theodotion,"[15] though nowadays the notion of Theodotion has evolved to become the *kaige* recension or, occasionally, *kaige*-Theodotion.[16] The origin of this change in terminology was the publication of D. Barthélemy's research on the Minor Prophets Scroll discovered at *Nahal Hever*.[17] Barthélemy is credited with iso-

---

15. We will employ the name Theodotion in this volume for the sake of convenience. The use of this term to designate the readings in the sixth column of the Hexapla and other translation work attributed to him does not imply any connection to the putative Theodotion of the third century C.E. There is no firm evidence that there was a historical Theodotion. These issues are discussed more thoroughly in the chapter on Transmission History.

16. As far as I know Tov first employed the term *kaige*-Theodotion in "Transliterations of Hebrew Words in the Greek Versions of the Old Testament," *Textus* 8 (1973): 78-92.

17. D. Barthélemy, *Les devanciers d'Aquila: première publication intégrale du texte des fragments du Dodécaprophéton*, VTSupp 10 (Leiden: Brill, 1963). The Minor Prophets Scroll has now appeared in the *DJD* series. See E. Tov, R. A. Kraft, and P. J. Parsons, *The Greek Minor Prophets Scroll from Nahal Hever (8HevXIIgr)*, *DJD* VIII (Oxford: Clarendon; New York: Oxford University Press, 1989).

lating eight techniques whereby the Oldest Greek (OG) translation of the Twelve Minor Prophets was revised in the scroll in order to make the wording of the Greek translation reflect the Hebrew text more closely. He also argued that the same techniques that were used to make the Greek translation of the Twelve Minor Prophets mirror the Hebrew text could be found in other Greek texts, and that these texts were the product of a group of translators working in Palestine. Eventually, according to Barthélemy, the practice of providing strict word-for-word equivalencies between the Greek and the Hebrew culminated in another recension of the OG that was carried out by Aquila. Chief among these books associated with what Barthélemy named the *kaige* recension were the books that were translated into Greek that were designated with the siglum θ′ (traditionally attributed to the individual *Theodotion*) in the sixth column of the Hexapla, Lamentations, Ruth, Cantica, two sections of Kings, the B text of Judges, the Theodotionic additions to Job and Jeremiah, TH Daniel, and the Quinta of the Psalter.[18] Barthélemy suggested the revision of the scroll was completed between 30 and 50 C.E. and identified the translator with Jonathan ben 'Uzziel, who has traditionally been associated with the authorship of an Aramaic Targum in the mid-first century C.E.[19] It would be fair to say that Barthélemy's description of the revisional activity in Palestine has never attained a consensus. For example, O. Munnich has cogently demonstrated that the links between *kaige* and rabbinic exegesis are tenuous at best.[20] A more detailed explanation of the origin of the Greek Jewish Scriptures and the later revisions is provided in chapter four.

The characteristics of the *kaige* recension that Barthélemy isolated took on a life of their own, however, and have been an integral part of Septuagint research ever since. A significant proportion of research on the Septuagint followed the publication of work on the Minor Prophets Scroll and was de-

18. Barthélemy delineated the main characteristics of this group as the translation of the Hebrew word וגם/גם by καίγε (hence the name *kaige* recension) coupled with the nontranslation of the word את by σύν. See Barthélemy, *Les devanciers d'Aquila,* pp. 15-46. He added eight more characteristics as well (pp. 48-80).

19. Barthélemy, *Les devanciers d'Aquila,* pp. 144-57. E. Tov (*Textual Criticism of the Hebrew Bible* [Minneapolis: Fortress, 1992], p. 145) now dates the scroll to ca. 50 B.C.E.

20. Though P. Grelot ("Les versions grecques de Daniel," *Bib* 47 [1966]: 393-96) accepts Barthélemy's conclusions, S. Jellicoe ("Some Reflections on the KAIGE Recension," *VT* 23 [1973]: 15-24) follows the suggestion of Thackeray and argues for Ephesus as the place where *kaige* originated. For a thorough critique of the proposed Palestinian influence see O. Munnich, "Contribution à l'étude de la première révision de la Septante," *ANRW* II.20.1 (1986): 190-220. See also L. Grabbe, "Aquila's Translation and Rabbinic Exegesis," *JSS* 33 (1982): 527-36.

voted to the readings traditionally attributed to Theodotion.[21] For our purposes it is important to note that a great deal of this research was carried out by students of Frank Cross at Harvard University. The reason for this will become evident shortly. The presence of some common agreements with the characteristics that Barthélemy identified was enough justification for these scholars to identify the TH readings in the biblical book in which they were working as belonging to the *kaige* recension. Once the TH readings of a given book were identified as belonging to *kaige*-Theodotion, each of these scholars was then free to discover further *kaige* characteristics, which ultimately ballooned to nearly one hundred.[22] Thus, there developed a kind of *kaige*-fad where these students attempted to identify more and more characteristics of the *kaige* recension.

Despite the fact that Barthélemy himself never referred to a "*kaige* recension," this terminology is now common[23] and is in large part due to the influence of the Harvard school. Furthermore, the growth of the list of *kaige* traits is attributable to the common assumption by these scholars that the *kaige* recension is in most books of the Septuagint a homogenous recension of the OG towards the developing MT[24] by an individual or school of transla-

21. One can trace the development of *kaige* research through the following theses: A. Schmitt, "Stammt der sogennante θ' Text bei Daniel wirklich von Theodotion?" *MSU* 9 (1966): 281-392; J. D. Shenkel, *Chronology and Recensional Development in the Greek Text of Kings*, HSM 1 (Cambridge, Mass.: Harvard University Press, 1968); K. G. O'Connell, *The Theodotionic Revision of the Book of Exodus*, HSM 3 (Cambridge, Mass.: Harvard University Press, 1972); W. Bodine, *The Greek Text of Judges*, HSM 23 (Chico, Calif.: Scholars Press, 1980); W. Bodine, "*Kaige* and Other Recensional Developments in the Greek Text of Judges," *BIOSCS* 13 (1980): 45-57; L. Greenspoon, *Textual Studies in the Book of Joshua*, HSM 28 (Chico, Calif.: Scholars Press, 1983); O. Munnich, "Étude lexicographique du Psautier des Septante," Ph.D. diss., Université de Paris-Sorbonne, 1982; P. J. Gentry, *The Asterisked Materials in the Greek Job*, SCS 39 (Atlanta: Scholars Press, 1995); T. McLay, *The OG and Th Versions of Daniel*, SCS 43 (Atlanta: Scholars Press, 1996).

22. See the list Greenspoon provides (*Textual Studies in the Book of Joshua*, pp. 270-73). Two more recent contributions on *kaige* are T. Janz, "The Second Book of Ezra and the 'Καίγε Group,'" and S. Olofsson, "The Kaige Group and the Septuagint Book of Psalms," both in *IX Congress of the IOSCS*, ed. B. Taylor, SCS 45 (Atlanta: Scholars Press, 1997).

23. See the discussion of this issue in J. W. Wevers, "Barthélemy and Proto-Septuagint Studies," *BIOSCS* 21 (1988): 23-34.

24. For views on the nature of the HB and its development, see F. M. Cross, "The Evolution of a Theory of Local Texts," in *Qumran and the History of the Biblical Text*, ed. F. M. Cross and S. Talmon (Cambridge, Mass.: Harvard University Press, 1975), pp. 306-20. Talmon proposes an alternative view in the same volume. For an example and critique of how Cross's theories have influenced his students see D. W. Gooding, "A Recent Popularization of Professor F. M. Cross' Theories on the Text of the Old Testament," *TynBul* 26 (1975): 113-32. In more recent years Tov has been very influential in discussions concerning

tors.[25] However, in very recent years there has been significant criticism of both the view that *kaige* represents a monolithic recension and the methodology employed to isolate all of the proposed *kaige* characteristics. It has also been argued in detail that the Theodotionic revisions of Job or Daniel neither can be connected with *kaige* nor are revisions of the OG text at all.[26] The primary criticism of the research on the supposed *kaige* recension is that *kaige* research was biased in its approach. The characteristics that were adduced for *kaige* are not shared consistently by all the so-called members of the recension, nor was there any significant recognition of the differences among the texts that contain the so-called *kaige* traits. Many of the so-called characteristics appear in only one book! Overall, the methodology was almost exclusively guided by the concern to isolate similarities among the texts, while the implications of significant differences within the same texts were not taken into account.

Although I have criticized aspects of *kaige* research, it is important to note that these criticisms have had the benefit of hindsight. Throughout the history of academic research it has frequently been the case that "the assured results of critical research" of one generation are seriously undermined or

textual criticism and the origins of the Hebrew text. See, for example, E. Tov, "The Nature of the Hebrew Text Underlying the Septuagint: A Survey of the Problems," *JSOT* 7 (1978): 53-68; "A Modern Textual Outlook Based on the Qumran Scrolls," *HUCA* 53 (1983): 11-27. Tov's views are most easily accessible in *Textual Criticism of the Hebrew Bible*.

A discussion of the origins of the Hebrew Bible by Cross, Tov, and Ulrich can be read in the first of two volumes edited by J. T. Barrera and L. V. Montaner, *The Madrid Qumran Congress* (Leiden: Brill, 1992). The divergent character of the textual witnesses at Qumran indicates that the biblical text at the time was very fluid. There were authoritative books but a plurality of texts (see "Pluriformity in the Biblical Text, Text Groups, and Questions of Canon" by Ulrich in the volume mentioned above). A useful introduction to the differences between the views of Cross and Tov is provided in T. H. Lim, *Holy Scripture in the Qumran Commentaries and Pauline Letters* (Oxford: Clarendon, 1997), pp. 14-22.

25. Shenkel, *Chronology and Recensional Development*, pp. 11-13; O'Connell, *Theodotionic Revision of the Book of Exodus*, p. 291; Bodine, *Greek Text of Judges*, pp. 2-4; Greenspoon, *Textual Studies in the Book of Joshua*, p. 2.

26. See A. Pietersma, "Septuagint Research: A Plea for a Return to Basic Issues," *VT* 35 (1985): 304-5; and A. Schmitt, "Die griechischen Danieltexte (θ und ό) und das Theodotionproblem," *BZ* 36 (1992): 1-29. For the book of Job see the thorough evaluation by Gentry, *Asterisked Materials in the Greek Job*, pp. 406-10. Gentry concludes that "while R [Theodotion Job] is related somehow to the *kaige* group, the differences are by no means insignificant and should not be ignored in a blind attempt to connect R to a so-called Kaige Recension" (p. 410). For the argument that TH Daniel is an independent translation, as well as criticisms of the methodology employed to isolate *kaige*, see my work noted in n. 21 above; cf. T. McLay, "*Kaige* and Septuagint Research," *Textus* 19 (1998): 121-34.

overturned by the next. This is the product of our growing knowledge and the nature of research. It should also be observed that each of these scholars in their methodology of discovering further characteristics of the *kaige* recension followed a trail that had been blazed before them. The point of this example for our present discussion is that it is precarious to make assertions about the *kaige* recension or to construct a picture of Judaism in the first century and then to form conclusions about the use of the Greek versions of the Hebrew Bible in the Early Church without an awareness of such problems.

The difficulties surrounding the so-called *kaige* texts and the other Greek versions of the Jewish Scriptures that also arose in the early centuries of the Common Era serve to highlight an issue that is fundamentally of greater significance for Septuagint research: we do not possess critical editions for all of the books of the LXX. By "critical edition" we mean an eclectic text as opposed to a diplomatic text. An eclectic text is produced through a comparison of all the available texts of a particular book and represents in the judgment of the scholar or scholars the closest approximation to what was originally written since no single manuscript contains a pristine copy of the original writing. Even if a pure copy of a book of the Bible existed, we would have no means to identify it. An eclectic text provides the basis for comparing the texts and manuscripts to one another as well as to the variant traditions and later recensions. The most important issue in Septuagint research, then, is the ongoing need for critical editions for all the books of the LXX. A significant corollary of completing this endeavor will be that we will have a solid textual basis for examining the other Greek versions and determining their relationships to one another, not to mention how this will help increase our knowledge of the NT use of the Scriptures. Given the importance of this issue for LXX research and its impact on our understanding of the use of the LXX in NT research, we will pay considerable attention to the relationship of the Hebrew and Greek texts to one another throughout this volume. Hopefully, our discussion will demonstrate the significance of this issue for the reader.

A second issue in LXX research is the evaluation of Translation Technique (TT), that is, how we understand the process by which a Greek translator worked to provide a translation of a Hebrew text into Greek. There has been some debate over this issue, and we will deal with it over the course of two chapters. In general, there have been two types of approaches to describing TT. The first is represented by scholars who have been concerned with describing translations in terms of how literally they have been translated.[27]

---

27. The emphasis on literalism has been influenced by two major scholars who have set forth most clearly the means for defining literalism: James Barr and Emanuel Tov.

Typically, this approach has relied on computer-generated statistics to compare various aspects of translation across several books. Here we would do well to remember the saying, "There are lies, damn lies, and statistics!" The second approach has tended to compare the way a particular syntactical construction is treated in a book or several books.[28] However, it would be fair to comment (at least in my opinion) that the proponents of the second approach have tended to be more thorough in their analysis and description of the phenomena they encounter from a linguistic perspective. Rather than being content to know that the computer tells them that a certain Hebrew construction is rendered three different ways in one book while only one way in another, they want to examine the various occurrences of the construction in both books to determine whether there might be an explanation for the different practices. It is not that those employing the first approach could not have done this, it is just a fact that by and large they have not.[29] Though the analysis of TT has more direct bearing on Septuagint research, the principles behind the methodology are applicable to the analysis of quotations in the NT and determining whether a quotation is based on the Hebrew text or a Greek translation.

The Use of Scripture in the New Testament

The reason why we will give such prominence to the Hebrew and Greek texts of the Jewish Scriptures and their relationship to one another is so that we can establish a solid textual basis from which to investigate the citations and the use of the Jewish Scriptures in the NT. It is a well-known fact that there are considerable differences among the texts of some of our Greek and Hebrew witnesses to the same book. For example, the text of OG Job is about one sixth shorter than the MT, while Jeremiah in the OG lacks about one seventh of the content of Jeremiah in the MT, and the chapters have a different order from the MT. Other books such as Exodus, Joshua, Samuel, and Proverbs also witness to widely different texts. There are two divergent Greek textual traditions that survive for the book of Daniel, and, though one is similar

28. I. Soisalon-Soininen and his students R. Sollamo and A. Aejmelaeus are usually identified as the leaders of this approach to analyzing TT, though the number of studies is growing. See I. Soisalon-Soininen, "Methodologische Fragen der Erforschung der Septuaginta-Syntax," in *VI Congress of the IOSCS*, ed. C. Cox, *SCS* 23 (Atlanta: Scholars Press, 1988).

29. This criticism does not apply to Barr, who, in setting forth his criteria for literalism, did not attempt to apply it to statistical analyses of complete books.

to the text of Daniel in the MT, they have significant common additional material that is not part of the MT. So, while we will devote much time to investigating the relationship of the Hebrew and Greek texts of the Scriptures to one another, the differing textual witnesses to various biblical books also illustrate the point we have already made concerning the books (as well as the content of those books) that later became canonized as Scripture: that is, they were not identical in all respects with the Scriptures of the Early Church. What do we do with these phenomena? Are citations of Scripture in the NT the same as the passage from which they are quoted in the HB? How did the NT writers cite Scripture? Did they quote from memory or copy from a manuscript? Does it make any difference if the writers were citing from a book written in Hebrew or Greek? These and many more questions come alive when we begin to scrutinize a passage and examine the texts that are involved.

Our journey into this fascinating world of the texts will begin with the citation of Amos 9:11-12 in Acts 15:16-18. This passage is an excellent example to initiate our study because it illustrates the complexities surrounding the use of the Greek Jewish Scriptures in NT research that the remainder of this volume will explore. We will not be able to solve every problem raised by the way that Scripture is cited in the NT or to provide an adequate answer for every concern, but we will be able to solve some of the riddles and provide a framework for understanding the issues.

In order to demonstrate the dynamic and complex relationship between the NT and the Jewish Scriptures in their Hebrew and Greek forms, this volume out of necessity will have to confine itself primarily to the analysis of explicit citations of Scripture. This method offers the surest results for an introductory volume of this nature, particularly when we are navigating some uncharted waters. For the purposes of this volume we understand a direct quotation in the NT to be restricted to those citations that have some type of introductory formula such as, but not limited to: *(just) as it is written, as the prophet* (x) *said,* and *in the law it is written.*[30]

A broad understanding of the textual situation in the time of the Early Church and the use of the Greek Jewish Scriptures in the NT will provide a foundation for our later examination of specific ways that the use of the Greek Jewish Scriptures influenced theology in the New Testament. It is my

---

30. For a discussion of introductory formulas, see H. M. Shires, *Finding the Old Testament in the New* (Philadelphia: Westminster, 1974); B. Metzger, "The Formulas Introducing Quotations of Scripture in the New Testament and the Mishna," *JBL* 70 (1951): 297-307; E. E. Ellis, "Biblical Interpretation in the New Testament Church," in *Mikra: Text, Translation, Reading and Interpretation of the Hebrew Bible in Ancient Judaism and Early Christianity,* ed. M. J. Mulder and H. Sysling (Philadelphia: Fortress, 1988).

hope that this initial venture will provide an impetus for others to improve and expand our understanding in this area of research.

As so often is the case, some of the subjects that we treat do not get the attention that they deserve, but to have given them that attention would have easily doubled the length of the text. Hopefully, the notes and references to the secondary literature will serve the reader who wants more information and the student who becomes fascinated by the world of the text. Indices are also provided in order to facilitate the use of the text.

Outline of Contents

We will follow this introductory chapter with our investigation of the citation in Acts 15:16-18. Chapter one will serve to introduce the reader to the complex world of the use of Scripture in the NT and to raise some of the issues that are involved. Chapter two will examine TT in the LXX and the problem of whether the NT writer is quoting a Hebrew or Greek text. Here we will begin defining the purpose of TT and discuss the problems of methodology for analyzing TT. This chapter contains some discussion that is quite technical in nature; it may be skimmed by students who are more interested in the impact of the Greek Jewish Scriptures on the NT. We will conclude the examination of TT in the following chapter by proposing a methodology for analyzing TT. Chapter four will outline the transmission history of the LXX and its recensions. Again, the knowledge gained from the study of specific texts will be applied to NT research. Chapter five will draw upon the arguments of the previous chapters as we examine more passages in order to determine how the NT writers' use of the Greek Jewish Scriptures is reflected in their theology. We will argue that the theology of the NT exhibits the distinct influence of the Greek scriptural tradition by its use of vocabulary, its citations of Scripture, and its theological concepts. The final chapter will offer concluding remarks.

Let the journey begin.

CHAPTER ONE

The Use of Scripture in the New Testament

The key to our gaining an appreciation of the use of the Greek Jewish Scriptures in the NT is to begin with a careful study of the texts. Obviously, this will not provide an answer to all of our questions or necessarily draw our attention to all of the issues. For example, a strict analysis and comparison of texts would not alert us to the fact that rabbinic rules of interpretation (explained later in this chapter) may be reflected in the way in which a NT writer employed a particular Scripture. Nor would we know whether the author actually had knowledge that a verse to which he alluded or from which he cited existed in multiple forms; thus, a specific reading from a number of available readings was chosen. However, if we begin with the texts and allow our understanding of the phenomena we encounter to be informed by the historical context, we will be in a better position to evaluate the relevance and use of the Greek Jewish Scriptures in the NT.

Although the way to an informed appreciation of the use of the Scriptures in the NT is through an examination of the texts, the relationship between the Jewish Scriptures and the NT is complicated. In order to introduce some of the issues with which we will be concerned in this volume, we will briefly examine the quotation of Amos 9:11-12 in Acts 15:16-18. This analysis will ask many questions and offer some answers, though primarily it will serve as the primer for the chapters that follow. Below the text of Acts 15:16-18, OG Amos 9:11-12, and MT Amos 9:11-12 are provided in parallel alignment, first in the original languages and then in English. Instances where the Greek Scriptures in the NT and OG are in agreement with one another and differ from the MT are <u>underlined</u>. *Italics* mark instances where the NT and OG only appear to differ from the MT. Square brackets [ ] highlight omissions

17

from the OG in the NT and **bold** focuses on additions or more substantial changes in the NT as compared to the OG.

The Texts

NT Acts 15:16-18	OG Amos 9:11-12	MT Amos 9:11-12
Μετὰ ταῦτα	ἐν τῇ ἡμέρᾳ ἐκείνῃ	בַּיּוֹם הַהוּא
ἀναστρέψω		
καὶ ἀνοικοδομήσω	ἀναστήσω	אָקִים
τὴν σκηνὴν Δαυὶδ	τὴν σκηνὴν Δαυὶδ	אֶת־סֻכַּת דָּוִיד
τὴν πεπτωκυῖαν	τὴν πεπτωκυῖαν	הַנֹּפֶלֶת
[ ]	καὶ ἀνοικοδομήσω	וְגָדַרְתִּי
[ ]	τὰ πεπτωκότα αὐτῆς	אֶת־פִּרְצֵיהֶן
καὶ τὰ κατεσκαμμένα αὐτῆς	καὶ τὰ κατεσκαμμένα αὐτῆς	וַהֲרֹסֹתָיו
ἀνοικοδομήσω	ἀναστήσω	אָקִים
καὶ ἀνορθώσω αὐτήν,	καὶ ἀνοικοδομήσω αὐτὴν,	וּבְנִיתִיהָ
[ ]	καθὼς αἱ ἡμέραι τοῦ αἰῶνος	כִּימֵי עוֹלָם
ὅπως ἂν <u>ἐκζητήσωσιν</u>	ὅπως <u>ἐκζητήσωσιν</u>	לְמַעַן יִירְשׁוּ
<u>οἱ κατάλοιποι τῶν</u>	<u>οἱ κατάλοιποι τῶν</u>	אֶת־שְׁאֵרִית
<u>ἀνθρώπων</u> τὸν κύριον	<u>ἀνθρώπων</u>	אֱדוֹם
καὶ πάντα τὰ ἔθνη	καὶ πάντα τὰ ἔθνη	וְכָל־הַגּוֹיִם
ἐφ᾽ οὓς ἐπικέκληται	ἐφ᾽ οὓς ἐπικέκληται	אֲשֶׁר־נִקְרָא
τὸ ὄνομά μου	τὸ ὄνομά μου	שְׁמִי
ἐπ᾽ αὐτούς,	ἐπ᾽ αὐτούς,	עֲלֵיהֶם
λέγει κύριος	λέγει κύριος	נְאֻם־יְהוָה
ποιῶν ταῦτα	ὁ ποιῶν ταῦτα	עֹשֶׂה זֹּאת
γνωστὰ ἀπ᾽ αἰῶνος		

NT Acts 15:16-18	OG Amos 9:11-12	MT Amos 9:11-12
After this	On that day	On that day
I will return		
and I will rebuild	I will raise up	I will raise up
the *dwelling* of David	the *dwelling* of David	the booth of David
that has fallen.	that has fallen	that is fallen
[ ]	and *rebuild*	and repair
[ ]	its *fallen parts*,	their breaches

I will rebuild	and raise up	and raise up
its ruins	its ruins	its ruins
and **will set it up,**	and rebuild it	and rebuild it
[ ]	as in the days of old;	as in the days of old;
<u>in order that the rest</u>	<u>in order that the rest</u>	in order that they
<u>of the peoples</u>	<u>of the peoples</u>	may possess
<u>may seek</u> **the Lord** —		the remnant of Edom
even all the nations	and all the nations	and all the nations
over whom my name	over whom my name	who are called
has been called,	has been called, <u>may</u>	by my name,
	<u>seek</u> [<u>me</u>],	
says the Lord,	says the Lord,	says the Lord,
who has been	who does	who does
making these things	these things.	these things.
known from the		
beginning.		

Comparing the OG and MT

When we compare the NT, OG, and MT of this passage, there are obvious similarities, but there are also differences. I would like to devote some time first to the relationship between the OG and MT before turning to examine the quotation as it appears in the NT. My intention at this point is to draw our attention to some of the questions and issues more than to provide answers.

Comparing the OG and MT of Amos 9:11-12, we notice that the Greek is, for the most part, a faithful rendition of a Hebrew text that was likely very similar to the text preserved in the MT. Several words are italicized *(dwelling, rebuild, fallen parts)* to indicate that despite the fact that there is a difference in our English translation, there is a direct relationship between the Greek and the Hebrew. For example, σκηνή *dwelling* is the most common *translational gloss* of סכה *booth* (26x) in the LXX. In the case of ἀνοικοδομέω *rebuild*, it occurs only 4/10x for גדר, but in this case the choice of the Greek word was also influenced by the appearance of the Hebrew verb בנה *to build* later in the verse, which was also translated by ἀνοικοδομέω. Once again, ἀνοικοδομέω is employed in some cases (12x) in the LXX to translate בנה, but the simple form of the verb (i.e., οἰκοδομέω) is preferred (over 300x). However, in the context it is obvious that the sense is to *rebuild* rather than *build*, and so ἀνοικοδομέω is the better translational choice for Greek. The translator chose the same Greek (ἀνοικοδομέω) word to render two different Hebrew words. In a similar way,

19

the translator chose *fallen parts* (πεπτωκότα, perfect accusative neuter participle of πίπτω) as a rendering for פרץ after employing *fallen* (πεπτωκυῖαν, perfect accusative feminine participle of πίπτω) for נפל.

The technique of employing one word in a language to translate two or more words from another language is called *lexical leveling*. Lexical leveling is frequent in the LXX. However, so is the opposite tendency, which is to employ more than one Greek gloss for the same Hebrew word. This is illustrated above where it was mentioned that both ἀνοικοδομέω and οἰκοδομέω translate בנה. We will discuss the methods employed by the Septuagint translators to translate the Semitic text, or *translation technique,* in the next chapter.

The most significant difference between the OG and the Hebrew is the portion of text that is underlined: *the rest/remainder of the peoples may seek [me]*[1] for *may possess the remnant of Edom*. Where did this translation come from? Is it totally due to a theological point *(Tendenz)* that the translator wished to introduce, or did the translator misread the *Vorlage* (the source text from which the translation was made), or was the source text for the OG different from what we have in the MT? We will deal with these matters in ascending order of difficulty. Though there is always the possibility that an alternative *Vorlage* is the source of a variant reading in the OG, it is also a question of probability. How likely is it that an alternative *Vorlage* is the best explanation? In this instance, the reading of the OG seems to be different because of an understanding of the Hebrew text rather than because the Hebrew text was different from the MT. The use of κατάλοιποι *the rest/remainder* to render שְׁאֵרִית *remnant* is a common equivalent in the LXX. However, the difficulty is that *remnant* is the object in the Hebrew whereas *the rest/remainder* has become the subject in the Greek. The second difficulty is that *the remnant of Edom* has become *the rest of the peoples*. Here the translator has read the Hebrew word אֱדוֹם *Edom* as if it were a plural form of אָדָם *people/humanity*. So, the translation *the rest of the peoples* is related very closely to the Hebrew text and could represent the translator's intention to provide a faithful rendition,[2] though there is the problem that *the rest of the peoples* has be-

---

1. Although it is not present in the Greek, *me* would be understood. However, the pronoun με is added in many witnesses after ἐκζητήσωσιν, though these reflect a strong (but not exclusively) Lucianic influence. See the textual evidence in J. Ziegler, *Duodecim Prophetae,* 3rd ed., *Septuaginta* 13 (Göttingen: Vandenhoeck & Ruprecht, 1984), p. 204.

2. In an *unvocalized text* the consonants would have been the same. It is also not certain whether the ו would have been present to indicate the vowel. Qumran mss. exhibit a mixed tendency, sometimes retaining and sometimes omitting the long vowels. See E. Tov, "Hebrew Biblical Manuscripts from the Judean Desert: Their Contribution to Textual Criticism," *JJS* 39 (1988): 5-37.

come the subject of the Greek subordinate clause. Turning to the verb we find that ἐκζητέω *seek* translates ירשׁ *possess*. This is a unique rendering in the LXX and is a departure from the sense of the Hebrew. Yet it is interesting to note that ἐκζητέω in the LXX most frequently renders דרשׁ *seek* (73x). The difference between the two Hebrew words ירשׁ *possess* and דרשׁ *seek* is only the first letter. There is also the possibility that the translator read בקשׁ, which is rendered by ἐκζητέω 29x, but that would require the translator to confuse two consonants, ב and ק for ד and ר.

The Meaning of the OG vs. the MT

There is a significant difference between the meaning of the OG and that of the MT. The Hebrew is referring to the decay of the Davidic empire and looks forward to a time when that empire will be restored. It envisions that the restoration of the kingdom will be followed by Israel's return to dominion over the nations that had been under its authority previously. Edom is singled out because of the history of hostility between the two nations (Amos 1:11-12), or, more specifically, because the passage is an allusion to the fall of Jerusalem and the exile (587/6 B.C.E.).[3] In contrast to the militaristic tones of the Hebrew, the OG imparts that the renewal of the Davidic kingdom will precipitate the remainder or remnant of humanity turning to Israel's God.

The question, then, is whether the translator read the Hebrew text slightly differently (דרשׁ *seek* for ירשׁ *possess;* אָדָם *people* for אֱדוֹם *Edom;* and the object as the subject) in order to create a theological rendering, or whether he misread the verb and *Edom* and rendered the text in a way that made sense to him.[4] There is also a third possibility that mediates between the two extremes. Perhaps the translator did not completely understand the meaning of the text and, based on reading *humanity* for *Edom* and combining it with *the rest/remainder,* assumed that the scribe who had copied the Hebrew text had made an error. Thus, he introduced a change that made sense to him. This would be an unintentional change on the part of the translator of what he assumed to be an error, as opposed to a deliberate change. Yet, if the translator introduced a change, then intentionally or not, his theology influenced the resulting translation as he attempted to provide a rendering both

3. S. Paul, *Amos* (Minneapolis: Fortress, 1991), pp. 290-91; J. L. Mays, *Amos* (Philadelphia: Westminster, 1969), p. 164.

4. See the analysis of Isaiah 23 by van der Kooij, who argues that the OG text reflects a fulfillment-interpretation (A. van der Kooij, *The Oracle of Tyre, VTSupp* 71 [Leiden: Brill, 1998]). The OG is very close to its *Vorlage* but was reapplied to the context of the translator.

that made sense in the context of the book and that reflected his own worldview and cultural context.

Why Is the OG Different?

How should we judge what has happened in the OG? It is not unusual to find variant readings that in the judgment of one scholar reflect a misreading of the *Vorlage*, but that in the eyes of another are the result of deliberate *Tendenz*. For this reason, it is essential to proceed cautiously and without prejudice in an examination of the texts; otherwise, we will only confirm our presuppositions. In my view, we cannot decide between these options for Amos given what we know up to this point, and there are times when we may not be able to harness the evidence to make a clear decision. However, there are means to achieve a better perspective.

The place to begin is to determine how likely it is that textual corruption took place in the transmission of the Hebrew or Greek texts. We have already suggested that it is possible that *Edom* could have been misread. There is also the question whether it is likely that the initial consonants of ירשׁ and דרשׁ could have been confused. This kind of information is available in almost any book on textual criticism of the Hebrew Bible.[5] However, Emanuel Tov has written a volume that is indispensable for anyone who desires to understand the relationship between the LXX and MT, and it treats such matters in detail: *The Text-Critical Use of the Septuagint in Biblical Research*.[6] Textual witnesses to Amos preserved in the *Dead Sea Scrolls* may also indicate whether אֱדֹום *Edom* is preserved in any texts without the marker for the vowel. Though they offer no evidence for this particular instance, the defective reading without the vocalic ו would not be unusual. As far as the OG text is concerned we should check the Göttingen edition. The other ancient versions such as the Old Latin, Coptic, and Peshitta may also shed light on the Greek text, and occasionally on the Hebrew.

On the one hand, the fact that certain Hebrew letters tended to be confused will at times lead to an easy resolution of a difference between the OG and MT. On the other hand, it is always better to err on the side of caution. Although letters could sometimes be confused, that does not mean that this

5. P. K. McCarter, *Textual Criticism: Recovering the Text of the Hebrew Bible* (Philadelphia: Fortress, 1986); E. Würthwein, *The Text of the Old Testament*, rev. ed., trans. E. F. Rhodes (Grand Rapids: Eerdmans, 1979).

6. E. Tov, *The Text-Critical Use of the Septuagint in Biblical Research* (Jerusalem: Simor, 1981).

actually happened in any particular case. Whether or not we think it is reasonable that the translator misread the consonants in Amos 9:12, or anywhere else, we can better assess the evidence if we determine whether or not the translator has confused/misread letters, particularly the ones that might have been confused in our passage, anywhere else in the unit of translation.[7] If there is evidence that this process occurs elsewhere, the probability increases that something similar has happened in 9:12. At the same time, if there is evidence that the translator employs *Tendenz* elsewhere, the possibility then increases that 9:12 is also a theological rendering. For some books of the Septuagint there are detailed monographs that have compared the OG and the MT, and we can readily find the answers to our questions.[8] Unfortunately, there is still a lot of work that needs to be done on the remaining books in order for conclusions to have integrity. With regard to Amos 9:12 we note that there are other cases where consonants have been confused in the translation of the Minor Prophets, but the fact that this variant involves three changes means that the alteration was probably not simply a case of misreading the consonantal text. In addition, the theology that *the rest/remainder of the peoples* would seek the Lord after the restoration of the people of Israel is a minor theme of the twelve prophets (see also Zech. 8:20-23; Mic. 7:17). Therefore, it is possible that reading the following clause *and all the nations over whom my name has been called* as parallel with the clause in question influenced the translator's understanding of the text.

In concluding our examination of the relationship between the MT and OG, it would seem that the translator produced a translation that was influenced by his theology, but it is questionable whether it was intentional.

---

7. I use the terminology "unit of translation" because different parts or sections of books were translated by different people. In the case of the Minor Prophets it is generally agreed that they were translated as a unit. See the next chapter for a full discussion of translation technique.

8. John Wevers has just completed his series on the Pentateuch published in Atlanta by Scholars Press: *Notes on the Greek Text of Genesis* (1993); *Notes on the Greek Text of Exodus* (1990); *Notes on the Greek Text of Leviticus* (1997); *Notes on the Greek Text of Numbers* (1998); *Notes on the Greek Text of Deuteronomy* (1996). Other useful works for other books are Gentry, *The Asterisked Materials in the Greek Job*, SCS 39 (Atlanta: Scholars Press, 1995); I. L. Seeligmann, *The LXX Version of Isaiah* (Leiden: Brill, 1948); Leslie C. Allen, *The Greek Chronicles: Part 1*, VTSupp 25 (Leiden: Brill, 1974).

Comparing the NT to the OG and MT

When we compare the quotation in Acts to the OG and MT, we find that the author is employing the OG, although there are changes that are introduced that are independent of both traditions preserved in the manuscripts of the LXX and MT. Our conclusion that the author is relying for the most part on the Septuagint tradition is based generally on the shared vocabulary between the OG and the NT and, more importantly, on the fact that there are distinctive agreements between them. For example, the NT follows the OG in employing ἀνοικοδομήσω *I will build* twice, and it includes the major change introduced by the OG against the MT: ἐκζητήσωσιν οἱ κατάλοιποι τῶν ἀνθρώπων *the rest of the peoples may seek*. In the latter case the NT author also inserts τὸν κύριον *the Lord* in order to make explicit whom the people will seek. Thus, the NT writer must have been reading the text as we have it in the OG; however, the meaning of the passage is very different in the context of the preaching of the Early Church. The restored house of David no longer refers to the Davidic kingdom because the promise to David has been fulfilled through the resurrection of Jesus.[9] It is because of Jesus' resurrection that the Gentiles will seek the Lord. We do not know whether the author was aware of the reading of the MT, but the OG text allowed the passage to be reinterpreted and applied as a prooftext to vindicate the mission to the Gentiles and their inclusion in God's people. (The context is the point at which James, acting as the leader of the council in Jerusalem, states that Simon's testimony of how God had poured out his spirit on the Gentiles [see 15:7-11] is in agreement with the words of the prophet that he cites in verses 16-18.)

There are several other changes introduced by the NT author against both the OG and the MT. The insertions are marked in **bold print** in the translation. In the first instance, following the introductory formula *as it is written,* the quotation begins Μετὰ ταῦτα ἀναστρέψω *After these things I will return.* This is a clear departure from the OG, yet it is not a translation of the Hebrew text. Besides the explanatory addition of τὸν κύριον *the Lord* in order to make explicit whom the people will seek, there is also the addition of γνωστὰ ἀπ᾽ αἰῶνος, which, with the omission of the article in OG, creates *who has been making these things known from the beginning.* Lastly, the verb ἀνορθώσω *I will set up* is an insertion. One other change is that καθὼς αἱ ἡμέραι τοῦ αἰῶνος *as in the days of old,* which is in the OG, is omitted in Acts.

---

9. E. Haenchen, *The Acts of the Apostles* (Philadelphia: Westminster, 1971), p. 448.

Why Is the NT Quotation Different from Both the MT and the OG?

The fact that frequently there are significant differences between what the NT author identifies as an explicit quotation of the Scripture and the text that is actually cited, whether one identifies the Hebrew or the Greek as the source of the quotation, raises several questions. First and foremost is the integrity of our textual witnesses. Are they reliable? We must remember that the same codices that are important witnesses for determining the original text of the NT, such as Sinaiticus (ℵ), Alexandrinus (A), and Vaticanus (B), are just as significant for reconstructing the text of the OG because they preserve a witness to the Jewish Scriptures in their Greek form. These manuscripts that are several hundred years removed from the original writing of the NT documents are even further removed from the period when the books of the Hebrew Bible were translated. So, our textual witnesses to the LXX are comparatively late when compared to textual witnesses to the NT. Moreover, since the Greek Scriptures of the Church were transmitted together, that is, both the LXX and the NT, there was a tendency to harmonize readings so that the text in the NT and the text of its source matched. The study of the critical apparatus in any Göttingen edition of an OG book reveals numerous variant readings, often with only one or very few supporting witnesses that were influenced by the text of the NT. For example, J. Ziegler notes that manuscript 764 has ἀνορθώσω instead of ἀναστήσω in Amos 9:11, which was obviously influenced by the presence of the quotation in Acts.[10] For the purpose of establishing a critical text of the OG we employ only the evidence that we actually possess, which is both fragmentary and corrupted. Occasionally, we might be able to justify an educated guess or *conjectural emendation* of what the text originally read, but the truth is that we do not know nearly as much as we might like; and in many cases we are reconstructing a *majority text* that may bear little resemblance to the original text.[11] Other reasons why the NT quotation may differ from both the OG and the MT will emerge in the following paragraphs.

---

10. Ziegler, *Duodecim Prophetae*, p. 204.

11. For example, in the book of Daniel where we have witnesses to two complete Greek translations there is ample evidence that the mss. witnessing to the OG translation have been corrupted by the TH version. See McLay, *The OG and Th Versions of Daniel*, SCS 43 (Atlanta: Scholars Press, 1996), pp. 245-47.

Do We Have and Can We Recognize All the Relevant Sources?

To this point our discussion has focused primarily on the MT and the OG/LXX, and this has been true of many similar investigations in the past. At the beginning of the twentieth century H. B. Swete declared that the majority of the "direct quotations from the O.T. in the Epistles of St. Paul are taken from the LXX, without material change."[12] Others have assumed this to be true in their investigations, consciously or unconsciously, as is evidenced by their uncritical use of the Greek Jewish Scriptures[13] or by restricting their research on quotations to the way in which the texts diverge from the MT or OG/LXX. For example, T. H. Lim justly criticizes the important study of Paul's quotations by D. A. Koch because Koch does not adequately account for the possibility that Paul employed alternative *Vorlagen* in some of his citations.[14] Lim argues that the *DSS* offer evidence for text forms that differ from the MT or OG/LXX and that Paul's citations sometimes reflect these texts. Given the existence of the *DSS* and the plurality of biblical texts to which they witness, it is wise to exercise a great deal of caution when examining the NT texts and quotations of Scripture.

How Was Scripture Cited?

The next question is, How did the authors cite Scripture? Did they quote their sources directly or quote from memory? Quoting from memory would be one way to explain the way in which the NT authors sometimes blended several Scriptures together.[15] For example, it might explain the use of ἀνορθώσω in Acts 15:16. The verb is not that common in the LXX (only 16x), but it does occur in 2 Reigns (Samuel) 7:13, 16 where the prophet Nathan tells King David

12. H. B. Swete, *An Introduction to the Old Testament in Greek,* rev. R. R. Ottley (Cambridge: Cambridge University Press, 1914), p. 400.

13. See the review by J. Barr, "Paul and the LXX: A Note on Some Recent Work," *JTS* 45 (1994): 593-601.

14. T. H. Lim, *Holy Scripture in the Qumran Commentaries and Pauline Letters* (Oxford: Clarendon, 1997), p. 143. See D. A. Koch, *Die Schrift als Zeuge des Evangeliums: Untersuchungen zur Verwendung und zum Verständnis der Schrift bei Paulus* (Tübingen: Mohr, 1986). The same is true of C. Stanley's research in *Paul and the Language of Scripture: Citation Technique in the Pauline Epistles and Contemporary Literature* (Cambridge: Cambridge University Press, 1992).

15. For example, see E. E. Ellis, *Paul's Use of the Old Testament* (Edinburgh: Oliver & Boyd, 1957), pp. 14-15.

that he is not to build the temple, but where the Lord says that David will οἰκοδομήσει *build* it through his seed and "I will ἀνορθώσω *establish* his throne." The similar themes and vocabulary regarding the kingdom of David are probably responsible for the author's choice of vocabulary, particularly since 2 Reigns 7:13-14 was a very important messianic text. Memory might also account for the different introduction *After these things I will return* and, perhaps, for the omission of the second reference to the *fallen parts.* However, it is noticeable that while Acts 15:16 departs quite significantly from Amos 9:11, the next verse in Acts is almost identical to that in Amos. It would be difficult to believe that one could make mistakes in one verse and then be so accurate in the next.[16] Thus, it seems unlikely that lack of memory could account for the differences in this particular case.

How Did the NT Writers Use Their Sources?

Although quoting from memory may explain some instances in which the NT deviates from its presumed source, there are many instances, such as Acts 15:16-18, where it cannot. However, unless we are willing to believe that the transmission of the texts was totally unreliable or that the quotation reflects a divergent tradition, it is obvious that our passage is not a direct quotation from a Greek manuscript of Amos. As we have already argued, there are instances in which one or both of these factors is the reason that a quotation appears to depart from its source, but we will argue that neither explanation is satisfactory in this particular passage. The quotation in Acts is introduced with the words: *This agrees with the words of the prophets, as it is written.* This may refer to a scroll containing the Minor Prophets. However, the introduction to the quotation contrasts with Acts 2:16 where the quotation is specifically attributed to Joel and, apart from some introductory words, basically follows Joel 2:28-29 in the OG. Another example of attributing the quotation to a specific prophet would be the citation of Isaiah 6:9-10 in Acts 28:26-27. Yet, the quotations in Acts 7:42-43 and 13:41 are also introduced as derived from the *prophets,* and both basically follow the OG texts of Amos 5:25-27 and Habakkuk 1:5, respectively. So, there are various introductory formulas that are employed, but, for the most part, it would appear that the author of Acts — and the same is evident in the remainder of the NT books — used written

---

16. The ability to memorize was quite highly developed among ancient individuals. See W. Harris, *Ancient Literacy* (Cambridge, Mass.: Harvard University Press, 1989), pp. 30-33, 301.

sources and followed them quite closely in most instances.[17] The differences in our passage alert us to the freedom that the NT writers exercised in their treatment of their sources when they employed a citation.[18]

What Accounts for the NT Authors' Freedom with Respect to Their Sources?

There is no one single explanation for all the differences between the quotation in Acts and its source. For example, the omission of *its fallen parts* is probably due to the author's choice to simplify the text and eliminate some elements that were redundant. The retention of *I will rebuild* twice, plus *I will set up,* maintains the emphasis on the rebuilding of David's house with fewer words. We have also suggested that the insertion of *I will set up* probably is rooted in the similarities between Amos and 2 Reigns 7. The verbs ἀνορθώσω and ἀναστήσω begin with the same letters, and their meanings overlap; so, it is possible that the writer (or the scribe of the manuscript from which he was reading) employed ἀνορθώσω unintentionally because of these similarities and the occurrence of the verb in 2 Reigns.

Yet another reason must lie behind the differences in the opening words of the quotation *After this I will return.* It is suggested by some that the opening of the quotation has been influenced by Jeremiah 12:15,[19] but there is no linguistic justification for this connection. The only similarity between Jeremiah 12:15 and Amos 9:11 is the theology that expresses that the Lord will have compassion on the nations after Judah is restored. Is this similar theology sufficient ground for claiming that the writer of Acts was influenced by Jeremiah? A positive response would be based on extremely tenuous reasoning given the fact that there is no demonstrable lexical dependence of the quote in Acts upon Jeremiah.[20]

17. In his analysis of Paul's citation technique, which includes an examination of comparative Jewish and Roman literature, Stanley notes that "in none of the materials surveyed does there appear to be any correlation between the way a quote is introduced and the degree to which it adheres to the wording of the source text" (*Citation*, p. 340).

18. See C. Stanley, "The Social Environment of 'Free' Biblical Quotations in the New Testament," in *Early Christian Interpretation of the Scriptures of Israel,* ed. C. A. Evans and James A. Sanders (Sheffield: Sheffield Academic Press, 1997).

19. E.g., H. Conzelmann, *Acts of the Apostles* (Philadelphia: Fortress, 1987), p. 117. It is also given as a marginal reference in NA.

20. Even the verb *I will return* is ἀναστρέψω in Acts 15:16, whereas Jer. 12:15 employs the more common ἐπιστρέψω. The D text of Acts does have the variant reading ἐπιστρέψω, but even that is very little evidence to argue for linguistic influence.

How then do we account for the author's choice of beginning the quotation with *After this I will return?* The words do not stem from either Amos 9 or Jeremiah 12. It is probable that μετὰ ταῦτα *After this* is merely a matter of the author's style because the same combination is found in Acts 7:7; 13:20; 18:1. The difficulty with this suggestion, however, is that none of these other passages are quotations. The verb ἀναστρέψω may be the result of an unintentional error on the part of the author because it is orthographically similar to ἀναστήσω. In other words, we do not know for certain what might have prompted this particular choice.

We have argued above that the writer of Acts capitalized on the theology of the OG reading and reinterpreted it in the light of the Christ event. This accounts for the addition of *the Lord,* but also for the omission of *just as in the days of old* from the quotation. Obviously, the new situation brought about through Christ could not have existed in a former time, and so the reference to *the days of old* would not have contributed to the point being made by the quotation. The final difference between Acts and Amos is the addition of **known from the beginning** in verse 18. As in the initial words of the quotation, the editors of NA again provide a marginal reference for the added words (Isa. 45:21). Unfortunately, this reference suffers from difficulties similar to those in the initial reference to Jeremiah 12:15. According to the critical edition there is no Greek manuscript of Isaiah 45:21 in existence that reads ποιῶν ταῦτα γνωστὰ ἀπ' αἰῶνος.[21] The portion of text that we are concerned with in Isaiah 45:21 reads ἐποίησε ταῦτα ἀπ' ἀρχῆς *he did these things from the beginning,* and there are no significant textual variants. Like Jeremiah 12:15, the words in OG Isaiah 45:21 express a thought similar to the quotation in Acts, but apart from the vocabulary ἀπ' ἀρχῆς *from the beginning* the wording is different.[22] One could also argue that there is a connection between the participle ποιῶν *making* and the verb ἐποίησε *he did/made,* but this is not enough to argue for dependence upon OG Isaiah 45:21. Unless there was a manuscript of Isaiah 45:21 that the NT writer employed and to which we no longer have access, there is very little textual evidence to connect the end of the quotation in Acts to Isaiah 45:21, though one may assume that the author's knowledge and familiarity with the Scriptures became part of his expression. In the end, the writer of Acts has retained the majority of the text from the OG of Amos 9:11-12, but has also acted as an author, creatively reinterpreting

21. J. Ziegler, *Isaias,* 3rd ed., *Septuaginta* 14 (Göttingen: Vandenhoeck & Ruprecht, 1983).

22. The Hebrew of Isa. 45:21 is unlike that of Amos 9:12 and would not have been the source of the Greek translation in Acts either.

the Scriptures for his audience through subtle substitutions and additions to, as well as omissions from, the cited Scripture.

Theories on the Use of Scripture in the NT

Already in just this one quotation that we have examined we have discovered a variety of reasons why the text of a NT quotation might differ from its source. There is also no shortage of explanations that scholars have offered for the presence of these differences. It is worthwhile to survey the multiplicity of theories and issues that scholars have identified as relevant to an understanding of the use of Scripture in the NT.

Explicit Quotation vs. Allusion

Much of the research on the use of the LXX in the NT has been due to the focus on quotations. The study of quotations is important to our knowledge of the way in which the NT writers employed the Greek Jewish Scriptures, but it is not our exclusive concern.[23] The numerous allusions to sacred writings that do not fall within the corpus of books that now form the canon of the HB help us to recognize that the ancient writers' understanding of what constituted Scripture (as opposed to the later notion of canon) was quite broad; furthermore, these writings were all formative in shaping their theology. In addition, the adoption of vocabulary from the Greek Jewish Scriptures by the NT writers is another indication of the influence of the translation of the Hebrew Scriptures into Greek.[24]

23. There has been a great deal of research on quotations, but there is still no consensus concerning what constitutes a quotation. For example, we would accept that a direct quotation from the LXX of five or six words without any introductory formula should also be regarded as a quotation. It would detract from our discussion to treat this issue in detail. D. A. Koch and Stanley attempt to bring more rigor to the discussion, but see a recent article by S. Porter for an excellent discussion of the problem with terminology ("The Use of the Old Testament in the New Testament: A Brief Comment on Method and Terminology," in *Early Christian Interpretation of the Scriptures of Israel*, ed. C. A. Evans and James A. Sanders [Sheffield: Sheffield Academic Press, 1997]).

24. At one time it was believed that the LXX introduced changes to the meanings of many Greek words, but it is now recognized, chiefly through the discovery and study of more Greek manuscripts, that, for the most part, the vocabulary of the LXX does reflect the language of its time. See M. Silva, "Semantic Change and Semitic Influence in the Greek Bible: With a Study of the Semantic Field of Mind," Ph.D. diss., University of Manchester, 1972. Older studies on the use of the Greek language in the Scriptures are A. Deissmann, *The Philology of*

Identifying Sources

As we have discovered in our examination of Acts 15:16-18, it is no easy task to determine the relationship between the NT text and its possible source(s). In some cases a quotation seems to be a direct citation, more or less, from a Hebrew or Greek version. This judgment is based on the manuscript evidence that we have in our possession. In still other cases a quotation may reflect a direct citation from a Hebrew or Greek text that existed at the time of writing but to which we no longer have access. We cannot actually prove that this is the case. However, if the quotation is very similar to an existing text, it might be reasonable to suppose that a manuscript or a group of manuscripts existed with the variant reading. For example, John 1:23 has Εὐθύνατε τὴν ὁδὸν κυρίου *Make straight the way of the Lord* while other quotations of this verse from Isaiah 40:3 follow the OG with Ἑτοιμάσατε τὴν ὁδὸν κυρίου *Prepare the way of the Lord* (Matt. 3:3; Mark 1:3; Luke 3:4). Even though we have no other manuscript evidence for the reading in John 1:23, it is possible that there was a tradition or even one manuscript with the verb εὐθύνατε. However, it seems much more likely that the appearance of the verb εὐθύνατε *Make straight* is the result of the influence of εὐθείας ποιεῖτε *Make straight* in the OG of Isaiah 40:3b.[25]

In other cases where the differences are more substantial one cannot suppose that the cause of the variants is some type of unintentional error. For this reason, it has been argued that the apostles employed "testimonies," that is, collections of passages from the Scriptures that had been edited together. A prominent example of this linking of Scriptures is the use of the Psalms in Romans 3:10-18. There are also examples of testimonies in the *DSS*.[26] The testimony hypothesis may account for texts such as Acts 15:16-18, where portions from different passages are fused, and for other instances in which chains of references are present.[27] The fact that the NT writers tended to quote from

---

the Greek Bible: Its Present and Future (London: Hodder & Stoughton, 1908), p. 65; A. Thumb, *Die griechische Sprache im Zeitalter des Hellenismus* (Strassburg: Karl J. Trübner, 1901).

25. For an extended discussion of this variant, see B. Schuchard, *Scripture within Scripture: The Interrelationship of Form and Function in the Explicit Old Testament Citations in the Gospel of John* (Atlanta: Scholars Press, 1992), pp. 1-15.

26. *4QFlor* has 2 Sam. 7:6-16; Ps. 1:1; 2:1-2 together along with commentary, and *IQSb* 5:23-29 alludes to Ps. 61:2 and cites from Isa. 11:1-5 and Mic. 4:13.

27. E. Hatch, *Essays in Biblical Greek: Studies on the Value and Use of the Septuagint, on Origen's Revision of Job, and on the Text of Ecclesiasticus* (Amsterdam: Philo, 1899); H. Vollmer, *Die alttestamentlichen Citate bei Paulus* (Freiburg: Herder, 1896). Contrast K. Stendahl, *The School of Saint Matthew and Its Use of the Old Testament* (Philadelphia: Fortress, 1968); C. H. Dodd, *According to the Scriptures: The Substructure of New Testament Theology* (London: Nisbet & Co., 1952).

certain selected passages of Scripture would also suggest that they might have had certain passages written down for easy reference.[28] Though C. H. Dodd rejected the testimony hypothesis, in a similar vein he argued that the NT writers drew from certain blocks of material as opposed to specific verses. The three main building blocks for Christian theology were: (1) "apocalyptic-eschatological Scriptures"; (2) "Scriptures of the New Israel"; and (3) Scriptures of the Servant of the Lord and the Righteous Sufferer."[29]

Others have sought to uncover the differences among the NT citation and our known sources in some type of alternative Semitic source for the NT text. G. Dalman, C. C. Torrey, and M. Black are among those who have argued that an underlying Aramaic text could explain quotations in the Gospels as well as in Acts.[30] P. Kahle, on the basis of his theory that the origin of the OG lies in Greek targumim that arose in the synagogues, has postulated that quotations in the NT that are unrelated to the LXX derive from these Greek targums.[31] The Achilles heel of any theory that rests on an alternative Semitic source is the fact that we do not have textual evidence that such a beast ever saw the light of day. Furthermore, what might be explained as a *Semitism* in the NT, whether an *Aramaism* or a *Hebraism,* might just as easily be due to the prior influence of the Greek Jewish Scriptures on the style and language of the writer *(Septuagintism).*[32]

Exegetical and Hermeneutical Methods

Though resorting to the existence of an Aramaic gospel(s) to explain NT quotations is an unnecessary hypothesis, it is reasonable to assume, given the

28. See Koch, *Die Schrift als Zeuge des Evangeliums,* pp. 99-101; Stanley, *Citation,* pp. 73-79; Lim, *Holy Scripture,* pp. 150-56, who advocate some form of a collection or anthology of Scriptures. There are parallels in the Qumran literature to Paul's citations of several texts together. See J. Trebolle Barrera, *The Jewish Bible and the Christian Bible,* trans. W. Watson (Leiden: Brill, 1998), pp. 491-92.

29. Dodd, *According to the Scriptures,* pp. 61-108.

30. G. Dalman, *Die Worte Jesu: Mit Berücksichtigung des nachkanonischen jüdischen Schrifttums und der aramäischen Sprache,* vol. 1 (Leipzig: J. C. Hinrichs, 1898); C. C. Torrey, *The Translations Made from the Original Aramaic Gospels* (New York: Macmillan, 1912); M. Black, *An Aramaic Approach to the Gospels* (Oxford: Oxford University Press, 1967).

31. P. Kahle, *The Cairo Geniza* (Oxford: Blackwell, 1959).

32. M. Wilcox, *The Semitisms of Acts* (Oxford: Clarendon, 1965). A thorough discussion of Hebraisms is provided in I. Soisalon-Soininen, "Zurück zur Hebraismenfrage," in *Studien zur Septuaginta — Robert Hanhart zu ehren,* ed. D. Fränkel, U. Quast, and J. Wevers (Göttingen: Vandenhoeck & Ruprecht, 1990).

widespread use of Aramaic in Palestine and the interpretive tradition of the rabbis, that some quotations and/or use of Scripture in the NT reflect influence from Aramaic and Jewish sources.[33] It is only to be expected that the NT writers' use of Scripture would reflect the exegetical practices of their contemporaries. For example, scholars often note the importance of Hillel's seven rules of rabbinic interpretation and discuss the way in which these can be discerned in the use of Scripture in the NT. The seven rules are: (1) an inference drawn from a minor premise to a major premise and vice versa; (2) an inference drawn from analogy of expressions, that is, from similar words and phrases elsewhere; (3) a general principle established on the basis of a teaching contained in one verse; (4) a general principle established on the basis of a teaching contained in two verses; (5) an inference drawn from a general principle in the text to a specific example and vice versa; (6) an inference drawn from an analogous passage elsewhere; and (7) an interpretation of a word or passage from its context.[34] These seven principles provided the basis for midrashic interpretation, but the NT writings evidence a wider use of approaches to the Scriptures than midrash. A more refined understanding of the exegetical use of Scripture in the NT is provided by R. Longenecker, who examines the targums, Mishna, *DSS*, Jewish apocalyptic literature, midrashim, and Philo and on that basis outlines four types of exegesis employed during the period of the Early Church: literal interpretation, midrash, pesher, and allegory.[35] More recently, Koch, who limits his investigation to quotations in seven of the most widely acknowledged (or undisputed) books of the Pauline corpus,[36] divides Paul's use of Scripture into categories nearly identical to those of Longenecker: allegory, typology, midrash, and pesher.[37]

33. For a historical overview of approaches to the question, see E. E. Ellis, *The Old Testament in Early Christianity: Canon and Interpretation in the Light of Modern Research*, WUNT 54 (Tübingen: Mohr, 1991), pp. 54-74.

34. For examples of their application, see C. K. Barrett, "The Interpretation of the Old Testament in the New," in *Cambridge History of the Bible*, ed. C. F. Evans and P. R. Ackroyd (Cambridge: Cambridge University Press, 1970), 1:377-411; E. E. Ellis, "Biblical Interpretation in the New Testament Church," in *Mikra: Text, Translation, Reading and Interpretation of the Hebrew Bible in Ancient Judaism and Early Christianity*, ed. M. J. Mulder and H. Sysling (Philadelphia: Fortress, 1988), pp. 700-702.

35. R. Longenecker, *Biblical Exegesis in the Apostolic Period* (Grand Rapids: Eerdmans, 1975).

36. The seven books of the Pauline corpus that are most widely agreed as stemming from Paul are Romans, 1 & 2 Corinthians, Galatians, 1 Thessalonians, Philippians, and Philemon.

37. Koch also argues that Paul's use of Scripture follows the practices of diaspora Judaism as opposed to those of Alexandrian Judaism or the Qumran community.

While the categories like allegory (see Gal. 4:21-26) or typology (see 1 Cor. 10:4) are more readily grasped, the distinction between midrash and pesher can be confusing, especially when some scholars employ categories like midrashic pesher. The difference between them is that whereas midrashic interpretation sought to explicate the meaning of Scripture through the application of rules, such as Hillel's given above, pesher has a distinctly eschatological focus.[38] Pesher interpretation assumes that the meaning of the Scripture is being fulfilled in the context of the community, which is living in the period of the expected and imminent end of the age. Thus, the type of literature that pervades Christian bookstores throughout North America and interprets the Apocalypse of John and the book of Daniel as providing a blueprint for all the events leading up to Armageddon and the end of the world is utilizing pesher interpretation.

Acts 15:16-18 is an example of pesher interpretation because the author understands the words of Amos to be fulfilled in the situation of the Early Church. The words of the prophet that referred in the OG text to the decay of the Davidic empire and its renewal, which would precipitate the remainder of humanity turning to Israel's God, were seen to be fulfilled in the inclusion of the gentiles within the community of believers. The evidence for this inclusion was Peter's testimony that the Holy Spirit had been poured out on Cornelius and his men (Acts 15:7-11, 14; ch. 10, esp. vv. 44-45). Thus, the element of reapplication is key to the identification of pesher. In the NT, the Jewish Scriptures were seen to be fulfilled in new ways and reapplied to a new context — the Early Church community — because of Jesus.

The use of typology, midrash, or pesher does not exhaust the ways in which the NT writers employed Scripture because the Scriptures were also used to advance the particular message of the writers. At one level, this means that Paul may have employed midrash in his interpretation of a Scripture while he also utilized it to illustrate, establish, or conclude an argument that he was making. At a broader level the use of Scripture and the methods of citation employed served the theological purposes of the writers. It was part of the Jewish tradition of interpretation that the Scriptures were reinterpreted and applied to the new situation of the writers.[39] Such interpretation of the

---

38. Longnecker, *Biblical Exegesis*, p. 25.

39. A well-known example is the reinterpretation of Jeremiah in Daniel 9. See the excellent volume on the reinterpretation of Scripture within the HB and Jewish extrabiblical writings by M. Fishbane, *Biblical Interpretation in Ancient Israel* (Oxford: Clarendon, 1985). See also van der Kooij *(Oracle of Tyre),* who offers a careful comparison of the OG text of Isaiah to the version of Isaiah preserved in the MT and an analysis of how the text was reapplied. For the NT see D. A. Carson and H. G. M. Williamson, eds., *It*

Scriptures by the NT writers assumes both that they were knowledgeable of the Scriptures and that there was a fundamental continuity between the Jewish Scriptures and how they were being reapplied.

The worldview of the first-century Jew generally consisted in the belief that the one God who had created the world and sealed the election of Israel by means of the covenant at Sinai (Exodus 19–23) would act to deliver and redeem the people of Israel from her enemies. This basic belief was expressed in a variety of forms. For example, the inhabitants of Qumran believed themselves to be the true remnant of Israel, the "sons of light," and chose to live in a separate community. The same views, however, were held by those who took up arms against Rome in 66-70 and under Bar-Kochba in 135 in order to reestablish the nation of Israel. Likewise, the writers of the NT express the conviction that the fulfillment of Israel's hope for deliverance has come, but they argue and employ the Scriptures to affirm that the kingdom of God has come in the person and ministry of Jesus (Mark 1:15; Luke 1:20).[40]

The essential continuity with Jewish expectation is proclaimed by the NT writers because what God had accomplished through Christ was **according to the Scriptures**. The constant refrain that provides the interpretive framework of the NT is that the events of Jesus' life, passion, and resurrection are according to the Scriptures (1 Cor. 15:3-4), and this claim is supported by the citation of Scripture. Thus, the Scriptures were broadly interpreted and applied in their context through a Christological lens.[41] Moreover, we cannot forget that each writer brought his own unique perspective and understanding of the Christ event, which influenced the individual's use of the Jewish Scriptures in telling and interpreting the story of Jesus. The Christological reinterpretation and application of the available Scriptures, coupled with the theological purposes of the individual writers, account for a number of the differences that we find between the texts of passages in the NT and the texts of those same passages in our known sources of the Jewish Scriptures.

Is Written: Scripture Citing Scripture (New York: Cambridge University Press, 1988); and R. B. Hays, *Echoes of Scripture in the Letters of Paul* (New Haven: Yale University Press, 1989). Others would deny that Paul or the other NT writers would have introduced changes to Scripture. See W. Kaiser, *The Uses of the Old Testament in the New* (Chicago: Moody, 1985), p. 5.

40. For an extensive discussion of first-century Jewish and Christian worldviews, see N. T. Wright, *The New Testament and the People of God* (Minneapolis: Fortress, 1992), pp. 215-338, 349-464.

41. Longenecker, *Biblical Exegesis*, p. 104; Ellis, "Biblical Interpretation," p. 691.

Summary

1. We compared the citation of Amos 9:11-12 in Acts 15:16-18 to the version of the same text in the OG and the MT. Though the OG is a fairly faithful translation of a *Vorlage* similar to the MT, there are significant differences, and the NT quotation is dependent upon the Greek version.

2. Though the NT quotation is dependent upon the OG, it has differences as well. Various possible explanations for these differences were discussed: textual corruption, alternative sources, quotation from memory, and the author's freedom with respect to the use of the sources.

3. No one single explanation can account for the variety of differences between the NT citation and its sources. The investigation of the use of the sources for a quotation also has to consider the exegetical methods of the NT writers. The application of midrashic and pesher methods of interpretation of the Scriptures was consistent with the Jewish exegetical approaches of the time as evidenced in rabbinic literature and the *DSS*.

4. The Jewish tradition of interpretation inherited by the NT writers was one in which the Scriptures were reinterpreted and applied to the new situation of the writers. The new situation for the NT writers was what the writers proclaimed that God had accomplished through Christ according to the Scriptures. Thus, the Scriptures were broadly interpreted and applied in their context through a Christological lens. The citation in Acts 15:16-18 is an example of this process.

CHAPTER TWO

Identifying a Source as Greek or Hebrew

Our contention is that the LXX has not received the attention that it should in NT studies. However, it is just as unwarranted to make generalizations about the texts of the Greek Jewish Scriptures that Paul or any other NT writer might have used. As we have seen in the previous chapter, the focus of studies on NT quotations of the Scriptures has been their use of sources and exegetical methods. Some investigations have been more general in nature while others have considered more specifically the question of the *Vorlage* for a particular NT book or the Pauline corpus — though one of the weaknesses of some of these studies is that they have not always dealt adequately with the source texts. We can reasonably inquire, "How can one theorize about *how* exegetical procedures and pesher or midrashic exegesis are used in the NT without first discerning *what* texts the author is citing?"

The modest aim of this volume is to contribute to our ability to answer the above question by illuminating the ways in which the Greek writings of the Jewish Scriptures were employed in the NT. The examination of the quotation of Amos 9:11-12 in Acts 15:16-18 in the previous chapter has demonstrated that this is not an easy task. However, an introduction to the pertinent issues and problems will better equip the scholar and student. In this chapter we will look at the fundamental question of determining whether the author is citing the Hebrew or the Greek text.[1] What makes a quotation Septuagintal

1. An important and comprehensive aid to the study of the use of the LXX in the NT has been recently provided in Hans Hübner, *Vetus Testamentum in Novo*, vol. 2: *Corpus Paulinum* (Göttingen: Vandenhoeck & Ruprecht, 1997). In four parallel columns he presents: (1) passages from all thirteen epistles that tradition has ascribed to Paul that may contain a citation from or an allusion to the LXX; (2) passage(s) from the LXX (Göttingen

as opposed to the author's (or his source's) own translation of the Hebrew Scriptures or another version?[2] It is not within the bounds of this study to investigate every possible quotation, but to provide the tools for the reader to evaluate readings. Without arguing the case for each particular citation, it would also be irresponsible to classify which NT quotations are Septuagintal.

H. B. Swete, in his *Introduction to the Old Testament in Greek*, provides a list of quotations from the Old Testament present in the New Testament. Although he does not attempt a detailed discussion of these quotations, he does examine select passages as well as discuss the influence of the Greek versions on quotations from the LXX.[3] In general, Swete deems the LXX to be "the principal source from which the writers of the NT derived their quotations." A somewhat different view is espoused in the United Bible Societies Greek NT, which includes an index of quotations as well as what it refers to as allusions and verbal parallels. According to the index of quotations, there are seventy-three quotations from the Septuagint in the NT out of a total of approximately 350 passages that are quoted.[4] The definition of what actually constitutes a Septuagint quotation in the UBS is found elsewhere. According to the committee that edited the UBS text, "the Septuagint version (LXX) of the OT is cited only in those cases where it differs from the MT and it seems clear that the NT citation follows the LXX and not MT."[5] A quick check of this index indicates that most readers would be baffled if they attempted to use it. For example, on the one hand, the quotation of Amos 9:11-12 in Acts 15:16-17 is not marked as Septuagintal. On the other hand, the quotation in John 1:23, which

---

or Rahlfs) that may have been the source; (3) the corresponding text in MT; and (4) other possible sources and notes. Although Hübner cites the Göttingen edition where available, variant readings are not provided.

2. I am using the term Septuagintal to mean a reading that is dependent upon the OG and that is distinct from any other tradition, particularly, though not exclusively, the reading tradition of the MT. Terminology can become very confusing here because of our lack of knowledge about the transmission history of the Jewish Scriptures and the fact that not everyone uses terms in the same way.

3. H. B. Swete, *An Introduction to the Old Testament in Greek*, rev. R. R. Ottley (Cambridge: Cambridge University Press, 1914), pp. 381-403.

4. B. Aland et al., eds., *The Greek New Testament*, 4th rev. ed. (Stuttgart: United Bible Societies, 1993), pp. 898-900. The lists in the 4th and the 4th revised editions are the same.

5. R. Bratcher, *Old Testament Quotations in the New Testament*, 2nd rev. ed. (New York: United Bible Societies, 1984), p. viii. It is unclear whether this quotation reflects the committee's opinion or Bratcher's. The volume provides English translations of the texts of the quotations as well as allusions and paraphrases and their presumed sources in the LXX and MT that are cited in the index to the third corrected edition of UBS. The relationship of the "paraphrases" of this volume to the "verbal allusions" in the index of UBS[3] is also not clarified.

we discussed briefly in the previous chapter, is marked as Septuagintal despite the fact that there are no known manuscripts that read εὐθύνατε, and that there is nothing else distinctive in the quotation that would lead one to conclude that it depends upon the Greek text! It is obvious that one needs to use such tools carefully and that the question of what constitutes a quotation of the Greek Jewish Scriptures must be addressed more rigorously.[6]

Determining whether a quotation is Septuagintal will require us to become familiar with the study of translation technique (TT). This will be the aim of our next two chapters. The present chapter will focus on the purpose and presuppositions of the study of TT, while the following chapter will offer a model for analyzing TT. Familiarity with the ways in which the Greek scribes translated the Hebrew Scriptures will also inform our understanding of the LXX as the Scriptures of the NT community and help determine whether a quotation reflects a Greek or Hebrew/Aramaic source.

Is the Source Hebrew or Greek?

Although the question of whether the NT writer is citing some form of the Hebrew or a Greek text seems relatively simple and straightforward to answer, it has proved to be elusive for many. In order to illustrate the problem we will compare some texts. We will begin with two examples from the Gospel of Matthew. In each case we will first provide the NT quotation followed by the text of the OG and MT and then note whether any of the texts exhibit significant textual variants. We will then discuss the examples. The same procedure will be followed for two texts from the Pauline corpus.

1. Matt. 9:13; 12:7

    NT   Ἔλεος θέλω καὶ οὐ θυσίαν
                I desire mercy and not sacrifice.

    Hos. 6:6 OG   Ἔλεος θέλω καὶ οὐ θυσίαν
                I desire mercy and not sacrifice.

    Hos. 6:6 MT   חֶסֶד חָפַצְתִּי וְלֹא־זָבַח
                I desire steadfast love and not sacrifice.

There are no variants recorded for the NT and MT, and no significant variants in the OG.

---

6. I was informed at the annual meeting of the *Society of Biblical Literature* in November 2001 that a revised edition of Bratcher is being planned.

2. Matt. 21:13

NT   Ὁ οἶκός μου οἶκος προσευχῆς κληθήσεται
            My house shall be called a house of prayer.

Isa. 56:7 OG   Ὁ γὰρ οἶκός μου οἶκος προσευχῆς κληθήσεται
            For my house shall be called a house of prayer.

Isa. 56:7 MT   כִּי בֵיתִי בֵּית־תְּפִלָּה יִקָּרֵא
            For my house shall be called a house of prayer.

There are no variants recorded for the NT, OG, or MT.

There are those who would regard the OG as the source of the above citations in the NT based on the verbatim agreement between the two.[7] However, we must ask the question, "Does verbatim agreement require that one has borrowed from the other?" To put the question another way, "Is it possible for two or more translators to choose the same words to translate the *Vorlage?*" For example, if an English speaker were to read the French word *maison,* she or he would in most cases translate the word with *house.* Likewise, the Hebrew equivalent would be בַּיִת and the Greek would normally be οἶκος. It is not that we would always use any one of these words as the translation equivalent for the others, but they are the most common equivalents. Introductory language courses actually promote a one-to-one formal correspondence between the vocabulary of languages because students often learn only one translational gloss in their native language for each vocabulary term in the language they are acquiring.

The use of common translation equivalents by translators would seem to be a matter of common sense, but their implications for Septuagintal studies are far too frequently ignored. This principle will be illustrated from Matthew 9:13; 12:7; 21:13.

All three passages in Matthew follow the same basic pattern. In each case the OG and NT follow the word order of the MT. For example, in Matthew 9:13 (12:7) and OG Hosea 6:6 the noun Ἔλεος *mercy* precedes the verb θέλω *I desire,* just as חֶסֶד *steadfast love* precedes חָפַצְתִּי *I desire* in the MT. In all cases the *morphological* aspects of the Hebrew are also represented in the Greek translations. For example, the verb יִקָּרֵא in Isaiah 56:7 is a niphal imperfect, and so both Greek translations employ the future passive κληθήσεται *shall be called.*

---

7. All three examples have been taken from a recent volume by David New (*Old Testament Quotations in the Synoptic Gospels, and the Two-Document Hypothesis,* SCS 37 [Atlanta: Scholars Press, 1993], pp. 50, 52, 114). R. H. Gundry (*The Use of the Old Testament in St. Matthew's Gospel: With Special Reference to the Messianic Hope* [Leiden: Brill, 1967], pp. 149-50) and K. Stendahl (*The School of Saint Matthew and Its Use of the Old Testament* [Philadelphia: Fortress, 1968], p. 135) did not regard these as Septuagintal.

Furthermore, in each of these passages both the OG and NT provide expected translation equivalents for the MT. For example, the noun תְּפִלָּה *prayer* in Isaiah 56:7 occurs 77x in the MT. According to HR, προσευχή is the equivalent for תְּפִלָּה 69x in the LXX; therefore, it is the word that we would expect a Greek translator to employ. The noun זֶבַח *sacrifice* from Hosea 6:6 occurs 174x in the MT, and HR records that it is translated by θυσία 139x. The only agreement between the OG and MT that is even slightly questionable in these passages is the verb θέλω *I desire* for חָפַצְתִּי. There are a number of equivalents in the LXX for the verb חפץ, which is not totally unexpected. Greek has several words that overlap in meaning with θέλω, just as the English terms *desire, wish,* and *want* overlap in their meaning. חפץ is found 78x in the MT, and approximately half of these instances are translated by θέλω.[8] The next most common translation is βούλομαι (23x), followed by εὐδοκέω (4x). The fact that there are a number of equivalents for this verb employed in the LXX helps inform us that there is an increased possibility that two different translators might employ different equivalents when translating Hosea 6:6. However, we have to realize that θέλω is still the most likely choice if two people were translating the passage independently. When we consider that there is nothing unusual about the translations and that in each case the writers of the OG and NT are employing the most likely translation equivalents for the Hebrew, then our common sense should tell us that the agreements in vocabulary are insufficient grounds to claim that the NT quotation is dependent upon the OG. The NT quotations may in fact be dependent upon the OG, but one cannot just assume so.

There are numerous examples of NT quotations that may or may not be based upon the OG/LXX as opposed to the Hebrew. Two quotations from the Pauline letters are illustrative.

1. Gal. 3:6
   NT   Ἀβραὰμ ἐπίστευσεν τῷ θεῷ, καὶ ἐλογίσθη αὐτῷ εἰς δικαιοσύνην
   Abraham believed God and it was reckoned to him as righteousness.
   Gen. 15:6 OG   ἐπίστευσεν Ἀβραὰμ τῷ θεῷ καὶ ἐλογίσθη αὐτῷ εἰς δικαιοσύνην
   Abraham believed God and it was reckoned to him as righteousness.

8. In Ezek. 18:23 HR lists both θέλω and βούλομαι as equivalents for חפץ. The reason for this is that there is a difference between the readings of codices A and B and the concordance records where these mss. differ. HR is invaluable for research in the LXX, but it must be used with caution.

Gen. 15:6 MT וְהֶאֱמִן בַּיהוָה וַיַּחְשְׁבֶהָ לּוֹ צְדָקָה

He believed the Lord and he reckoned it to him as righteousness.

The same quotation is found in Romans 4:3, except in that case Paul has the order ἐπίστευσεν δέ Ἀβραάμ. There are two main differences between the Greek texts and the MT. First, the OG and NT texts substitute the proper name *Abraham* for the MT, which has only a verb in the third person.[9] The NT addition of the name does not necessarily depend upon the OG, however, because in both Romans and Galatians Paul is referring to Abraham as a model of faith for Israel. Second, the simple Hebrew verb וַיַּחְשְׁבֶהָ includes the object suffix. Thus, it is translated as *he reckoned it,* whereas both the NT and OG read *it was reckoned.* It could be argued that the OG transformed the active verb in the MT to a passive and that Paul copied the OG. However, the use of the passive voice in the Greek may also originate from both the OG translator and Paul reading ויחשב *it was reckoned* in an unvocalized Hebrew text. The only difference is the omission of the final ה, which could have occurred in the transmission of the Hebrew texts. Otherwise, the OG and NT follow the word order of MT and render the vocabulary with the expected equivalents.[10]

2. Rom. 13:9b

NT　　　　　Ἀγαπήσεις τὸν πλησίον σου ὡς σεαυτόν.
　　　　　　You shall love your neighbor as yourself.

Lev. 19:18 OG　Ἀγαπήσεις τὸν πλησίον σου ὡς σεαυτόν.
　　　　　　You shall love your neighbor as yourself.

Lev. 19:18 MT　וְאָהַבְתָּ לְרֵעֲךָ כָּמוֹךָ
　　　　　　You shall love your neighbor as yourself.

The same quotation also appears in Galatians 5:14; Matthew 19:19; 22:39; Mark 12:31; and James 2:8. There are variant readings of ἑαυτόν for σεαυτόν in both the LXX and NT manuscripts, though the external evidence argues for the latter. Apart from the textual variant, whose origin and influence are unclear, there is nothing distinctive about the Greek texts that would suggest that one

9. Note that NA does not even italicize Ἀβραάμ in Gal. 3:6 to indicate that it is part of the quotation.

10. C. Stanley (*Paul and the Language of Scripture: Citation Technique in the Pauline Epistles and Contemporary Literature* [Cambridge: Cambridge University Press, 1992], pp. 234-35) and D. A. Koch (*Die Schrift als Zeuge des Evangeliums: Untersuchungen zur Verwendung und zum Verständnis der Schrift bei Paulus* [Tübingen: Mohr, 1986], p. 106) assume that Paul quotes the OG.

is dependent on the other. The frequent appearance of this quotation in the NT, due no doubt to its theme, would also indicate that it was a well-known saying that had probably attained a fixed form prior to the NT writings. The communal use and understanding of Scripture is another intangible when it comes to examining the relationship between NT quotations and our known sources in the LXX, MT, and *DSS*.

The above quotations, then, may all be dependent upon the OG, but **the vocabulary agreements in these particular cases do not prove** this to be the case. We have already provided examples of inadequate conclusions drawn by some researchers regarding what represents a quotation from the LXX, and so it is important to stress that we need to exercise caution in our analysis.[11] There are times when the most we can suggest is a degree of probability that such agreements between the NT and OG/LXX texts are because the NT is dependent upon the OG. For example, in our view, the citation of Genesis 15:6 in Galatians 3:6 is the only citation from those above that exhibits a distinctive agreement with the OG and, therefore, is dependent upon the OG. The soundness of any conclusion is based on a careful comparison of the sources in the context of a thorough examination of all the quotations in a particular corpus (a Gospel, Luke-Acts, Pauline epistles). At the same time, the general agreement of NT quotations with the Greek Jewish Scriptures and the fact that both the NT and LXX are composed in Greek mean that some researchers may be predisposed to argue that agreements between the NT and the LXX occur because the former employed the Greek Jewish Scriptures as its source.[12] Hopefully, the cautious approach to analysis that

---

11. See M. Silva, "Old Testament in Paul," in *Dictionary of Paul and His Letters,* ed. G. F. Hawthorne and R. P. Martin (Downers Grove, Ill.: InterVarsity, 1993), p. 631, who has obviously taken such an approach to the evaluation of Paul's use of sources for his quotations. Silva has a table indicating Paul's use of sources for quotations, and according to his findings only 17 out of 107 quotations in Paul demonstrate a distinctive reading of the LXX. In contrast, 42 are judged to be Paul = LXX = MT, and in 31 Paul equals neither MT nor LXX. The table is a little confusing at some points though, since in the table 1 Cor. 2:16 is placed among quotations that do not agree with either LXX or MT, yet on p. 633 he states regarding 1 Cor. 2:16 that "Paul quotes the LXX of Isaiah 40:13a." The only difference is that different forms of the verb are found in the passages: συμβιβάσει in 1 Cor. 2:16 and συμβιβᾷ in OG Isa. 40:13. The text is based on the OG.

12. T. H. Lim, *Holy Scripture in the Qumran Commentaries and Pauline Letters* (Oxford: Clarendon, 1997), p. 26, states, "What is important to underscore here is that just because a biblical quotation is written in Greek is no reason for supposing that it is necessarily septuagintal." We agree with this statement in principle, as the discussion has shown, but there is also merit to the view that general agreement with the OG indicates substantial dependence unless proven otherwise.

we have advocated will provide the appropriate balance for conclusions in this area.

There are two other variables, however, that are inextricably connected to our decision as to whether the NT writer employed a Greek text or could have arrived at the same translation independently when the NT and OG/LXX show substantial or complete agreement. The first is, Do we believe that the NT writer could have read and translated a Semitic source? For example, it seems clear that Paul, on the basis of his testimony (e.g., Gal. 1:13-17; 2 Cor. 11:22; cf. Acts 23:6) and his use of the Scriptures, would have been comfortable reading either Hebrew or Greek. For the remaining NT writers there is only the internal evidence of the text and our own disposition with regard to the likelihood that the NT writers could have been bilingual or trilingual (Greek, Hebrew, Aramaic). The second is, How likely is it that even Paul would have had access to Greek and Hebrew versions of the Scriptures? Much of the discussion about whether a NT writer cited one text or another does not even consider the assumptions that are being made about access to and/or the use of the source texts. Thus, a reasonable working hypothesis would be that since Paul is the apostle to the Gentiles, he normally would have been working from the Scriptures in Greek.

Translation Technique

In the past quarter century a growing body of literature on the subject of TT has emerged. Our task in this chapter is to introduce the issues as well as the areas of debate among scholars. The discussion will begin by defining the purpose of TT. Then we will examine the studies on TT that have focused on features of literalism in a translation. Following this we will list and explain five presuppositions for TT. These presuppositions are informed by modern linguistics and are essential background for anyone wanting to analyze TT or the relationship between two or more texts. An appreciation for the ways in which the LXX translators rendered the Hebrew Scriptures into the Greek language is also necessary for our exegesis of the NT because of the NT writers' use of the Scriptures. There are instances where the differences between the Hebrew and Greek Scriptures are evident in their theology, and we will explore this phenomenon in a later chapter. In the next chapter we will offer a methodology for the analysis of TT.

Defining the Purpose

The purpose of the study of TT of the LXX is to describe the way in which individual translators engaged in the process of translating a unit of Scripture for a community.[13] There are five aspects of this definition that require comment. First of all, the definition is stated in terms of the translator's approach to the source text as a whole, but it is not meant to exclude employing TT as a description of the way in which the translator treated individual elements in a translation. Second, analysis of TT has to concern itself primarily with individual *units of Scripture* rather than with the entire corpus of the LXX.[14] Since various books and portions of Scripture were translated by different individuals, it only makes sense to treat the units separately. For example, our knowledge of the way in which the translator of Genesis rendered infinitive absolutes is not going to tell us about the way in which the translator of Isaiah approached them. An analysis of Genesis will provide possible renditions, but we have to examine Isaiah in order to know how the translator approached infinitive absolutes in that book. Thus, a *unit of Scripture* may describe more than one book, or a portion of a book in the case where two or more translators worked on separate parts of the same book.[15] Third, the reference to the *community* of the translator recognizes that these translations were not carried out in a sociological and historical vacuum. A translation of the Bible, whether the Greek translation of the Hebrew Scriptures or a modern-day version, is intended to meet the needs of a constituency. Therefore, it is the needs of the intended audience that will determine the kind of translation produced. For example, the later recensions of the LXX tended to be revised toward the developing MT, though Symmachus is a notable exception.[16] It is also to be expected that some

13. See also, T. McLay, *The OG and Th Versions of Daniel*, SCS 43 (Atlanta: Scholars Press, 1996), pp. 14-15.

14. See A. Aejmelaeus, "The Significance of Clause Connectors in the Syntactical and Translation-Technical Study of the Septuagint," in *VI Congress of the IOSCS*, ed. C. Cox, SCS 23 (Atlanta: Scholars Press, 1988), p. 377; A. Pietersma, "Septuagint Research: A Plea for a Return to Basic Issues," *VT* 35 (1985): 298.

15. H. St. J. Thackeray, *The Septuagint and Jewish Worship* (Oxford: Oxford University Press, 1920), pp. 16-39, and "The Bisection of Books in Primitive Septuagint MSS," *JTS* 9 (1907): 88-98; E. Tov, "The Literary History of the Book of Jeremiah in the Light of Its Textual History," in *Empirical Models for Biblical Criticism*, ed. J. H. Tigay (Philadelphia: University of Pennsylvania Press, 1985).

16. For a discussion of the different translation practices of the Greek translators within the context of ancient translation practices, see S. P. Brock, "Aspects of Translation Technique in Antiquity," *Greek, Roman, and Byzantine Studies* 20 (1979): 69-87, and "The Phenomenon of Biblical Translation in Antiquity," *Alta: The University of Birmingham Re-*

of the terminology and expressions employed will reflect the cultural background of the translator and the community in which she/he lives. As we have stated previously, in some cases of the ancient versions, we are dealing with the community's understanding of Scripture in the translation.[17] *Tendenz,* or theologically motivated translation, is the term used to describe those instances in which the historical context of the translator exerted a strong enough influence that the translation reflects a reapplication or new understanding of the text. Fourth, we speak of the attempt to describe *the way in which* the translator engaged in the task. It could be said that the study of TT attempts to expose the translator's discourse analysis of the parent text.[18] Our task is not to do a discourse analysis, but the analysis of TT ought to illuminate how the translator understood the *Vorlage.*[19] Finally, we refer to *individual translators* out of the belief that individuals worked alone on the task of translation. This view seems to be supported by the characteristic features evident throughout individual units. However, a methodology could be usefully employed in the analysis and description of a recension involving more than one editor or with any texts sharing a reciprocal relationship.

It need hardly be stated, but the whole process of analyzing TT must as-

---

view 2 (1969): 96-102. For examples of Sym's style see A. Salvesen, *Symmachus in the Pentateuch,* JSSM 15 (Manchester: Manchester University Press, 1991), pp. 220-54.

17. See M. Goshen-Gottstein, "Theory and Practice of Textual Criticism," *Textus* 3 (1963): 139-62; Salvesen, *Symmachus,* pp. 177-93; J. Weingreen, "Rabbinic-Type Commentary in the LXX Version of Proverbs," in *Sixth World Congress of Jewish Studies,* ed. A. Shinan (Jerusalem: Jerusalem Academic Press, 1977), pp. 407-15; also the more subtle examples of variant reading traditions witnessed to by the vocalization of the MT in E. J. Revell, "LXX and MT: Aspects of Relationship," in *De Septuaginta,* ed. A. Pietersma and C. Cox (Mississauga: Benben, 1984), pp. 41-51. James Barr has also recently restated his argument that some variant readings are the result of translators working from unvocalized texts and without access to the reading tradition. See J. Barr, "Guessing in the Septuagint," in *Studien zur Septuaginta — Robert Hanhart zu ehren* (Göttingen: Vandenhoeck & Ruprecht, 1990), pp. 19-34; cf. J. Barr, "Vocalization and the Analysis of Hebrew among the Ancient Translators," *VTSupp* 16 (1967): 1-11.

18. The translators of the LXX seem to have worked mainly with fairly small units of text (phrase and clause) and did not usually consider larger units. See the excellent discussion in I. Soisalon-Soininen, "Beobachtungen zur Arbeitsweise der Septuaginta-Übersetzer," in *Isac Leo Seeligmann Volume,* ed. A. Rofé and Y. Zakovitch (Jerusalem: Magnes, 1983), pp. 319-29.

19. The volume by A. van der Kooij, *The Oracle of Tyre,* VTSupp 71 (Leiden: Brill, 1998), is an excellent example of understanding the Greek translation in its own context. Aejmelaeus ("Significance of Clause Connectors," p. 362) speaks in a similar vein when she writes that the analysis of translation technique is an attempt "to see the translator behind it [the translation] and to appreciate his work." See also J. Barr, "The Typology of Literalism in Ancient Biblical Translations," *MSU* 15 (1979): 288.

sume that a direct relationship exists between the receptor text being analyzed and the source text to which it is being compared. The investigation of the TT of the ancient versions is complicated by the corruption of both the source and receptor texts in the course of transmission. However, in most units of the LXX and in other ancient versions the correspondence between the source and receptor texts is so close that we are justified in assuming that a relationship does in fact exist,[20] though there is no assumption that the *Vorlagen* for the OG and the MT are the same. As we have already mentioned, they are quite different in some books of the Jewish Scriptures. At the very least, the relationship between the LXX and MT provides the basis for the initial comparison. It is on this basis that we are able to use the LXX for textual criticism of the MT and to help reconstruct the complicated textual history of the Hebrew Bible.

The Focus on Literalism

The purpose of this section is to examine those studies that have focused on literalism as the means to describe TT.[21] In order to make the criticisms more intelligible there is an introductory section on defining a literal approach, followed by a section that explains the criteria for literalism.

Defining a Literal Approach

Scholars generally use the term literal to refer to a translation that mechanically reproduces each and every element of the source text while following the same word order and employing lexical equivalents consistently (stereotyping). Clarity to the definition of the term is given by G. Marquis, who defines a perfectly literal translation as one in which "it would be possible to retranslate from the Greek the original Hebrew [and Aramaic, presumably] words of the source."[22] In the traditional sense used in this discussion, then,

---

20. R. Hanhart, "Zum gegenwärtigen Stand der Septuagintaforschung," in *De Septuaginta*, ed. A. Pietersma and C. Cox (Mississauga: Benben, 1984), pp. 8-9.

21. Similar criticisms of literalism are expressed by Aejmelaeus and Soisalon-Soininen. See A. Aejmelaeus, "Septuagintal Translation Techniques — A Solution to the Problem of the Tabernacle Account," in *Septuagint, Scrolls and Cognate Writings*, ed. G. J. Brooke and B. Lindars, *SCS* 33 (Atlanta: Scholars Press, 1992); I. Soisalon-Soininen, "Zurück zur Hebraismenfrage," in *Studien zur Septuaginta — Robert Hanhart zu ehren*, ed. D. Fränkel, U. Quast, and J. Wevers (Göttingen: Vandenhoeck & Ruprecht, 1990).

22. G. Marquis, "Consistency of Lexical Equivalents as a Criterion for the Evalua-

"literal" is an adjective that describes a translation exhibiting *formal equivalence* to the source text from which it was translated. According to Eugene Nida, a translation that exhibits formal equivalence "is basically source-oriented; that is, it is designed to reveal as much as possible of the form and content of the original message."[23] This sense of a literal translation is to be distinguished from a translation that has successfully transferred the meaning and intention of the source text into the target language.[24] This latter type of translation is commonly described as one which exhibits *dynamic* or *functional*[25] *equivalence*. Nida describes a *dynamic equivalent* translation as one in which

> the focus of attention is directed not so much toward the source message, as toward the receptor response. A dynamic-equivalence (or D-E) translation may be described as one concerning which a bilingual and bicultural person can justifiably say, "That is just the way we would say it." It is important to realize, however, that a D-E translation . . . is a translation, and as such must clearly reflect the meaning and intent of the source.[26]

As Nida emphasizes, even if a translator uses the method of dynamic equivalence in his/her translation, the translation is intended to render the *meaning* of the parent text. The translator is just not as concerned with having a one-to-one, word-for-word relation between the *Vorlage* and the target language. At the same time, since the primary concern of a dynamic or functional translation is to render the meaning of the source text, it may have many of the characteristics of formal equivalence. The fact that formal and functional equivalence can overlap is one of the difficulties inherent in TT studies,

---

tion of Translation Technique," in *VI Congress of the IOSCS,* ed. C. Cox, SCS 23 (Atlanta: Scholars Press, 1988), p. 407; a similar meaning is assumed by E. Tov and B. G. Wright, "Computer-Assisted Study of the Criteria for Assessing the Literalness of Translation Units in the LXX," *Textus* 12 (1985): 149-87; and again by B. G. Wright, *No Small Difference: Sirach's Relationship to Its Hebrew Parent Text,* SCS 26 (Atlanta: Scholars Press, 1989), p. 29.

23. E. Nida, *Toward a Science of Translating* (Leiden: Brill, 1964), p. 165. In the words of Brock ("Aspects," p. 73), a literal translation "acts, as it were, as Aristotle's unmoved mover, and the psychological effect is to bring the reader to the original."

24. B. G. Wright also makes this distinction ("The Quantitative Representation of Elements: Evaluating 'Literalism' in the LXX," in *VI Congress of the IOSCS,* ed. C. Cox, SCS 23 (Atlanta: Scholars Press, 1988), p. 312.

25. Nida has changed his terminology from dynamic to functional.

26. Nida, *Toward a Science,* p. 166. Nida's discussion of formal vs. dynamic equivalence (pp. 22-26, 166-76) is set within the context of the approach to contemporary translation work.

which often treat these categories as mutually exclusive. As James Barr has already pointed out, the study of TT "has to concern itself much of the time with variations within a basically literal approach."[27] Likewise, a generally literal translation will often exhibit idiomatic renderings.[28]

A good example of the difference between formal and functional equivalence is provided by the opening adverbial phrase in Daniel 1:1:

TH = ἐν ἔτει τρίτῳ τῆς βασιλείας Ἰωακεὶμ βασιλέως Ἰούδα
in the third year of the reign of Joakim, king of Juda

OG = ἐπὶ βασιλέως τῆς Ἰουδαῖος Ἰωακεὶμ ἔτους τρίτου
during the third year of King Joakim, of Judea

MT = בִּשְׁנַת שָׁלוֹשׁ לְמַלְכוּת יְהוֹיָקִים מֶלֶךְ־יְהוּדָה
in the third year of the reign of Jehoiakim, king of Judah

TH adheres to the word order of the Hebrew exactly and, with one exception, renders every morphological element as well. The one morphological change occurs with the translation of לְמַלְכוּת *reign*. This word consists of three morphemes:[29] לְ is an inseparable preposition (bound morpheme) that specifies the particular third year, that is, of Jehoiakim's reign. מלכות is the stem (free morpheme) meaning kingdom/reign. Finally, מלכות is also in the construct state with the attributive genitive יְהוֹיָקִים, and the relation in this instance is marked by a zero morpheme. In this example, the לְ and the construct both serve to specify the particular reign being mentioned; so, the Greek genitive is sufficient to signal the same relationship. It would have been unnatural Greek to have added another element because of the word order. In contrast to TH, the OG rearranges the word order of the Hebrew, and this enables the translator to omit βασιλείας = מלכות as redundant. However, despite the fairly substantial differences between the two translations, both render the meaning of the *Vorlage*.[30]

---

27. Barr, "Typology," p. 281.

28. It is for this reason that Soisalon-Soininen prefers to distinguish between "slavish" (literal) renditions and "idiomatic" (free) ones. See Soisalon-Soininen, "Hebraismenfrage," pp. 37-38.

29. A morpheme may be defined as the minimal unit of grammatical meaning. Thus, a morpheme may be a word, but it may also be the letter "s," which is often added to words in English to mark the plural. A zero morpheme would refer to an instance where a grammatical meaning is evident without the presence of a morpheme to mark the meaning.

30. The above example is quite typical of what is encountered when comparing the translations of OG and TH in Daniel. TH uses a method of formal equivalence but makes

Both approaches to translation, functional and formal equivalence, are concerned with rendering the meaning and intent of the source text; they just set about the task differently. However, since the analysis of TT on the basis of literalism focuses on those aspects of the translation that mirror the formal aspects of the source text, a literal translation is frequently viewed more positively and assumed to be more faithful to the source text than is a free translation. Functionally equivalent translations are viewed more suspiciously than literal ones because freedom in translation is frequently, but incorrectly, associated with the notion that the translator took liberties with the source text. Once again, our common sense should tell us that although it is easier to compare a literal translation than a free one to its presumed source, facility of comparison has no logical connection with the intentions of the translator and fidelity to the *Vorlage*. A translator employing formal equivalence could just as easily omit or add elements to the text or misunderstand and mistranslate the source text as could one employing dynamic equivalence.

One suspects that the prejudice against free translations is rooted in some biblical scholars' unconscious, fundamentalist-type view of Scripture, a view that associates a formal approach to translation with a concern to preserve every jot and tittle of the HB. Certainly, there was a developing tendency towards preserving the biblical text within Judaism and Christianity, and it is possible that such practices existed prior to the first century of the common era.[31] However, employing a formal approach is a far cry from the intent to produce a translation from which one can reproduce the *Vorlage*. It is also anachronistic to attribute less honorable intentions or a lack of reverence for the text to the translator who attempted to produce functional equivalence. Most modern scholars would be offended if they were accused of having no respect for the Scriptures just because they did not use the Authorized Version.

It must be admitted, however, that the analysis of what is meant by a literal or free translation takes literalism as the more natural starting point because the majority of the LXX books are "more or less" literal.[32] The basically

---

minor adjustments in the translation in order not to commit grievous grammatical errors. OG writes more in keeping with Greek idiom. However, our example is atypical in the sense that OG does not depart from the style of the *Vorlage* nearly so often as it could. Although we prefer the use of the designations formal vs. dynamic/functional equivalence in this discussion, we will continue to use literal vs. free for stylistic variation.

31. See the articles by S. Brock in the bibliography.

32. E. Tov, *The Text-Critical Use of the Septuagint in Biblical Research* (Jerusalem: Simor, 1981), p. 53; I. Soisalon-Soininen, "Methodologische Fragen der Erforschung der Septuaginta-Syntax," in *VI Congress of the IOSCS*, ed. C. Cox, *SCS* 23 (Atlanta: Scholars Press, 1988), p. 428.

literal approach of the translators means that we can see that many books in the LXX follow their *Vorlagen* so closely that they can be loosely characterized as Hebrew written in Greek characters. Therefore, studies focusing on formal equivalence are helpful if for no other reason than the fact that they reveal the degree to which the different translators followed their *Vorlagen*. With the advent of computers and the Computer Assisted Tools for Septuagint Studies (CATSS)[33] database the process of examining the features of literalism has been greatly simplified, and the degree of literalness/formal equivalence in specific features of the individual translations can even be expressed statistically.[34]

The Criteria for Literalism

The focus on measuring literalism has been influenced mainly by James Barr and Emanuel Tov. In separate works, first Barr and then Tov proposed criteria for literalism that were very similar in content.[35] Here we will refer more often to Tov for the sake of convenience. Tov proposes five criteria for literalness in a translation: consistent representation of terms in translation ("stereotyping"); segmentation and representation of the constituent elements of the Hebrew words; word order; quantitative representation; and availability and adequacy of lexical choices.[36] All of the aforementioned criteria, save the last, are capable of being measured relative to how consistently they formally reproduce the elements in the source text, and thus determine the literalness of a translation.[37] The translation of vocabulary, what Tov refers to as the availability and adequacy of lexical equivalents, is the most difficult area to research for the analysis of TT and is usually not treated in any depth; but this volume will pay special attention to the subject.[38] The primary tool that

33. See E. Tov, "The CATSS Project: A Progress Report," in *VII Congress of the IOSCS*, ed. C. Cox, *SCS* 31 (Atlanta: Scholars Press, 1991); G. Marquis, "CATSS-Base: Computer Assisted Tools for Septuagint and Bible Study for All — Transcript of a Demonstration," in *VII Congress of the IOSCS*, ed. C. Cox, *SCS* 31 (Atlanta: Scholars Press, 1991).

34. See Wright, *No Small Difference*, pp. 19-118, for a classification of books in the LXX according to four criteria for literalism.

35. Tov, *Text-Critical Use*; Barr, "Typology." S. Olofsson has written *The LXX Version: A Guide to the Translation Technique of the Septuagint, ConBib.OT* 30 (Stockholm: Almqvist & Wiksell, 1990), but it basically presents the approach of Barr and Tov with updated bibliography.

36. Tov, *Text-Critical Use*, pp. 54-60.

37. Wright, *No Small Difference*, pp. 27, 30-31.

38. The exception is the article by Marquis ("Consistency"), though the attempt to predict textual variants based on the number of times that a translator departs from an SE is not linguistically defensible.

facilitates the analysis of the formal features of the LXX is the CATSS database. Indeed, the focus on formal criteria for analyzing TT was greatly influenced in the work of B. G. Wright and G. Marquis by the actual format of the CATSS database, because the parallel alignment file presupposes a formal relationship between the LXX and MT.[39] In order to understand the criteria for literalism and the criticisms that will be made of the methodology it is useful to provide a brief overview of the way in which these criteria are generally defined.

Stereotyping Stereotyping[40] describes the tendency of translators to use consistently the same Greek term to render a term in the HB,[41] though there is some disagreement regarding the degree to which the Greek term must be employed as an equivalent in order to qualify as a "stereotyped" equivalent (SE). R. Sollamo suggests that if a term is used to render the same word in 50 percent of its occurrences in a book, then it should be considered a SE.[42] Wright chooses 75 percent, which seems more reasonable,[43] though statistics are not always a reliable means of determining the importance of the translators' choices of particular constructions. The fact that one word is employed in three of four places for the same Hebrew term should be regarded differently than a word that is used 30 times out of 40.

There is no doubt that translators often chose to translate a word in the *Vorlage* with the same Greek word. C. Rabin suggests that a stimulus-response reaction took place as the translators would tend to render words or phrases with the words they used first.[44] Tov has also argued that the later

39. Such an alignment is understandable and useful for comparing the texts, but it leads, as we later argue, to an inappropriate methodology for the study of TT.

40. The term was first coined by M. Flaschar, "Exegetische Studien zum Septuagintapsalter," *ZAW* 32 (1912): 105. Other terminology employed has been "verbal linkage" by Rabin and "systematic representation" by Rife. See C. Rabin, "The Translation Process and the Character of the Septuagint," *Textus* 6 (1968): 1-26; J. M. Rife, "The Mechanics of Translation Greek," *JBL* 52 (1933): 244-52.

41. Tov, *Text-Critical Use*, p. 54.

42. R. Sollamo, *Renderings of Hebrew Semiprepositions in the Septuagint*, AASF, DHL 19 (Helsinki: Suomalainen Tiedeakatemia, 1979), p. 13.

43. Wright, "Quantitative Representation," p. 105. Since Wright attempts to reconstruct the Hebrew from the Greek, he also starts from the Greek usage rather than the Hebrew (p. 92).

44. Rabin, "Translation Process," p. 7. We find less compelling his suggestion that the translators had a primitive word list that they used as a lexicon (p. 21), though it was accepted by Marquis ("Consistency," p. 409) and Wright ("Quantitative Representation," pp. 92, 279, n. 80). The belief that the translators worked from some kind of word list is rooted in Elias Bickerman's suggestion that the translators may have borrowed the tech-

translators consulted the Pentateuch as an aid to their work.[45] An additional consideration about stereotyped equivalents noted by S. Olofsson is that it is more significant when a SE is "doubly consistent,"[46] that is, when a Greek term is used consistently for only one Semitic word and the Semitic word is rendered by only the one Greek term. Olofsson also stresses the role of semantics in translators' choices.[47]

Segmentation and Quantitative Representation The difference between segmentation and quantitative representation is not clearly defined either by Tov or Barr. Tov explains "the representation of the constituents of Hebrew words by individual Greek equivalents" (segmentation) as the translators' tendency "to segment Hebrew words into meaningful elements, which were then represented by their individual Greek equivalents."[48] Yet, on the very next page, he defines quantitative representation with the words "literal translators did their utmost to represent each individual element in MT by one equivalent element in the translation."[49] Since Tov entertains only a brief discussion of his criteria, it is difficult to know the means by which he would differentiate between the two. Barr, who actually employs the term segmentation, defines it as the division of the Hebrew text into elements or segments. For example, the Hebrew morpheme ה marks something as definite, and thus the word הַמֶּלֶךְ *the king* consists of two elements. In practice, Barr uses quantitative addition to refer to the addition of elements by the translator for the

---

niques of the Aramaic dragomen (E. J. Bickerman, "The Septuagint as a Translation," in *Proceedings of the American Academy of Jewish Research* 28 [1959]: 1-39). Van der Kooij (*Oracle of Tyre,* pp. 112-23) has recently examined this issue and has argued that the translators of the biblical books are better understood as learned scribes rather than as ancient dragomans as advocated by Rabin and Bickerman.

45. E. Tov, "The Impact of the LXX Translation of the Pentateuch on the Translation of the Other Books," in *Mélanges Dominique Barthélemy,* ed. P. Casetti, O. Keel, and A. Schenker (Göttingen: Vandenhoeck & Ruprecht, 1981). See also P. Walters, *The Text of the Septuagint, Its Corruptions and Their Emendations* (Cambridge: Cambridge University Press, 1973), pp. 150ff.; O. Munnich, "Étude lexicographique du psautier des Septante," Ph.D. dissertation, Université de Paris-Sorbonne, 1982; S. Olofsson, "The Kaige Group and the Septuagint Book of Psalms," in *IX Congress of the IOSCS,* ed. B. Taylor, *SCS* 45 (Atlanta: Scholars Press, 1997). However, see the cautious assessment by P. Gentry, *The Asterisked Materials in the Greek Job,* SCS 39 (Atlanta: Scholars Press, 1995), pp. 281-370.

46. See Olofsson, *LXX Version,* pp. 18-19; Barr, "Typology," p. 311.

47. S. Olofsson ("Consistency as a Translation Technique," *SJOT* 6 [1992]) points out various difficulties in analyzing stereotyping as a criterion for consistency.

48. Tov, *Text-Critical Use,* p. 57.

49. Tov, *Text-Critical Use,* p. 58.

purpose of clarity (e.g., making the subject explicit) or exegetical comment, though we could say that the same elements that are added to or subtracted from the Hebrew are the ones that are segmented.[50]

Wright notes the ambiguities in the work of Barr and Tov,[51] and so he restricts the usage of the term segmentation to "the translator's technique of dividing Hebrew *words* into their constituent parts in order to represent each part in the Greek translation."[52] Quantitative representation, however, "concerns the one-to-one representation (or lack of it) of multi-word Hebrew *phrases, clauses* and *sentences*."[53] On this basis Wright is able to analyze a target text at both the word and multi-word level for how well it formally reproduces its source.[54]

Word Order Adherence to word order[55] can reveal the extent to which the translators followed their *Vorlagen* because there are certain aspects of Hebrew word order that are fixed. For example, adjectives and demonstrative pronouns follow substantives, and genitives follow their constructs.[56] Since Greek allows for great freedom in word order, it could reconstruct Semitic syntax quite easily, though this would not necessarily yield typical Greek usage. As Wright points out, "Variations in Greek from these [types of constructions that have a fixed word order in Hebrew] must be stylistic in nature," though that in itself does not remove the necessity of examining the differences to see if there are other factors involved as well.[57]

One grammatical feature of Greek that would always introduce a change in the word order of Hebrew (or Aramaic) is the use of postpositive conjunctions. In fact, it is generally agreed that this accounts for the relatively infrequent appearance of postpositives in the LXX.[58] On the surface, the eval-

---

50. Barr's discussion of quantitative addition and subtraction dwells mainly on Targummic material ("Typology," pp. 303-5). However, the kind of interpretive comment we find in the Targums is not characteristic of the LXX. The only example he gives of omissions is the Greek text of Job (p. 304).

51. Wright, "Quantitative Representation," p. 314.

52. Wright, *No Small Difference*, pp. 55-56.

53. Wright, *No Small Difference*, p. 56.

54. For his discussion and statistics see *No Small Difference*, pp. 55-91.

55. G. Marquis, "Word Order as a Criterion for the Evaluation of Translation Technique in the LXX and the Evaluation of Word-Order Variants as Exemplified in LXX-Ezekiel," *Textus* 13 (1986): 59-84; Wright, *No Small Difference*, pp. 35-54.

56. See Rife, "Mechanics."

57. Wright, *No Small Difference*, pp. 37-38.

58. Aejmelaeus, "Significance of Clause Connectors," pp. 364-69; R. Martin (*Syntactical Evidences of Semitic Sources in Greek Documents*, SCS 3 [Missoula, Mont.: Scholars

uation of word order would appear to be the easiest of the criteria of formal equivalence for which to determine statistics.

Reservations concerning the Focus on Literalism

Although there is much to be gained from the investigation of the features of literalism in the LXX, serious questions can be raised about the adequacy of the methodology as a means to analyze TT.[59] Part of the problem is that the focus on literalism is concerned with *the description of the literalness of a particular book in comparison to other books,* rather than with a method to describe TT. However, if for no other reason than the fact that there is a considerable volume of secondary literature devoted to using the focus on literalism as a means to investigate TT, it demands that we address some of the shortcomings of the approach.[60] In the following, rather than selecting specific instances where the presentation of material or statistics dealing with literalism has been inaccurate or misleading,[61] we will concentrate on the methodology as a whole. The criticisms will be balanced by the presentation of the proposed methodology in the next chapter.

The Assumption of Literal Intentions

The basic difficulty of the literal approach has been the assumption that the translator **intended** to produce a literal translation.[62] This assumption is clear in the following comment by Wright:

Press, 1974]) uses the frequency of δὲ as one of his criteria to distinguish translation Greek from original composition.

59. So also A. van der Kooij, "The Old Greek of Isaiah in Relation to the Qumran Texts of Isaiah: Some General Comments," in *Septuagint, Scrolls and Cognate Writings,* ed. G. J. Brooke and B. Lindars, *SCS* 33 (Atlanta: Scholars Press, 1992), pp. 202-5.

60. For example, Olofsson *(LXX Version)* presents the criteria for literalism as the means to evaluate TT.

61. Specific criticisms of the use of some of the statistics as well as other concerns that overlap to some degree with our own have been expressed elsewhere by Ilmari Soisalon-Soininen and his former student, Anneli Aejmelaeus (see n. 21). See Soisalon-Soininen, "Methodologische Fragen," pp. 425-44; Soisalon-Soininen, "Hebraismenfrage," pp. 46-51; Aejmelaeus, "Significance of Clause Connectors," pp. 361-80; and A. Aejmelaeus, "Translation Technique and the Intention of the Translator," in *VII Congress of the IOSCS,* ed. C. Cox, *SCS* 31 (Atlanta: Scholars Press, 1991), pp. 23-36. See also Olofsson, "Consistency," pp. 14-30; A. Lübbe, "Describing the Translation Process of 11QtgJob: A Question of Method," *RevQ* 52 (1988): 583-93.

62. See also Aejmelaeus, "Translation Technique."

... a translation could be described as "literal" if the translator has attempted to reproduce in a rigid way in Greek the actual form of the various elements of the parent text.[63]

The problem with this view is that the fact that a translation reproduces a great deal of the formal features of the source text does not mean that the translator *intended* that the reader could retranslate back from the Greek to the Hebrew. Translators' reverence for the text is evident in their desire to follow the word order and represent the various elements of the words in the source text, but they were able to do this while faithfully attempting to translate the *meaning* of the text as they understood it.[64] Thus, there was an overlap between formal and functional equivalence. As we have already stated, it was only at a later period, partly due to the debates over the use of Scripture between Christians and Jews and partly due to the belief of the inspiration of Scripture, that literalism became more of a conscious methodology.[65] For example, even though TH exhibits a high degree of formal equivalence to the parent text for many books of the LXX, it does not leave the impression that it was intended to provide a one-to-one equivalence between the translation and the parent text.[66]

There are also instances in which the translators seemed to exercise a

---

63. Wright, *No Small Difference*, pp. 29, 32, 36.

64. H. M. Orlinsky, "The Septuagint as Holy Writ and the Philosophy of the Translators," *HUCA* 46 (1975): 89-114. That the translators regarded the LXX as authoritative and therefore were concerned with accuracy is discussed in J. Wevers, "A Study in the Narrative Portions of the Greek Exodus," in *Scripta Signa Vocis: Studies about Scripts, Scriptures, Scribes and Languages in the Near East*, ed. H. L. J. Vanstiphout (Groningen: E. Forsten, 1986), pp. 295-303. The tension that existed for the individual translators between using formal expressions (i.e., those faithful to the language of their literary source) and using more dynamic expressions (i.e., those faithful to their own language) is evident in the use of Hebraisms. See Soisalon-Soininen's discussion of what constitutes a Hebraism and the importance of determining Hebraizing tendencies in the analysis of TT ("Hebraismenfrage," pp. 39-43).

65. Barr, "Typology," p. 324. E. Tov also notes that "Jer-R's revision is remote from the slavish literalness of *kaige*-Th and Aquila" (*The Septuagint Translation of Jeremiah and Baruch* [Missoula, Mont.: Scholars Press, 1976], p. 167). Aejmelaeus ("Translation Technique") emphasizes that the translators "had no conscious method or philosophy of translation." For the developing trend toward literalism, see S. P. Brock, "The Phenomenon of the Septuagint," *OTS* 17 (1972): 20-27, and "To Revise or Not to Revise: Attitudes to Jewish Biblical Translation," in *Septuagint, Scrolls and Cognate Writings*, ed. G. J. Brooke and B. Lindars, *SCS* 33 (Atlanta: Scholars Press, 1992), pp. 301-38.

66. This is obvious in the book of Daniel, for example. See my *OG and Th Versions of Daniel*.

great deal of freedom with respect to their sources by adding and omitting elements or employing theological renderings, so that the resulting translation is significantly different from the *Vorlage*. One always needs to be careful with such judgments because differences between the translation and the presumed source text may stem from an alternative *Vorlage*, but Isaiah and Proverbs offer examples of translations that exhibit a tendency to depart from the source.[67]

If the translators did not strive for literalism, why are the translations generally literal? Barr, referring to the fact that the LXX frequently follows the Semitic word order, suggested that it was "probably to be attributed to habit and the quest for an easy technique rather than to any literalist policy."[68] I. Soisalon-Soininen and A. Aejmelaeus, whose views are somewhat opposed to the literalist approach, have emphasized that the translators generally worked instinctively by choosing in an *ad hoc* manner the rendering that they believed suited the context best.[69] We would agree with this point of view, with one qualification drawn from Barr's perspective. The individual translators, in varying degrees, also tended to repeat grammatical constructions and had a tendency toward stereotyping because it was easier.

Since the translators of the LXX were generally not intentionally striving for literal translations, we must question the validity of using this gauge to measure how well they achieved the standard. The following criticisms will place the preceding comments in perspective.

The Focus on Literalism Fails to Account for Dynamic Features of Translation

Since all of the books of the LXX are more or less literal, there is more to be learned about the individual translators from those instances in which the

67. For Isaiah, see I. L. Seeligmann, *The LXX Version of Isaiah* (Leiden: Brill, 1948), and van der Kooij, *Oracle of Tyre*, pp. 48-161. Johann Cook has taken issue with the recent tendency to emphasize the fidelity of the translators of the LXX to their *Vorlagen,* and he employs Proverbs as an example of a different approach. See J. Cook, *The Septuagint of Proverbs — Jewish and/or Hellenistic Proverbs (Concerning the Hellenistic Colouring of LXX Proverbs),* VTSupp 69 (Leiden: Brill, 1997); "The Hexaplaric Text, Double Translations and Other Textual Phenomena," *JNSL* 22 (1996): 129-40; "Aspects of the Translation Technique Followed by the Translator of Proverbs," *JNSL* 22 (1996): 143-53; and "Aspects of the Relationship between the Septuagint Versions of Proverbs and Job," in *IX Congress of the IOSCS,* ed. B. Taylor, *SCS* 45 (Atlanta: Scholars Press, 1997).

68. Barr, "Typology," p. 26.

69. Soisalon-Soininen, "Hebraismenfrage," p. 36; Bickerman, "Septuagint," pp. 30-39.

translation departs from the technique of formal equivalence. Why did a particular translator forsake a formal correspondence in favor of a more idiomatic Greek expression only with certain constructions or only in some of the instances of a given construction? In linguistic terminology, why is it that the translator departed from his normal or "unmarked" usage to employ a different or "marked" rendering? The answers to these kinds of questions are crucial to understanding the way in which the translator went about his work. At the very least, we realize that focusing on features of formal equivalence neglects significant features of translation.

A very different kind of analysis and description of TT emerges if we turn the focus on literal features upon its head. In other words, if it is the features of dynamic equivalence that reveal the most important tendencies of the translator, then we can state the axiom: **it is the type and frequency of nonliteral renderings in the translation units that provide the most distinguishing characteristics of TT.**[70] A relatively minor lexical example is provided in OG Daniel 3:12, in which A. McCrystall has argued that τῷ εἰδώλῳ *the idol* is used instead of τοῖς θεοῖς *the gods* because of the translator's desire to identify the statue, which the three friends of Daniel are to worship, as an effigy of Nebuchadnezzar.[71] However, the rendering of אלוה (אלוהים) by εἴδωλον is not without precedent in the LXX.[72] Furthermore, εἴδωλον is employed in four other passages by OG Daniel to designate idols in contrast to the one true God of Israel and renders אלוה (אלוהים) in every case.[73] In 3:12 and 3:18 OG employs εἴδωλον when the three refer to Nebuchadnezzar's "idol," whereas in 3:14 OG has θεοῖς when the king commands them to serve his "gods." OG's translation preserves a nice distinction between the two parties and their conception of what the statue represents. The king views the statue as a god, while the three refer to it as an idol. If OG's translation were intended to carry the significance discerned by McCrystall, then we might also expect OG to use the first person pronoun in 3:14 when the king asks, "Why do you not worship the [**my?**] image which I set up?"

---

70. Aejmelaeus, "Significance of Clause Connectors," p. 362. Aejmelaeus states, "Free renderings are like fingerprints that the translators have left behind them."

71. A. McCrystall, "Studies in the Old Greek Translation of Daniel" (Ph.D. diss., Oxford University, 1980), pp. 5-6. He also notes (following Delcor) the addition of the personal pronoun σου after εἰκόνι as further evidence that the OG changes the meaning of the MT. See M. Delcor, "Un cas de traduction 'Targumique' de la LXX à propos de la statue en or de Dan. III," *Textus* 7 (1969): 30-35.

72. Num. 25:2 (twice); 3 Reigns 11:2, 7, 33; Isa. 37:19.

73. Dan. 3:18; 5:4, 23. Dan. 6:28(27), where MT = 0, is the exception. εἰδωλείῳ *idol's temple* (1-5 in LXX) is also used in 1:2.

The Focus on Literalism Cannot Account for the Detailed Aspects of Translation

It is not just the type and frequency of dynamic translations that illuminate the TT of the individual translators. In a similar fashion, we have to consider favorite renditions and syntactical constructions employed by the translator in his work. For example, one translator may employ a formally equivalent expression to render a particular syntactical construction in the *Vorlage,* but it may be different from the way any other translator reproduced the same expression.[74] However, the global statistics for literalism in a translation will provide only a general indication of what the translator might have done in any specific instance.

The ability to isolate the individual traits of the translator within his overall approach to translating presupposes a thorough analysis of both the source and target texts. In most cases where we examine the idiosyncratic traits that characterize a translator we are dealing with a small percentage of the actual renderings for a given expression. Therefore, by grouping the various ways in which a construction has been translated we can examine the differences in usage. Then we can both attempt to explain the deviations that might stem from the TT of the translator and discern the characteristics that differentiate the individual translators.[75] Indeed, it may be that there is no apparent reason for the change(s) other than stylistic variation, but often there is. Thus, to expand upon the previously stated axiom, we must say that it is **the idiosyncrasies of the individual translators that provide the most distinguishing features of TT.**

A good example of the subtle distinctions made by translators is given by J. W. Wevers in a recent article. He notes that the phrase "sons of Israel" occurs 53 times in Exodus in the nominative, dative, and accusative, and it has the article in every case. However, in 12 of 35 cases in the genitive (τῶν υἱῶν Ἰσραήλ) the article is omitted. The difference in the twelve cases is that

---

74. See Soisalon-Soininen, "Methodologische Fragen," pp. 431-32, where he criticizes Tov and Wright's use of consistency as the means to indicate literalness. Wright (*No Small Difference,* pp. 31-32) has responded by stating that it is the "mechanicalness or woodenness of representation combined with the consistency of that mechanical approach [which is] a major exponent of literalness." However, Wright does not really deal with the heart of Soisalon-Soininen's criticism, that is, the inadequacy of the purely formal approach when comparing the OG to MT.

75. See Soisalon-Soininen, "Methodologische Fragen," pp. 435-43, which expands on the introduction to his volume, *Die Infinitive in der Septuaginta* (Helsinki: Suomalainen Tiedeakatemia, 1965), pp. 5-16. This type of methodology is evident in the work of Aejmelaeus and Sollamo.

the phrase is used in the context to modify "assembly" (i.e. συναγωγὴ υἱῶν Ἰσραήλ).[76]

If we were concerned only with measuring literalness according to a strict set of criteria, then we might fail to take sufficient note of the reason why the translator of Exodus omitted the article for the construct-genitive in 12 cases and that the translator of Daniel rendered אלוה (אלוהים) with εἴδωλον. To borrow from a well-known expression, the focus on literalism for the analysis of TT can be like counting the fir and pine trees in order to describe the forest in which they grow. Obviously, there is more to a forest than these particular trees.

The Inadequacy of Literalism's Statistics for Textual Criticism

The primary reason for the research of the LXX and the attempt to reconstruct the OG of each book has been text-critical. We have also noted that the understanding of the TT in the individual book/unit is essential for the critic to attempt to reconstruct the *Vorlage* of the OG. Since the statistics produced by those focusing on formal correspondence measure literalism, by definition these statistics are chiefly concerned with quantifying the degree to which the translation faithfully reproduces the *Vorlage*. Now, it may be helpful to know as a general rule that one translator used formal equivalents more often than another, but the use of the LXX for textual research primarily concerns those instances where it does not literally reproduce its *Vorlage*.[77]

Part of the problem with the formal approach is that it does not really account for the complexity of languages and the act of communicating. This may be due, as we have stated above, to the conscious or unconscious presupposition that the translators intended to produce a translation whereby one could easily retrovert back into the source language. Language is a means of communication, which "consists of words (or other units) which are organized, according to 'the rules of grammar,' into particular types of combinations."[78] The symbols (words) of a language that a speaker uses in a given situation depend both on the type of situation (we would not employ the same vocabulary writing to our auto mechanic as we would to a politician) and on the particular speech event, including among other factors the whole discourse, the paragraph, the clause, and the preceding and following words, that

76. J. Wevers, "The Göttingen Pentateuch: Some Post-Partem Reflections," in *VII Congress of the IOSCS*, ed. C. Cox, SCS 31 (Atlanta: Scholars Press, 1991), p. 56.

77. For the present purpose we put aside the fact that in some cases (e.g., Jeremiah and Job) the OG witnesses to a much shorter *Vorlage*.

78. Nida, *Toward a Science*, p. 30.

is, the context.[79] So, in a discourse our choice of words is limited by the subject about which we are speaking/writing. However, there are still an infinite number of ways in which we can combine these remaining words to communicate our message. The choice of a particular word or construction by a particular writer in a particular context is the result of a complex series of competing choices in that particular speech event, which in turn is influenced by prior experiences (i.e., habit and the easiest technique for a translator) of the speaker/writer. Thus, the very fact that the Greek translators were engaged in translating meant that they were constrained by their linguistic context. Formal equivalence describes the results of those translators who allowed or chose to allow their lexical and grammatical choices to be constrained more narrowly by the source text. At the same time, attention to the particular social and linguistic context may also alert the analyst of TT to instances where the translator has employed language that reflects the circumstances of the translator. For example, R. Glenn Wooden has argued that the translator of OG Daniel employed the terms σοφιστής (1:20), φιλολόγων (1:20), and γραμματική (1:17) in chapter one in order to emphasize that the Jews and the texts that they studied produced better scholars than the Alexandrian academics (φιλόλογοι) who immersed themselves in the study of Greek culture and literature.[80] In the book of Daniel in the MT the contrast is between their skills of divining.

Five Presuppositions for Translation Technique

If the criteria for literalism are not fully adequate as a means to analyze TT, then by what means should this analysis be accomplished? We will begin to answer that question in this section by setting forth five presuppositions for the analysis of TT. The first four derive from the study of linguistics proper, while the last is specific to TT. There is some overlap in the discussion of these five presuppositions because they are interdependent.

TT Is Descriptive

By descriptive we mean that the analysis of TT is concerned with *describing* the way in which a translator rendered the source text into the receptor language

---

79. Nida, *Toward a Science,* pp. 37-43; M. Silva, *Biblical Words and Their Meaning* (Grand Rapids: Zondervan, 1983), pp. 137-48.

80. See the forthcoming article by R. Glenn Wooden, "Recontextualization in OG Daniel 1," in *Of Scribes and Sages: Studies in Early Jewish Interpretation and Transmission of Scripture,* ed. C. A. Evans (Sheffield: Sheffield Academic Press).

as opposed to *evaluating* the grammatical correctness of the translation.[81] The difficulties that beset the translators in their task are well stated by Aejmelaeus:

> With the source language and the target language differing as greatly from one another, particularly with regard to their syntactical structures, as Hebrew and Greek, a Semitic and an Indo-European language, the translators must have often faced a conflict between two requirements, the requirement of rendering the contents of the Scriptures in intelligible and fluent Greek and the requirement of following the original as closely as possible. Some of the translators more than others have yielded to the former by use of various free renderings, whereas literal and even Hebraistic renderings are the result of the latter. The study of the translation techniques aims at describing the translators exactly from this point of view and finding criteria by which to measure their freedom or literalness.[82]

Unless a grammatical anomaly resulted from the translator's misunderstanding of the *Vorlage* (due to textual difficulty, error, or ignorance), it does not matter that it exists in the target text because the objective of TT is to describe what the translator has done.

TT Is Primarily Synchronic

"Synchronic linguistics investigates the way people speak in a given speech community at a given point of time,"[83] as opposed to diachronic linguistics, which focuses on the change of language through time.[84] The primary impli-

---

81. Linguists describe how language is used as opposed to *prescribing* how it ought to be used. For example, in North America one frequently hears statements like, "He did good." Traditional grammars teach that the adjective "good" is incorrect in this position, and that the adverb "well" would be proper English. Another example would be the so-called split infinitive. See H. A. Gleason, *An Introduction to Descriptive Linguistics*, rev. ed. (London: Holt, Rinehart and Winston, 1961), pp. 195-209; J. Lyons, *Language and Linguistics* (Cambridge: Cambridge University Press, 1981), pp. 46-54.

82. A. Aejmelaeus, "What Can We Know About the Hebrew *Vorlage* of the Septuagint?" *ZAW* 99 (1981): 63; Soisalon-Soininen ("Methodologische Fragen," p. 426) notes, ". . . der Character der Übersetzung wird von zwei ganz verschiedenen Faktoren bestimmt: erstens vom Stil des hebräischen Urtextes, der in den verschiedenen Büchern des ATs sehr unterschiedlich ist, zweitens von der unterschiedlichen Arbeitsweise der Übersetzer."

83. J. Lyons, ed., *New Horizons in Linguistics* (Middlesex: Penguin, 1970), p. 14. Descriptive and synchronic are often used interchangeably, but for our purposes it is useful to distinguish between them.

84. The distinction between the two approaches and the primacy of the synchronic

cation of this principle for TT is that TT is a description of a particular written communication given at a particular time. The orthography, morphology, lexical choices, and the syntax of the translation will reflect the conventions of the language in the time and place in which it was produced. At the semantic level, the meaning of the translation for its intended audience is determined by the context, both the linguistic context and the socio-historical context, as far as it can reasonably be reconstructed.[85]

There are two consequences of a synchronic description when it comes to the evaluation of the meaning of the translation. From the perspective of the reader of the target language there is no difference in meaning (though she/he may at times be confused), because this reader has no direct access to the source text from which the translation was made.[86] In our case, the Greek Jewish Scriptures were eventually read and understood by Greek-speaking Jews and Christians without reference to the Hebrew Scriptures.[87] However,

---

approach traces itself to the father of modern linguistics, Ferdinand de Saussure. See F. de Saussure, *Cours de linguistique générale*, ed. C. Bally and A. Sechehaye, 5th ed. (Paris: Payot, 1955), pp. 79-81. There is an English translation by Wade Baskin, *Course in General Linguistics* (New York: McGraw-Hill, 1966). See also S. Ullmann, *The Principles of Semantics* (Glasgow: Jackson, Son & Co., 1951), pp. 50-62; Lyons, *Language and Linguistics*, pp. 54-58.

85. Context is everything when it comes to determining meaning. Understanding the meaning of a given communication involves far more than determining linguistic reference, however. Referential meaning (e.g., the identity of the little horn in Daniel 7) and emotive meaning (e.g., the reaction to so-called "four letter words") require understanding the historical context. See Ullmann, *Principles of Semantics*, pp. 60-82; Nida, *Toward a Science*, pp. 37-43, 57-144; the detailed treatments by A. Lehrer, *Semantic Fields and Lexical Structures* (London: North-Holland, 1974); J. Lyons, *Semantics*, 2 vols. (Cambridge: Cambridge University Press, 1977). In biblical studies the work of Barr is a classic. See J. Barr, *The Semantics of Biblical Language* (Oxford: Clarendon, 1961); Silva, *Biblical Words*, pp. 137-69; E. Nida and J. P. Louw, *Lexical Semantics of the Greek New Testament* (Atlanta: Scholars Press, 1992).

86. H. M. Szpek, *Translation Technique in the Peshitta to Job*, SBLDS 137 (Atlanta: Scholars Press, 1992), pp. 59-60. Most discussions of the meaning of the LXX have taken problems of lexicography as their point of departure. See T. Muraoka, ed., *Melbourne Symposium on Septuagint Lexicography*, SCS 28 (Atlanta: Scholars Press, 1990); T. Muraoka, "Hebrew Hapax Legomena and Septuagint Lexicography," in *VII Congress of the IOSCS*, ed. C. Cox, SCS 31 (Atlanta: Scholars Press, 1991), pp. 205-22; J. A. L. Lee, *A Lexical Study of the Septuagint Version of the Pentateuch*, SCS 14 (Chico, Calif.: Scholars Press, 1983). Tov has been the main proponent of the view that the Hebrew meaning of words sometimes has to be considered in Septuagint lexicography. See E. Tov, "Three Dimensions of LXX Words," *RB* 83 (1976): 529-44. What the original writer may have intended is at times different from what a Greek reader would understand.

87. The literary critical comparison of Daniel 2–7 in the MT and LXX by T. J. Meadowcroft (*Aramaic Daniel and Greek Daniel: A Literary Comparison* [Sheffield: Shef-

the perspective of the translator and the evaluator of the translation is different from that of the translator and the intended/presumed reader because both the translator and the evaluator have access to the source text.

The possibility that a variant reading stems from an alternative *Vorlage* must always be considered, but there are instances where questions about the text from which a particular translation equivalent was derived are unwarranted. Besides the types of corruptions that can enter the text during its transmission and the various ways that the translators could have misread the text they translated, many renderings, which at first appear to be inexplicable, can be explained when we consider the synchronic and diachronic nature of language. A synchronic view of language ensures that we are aware that some puzzling translation equivalents are present in the translation, because the translators encountered words or concepts for which there was no adequate translation equivalent in the target language.[88] In such cases the translators could attempt to restate or paraphrase the meaning of the source text or resort to one of three options: loan translation, shifts in application, or transliteration.

Loan Translation, Shifts in Application, or Transliteration

The process of loan translation is one way of introducing a change in a language because it often involves creating new words *(neologisms)*.[89] Loan translations are words that are created by combining the translation equivalents of individual components of a word from the source language together in the target language to create a new word. For example, the compound word ἀρχιευνοῦχος *chief eunuch* in Daniel most likely originated from the combination of the usual equivalents for שַׂר (ἄρχων) and סָרִיס (εὐνοῦχος) in the Hebrew.[90] The two words appear together in construct as a designation of

---

field Academic Press, 1995]) offers a good example of the fruitfulness of examining the meaning of the Greek text in its own right, though his decision to use Rahlfs' edition as representative of the OG text is hardly defensible.

88. Cultural differences are particularly fertile ground for these kinds of differences because "a particular language will reflect in its vocabulary the culture of the society for which it is the medium of expression." See J. Lyons, *Structural Semantics* (1963), pp. 40-41; E. Nida, *Exploring Semantic Structures* (Munich: Fink, 1975), pp. 66-78, 121-24.

89. For a discussion of the phenomenon, see Silva, *Biblical Words,* p. 87. For examples, see H. St. J. Thackeray, *A Grammar of the Old Testament in Greek,* vol. 1 (Cambridge: Cambridge University Press, 1909), pp. 34-36; E. Tov, "Compound Words in the LXX Representing Two or More Hebrew Words," *Bib* 58 (1977): 189-212; Lee, *Lexical Study,* pp. 113-18.

90. The rendering of שַׂר with ἄρχων is the most frequent in the HB. Outside of Daniel the equivalent is used over 240 times. Εὐνοῦχος as a translation equivalent is employed strictly for סָרִיס.

an official in Nebuchadnezzar's court in Daniel, and the translator coined the word ἀρχιευνοῦχος as a translation equivalent. The word ἀρχιευνοῦχος does not appear in earlier Greek literature. Since Greek is a highly inflected language, it lent itself to the creation of neologisms by combining affixes, such as prepositions with lexemes or two lexemes together, in order to provide a lexeme for the word in the *Vorlage*.[91] Loan translations should not present any difficulty for the evaluation of variant readings, but a "shift in application" may be more challenging. By a "shift in application" we mean that the translator used a familiar word in an innovative way and, thereby, added a new sense to the lexeme.[92] Such "shifts in application" occur mainly through metonymy or metaphor and may result in polysemy. An example of a shift in application would be the Greek lexeme διαθήκη, which came to mean *covenant,* because it was a SE for בְּרִית. The difficulty for the textual critic is deciding whether the translator has merely extended the meaning of a word as a translation equivalent for a term in the *Vorlage,*[93] or whether that word is employed because the *Vorlage* of the translation was different. Finally, the translators sometimes chose to transliterate, particularly in the case of technical terms or proper names.[94]

The diachronic nature of language also has bearing on the analysis of TT and has corresponding implications for textual criticism because the temporal distance of the translator from the environment in which the source text was produced may have been a cause of confusion or misunderstanding. Lexical items in a language are continually being added and deleted, or their semantic range is changing. Therefore, a translator who knows the source language very well at a given point in time may not have access to the mean-

---

91. This practice is related to "etymological" renderings, i.e., translating a word on the basis of an understanding of its etymology or root meaning.

92. See Ullmann, *Principles of Semantics,* pp. 114-25; Silva, *Biblical Words,* pp. 82-85, 92-94. For examples, see the extensive list in Thackeray, *Grammar,* pp. 39-55; also those noted by Tov for the translation of causatives in E. Tov, "The Representation of the Causative Aspects of the *Hiph'il* in the LXX: A Study in Translation Technique," *Bib* 63 (1982): 417-24.

93. Silva ("Semantic Change and Semitic Influence in the Greek Bible: With a Study of the Semantic Field of Mind," University of Manchester, 1972, pp. 103-34) notes that metaphor is by far the most common cause of semantic change in his study of the vocabulary of the NT. He also warns that since these changes involve slight extensions of meaning, it is always possible that the semantic development was already present within the native language. This is just as true for the LXX as the NT.

94. Thackeray, *Grammar;* E. Tov, "Transliterations of Hebrew Words in the Greek Versions of the Old Testament," *Textus* 8 (1973): 78-92; E. Tov, "Loan-Words, Homophony, and Transliterations in the Septuagint," *Bib* 60 (1979): 216-36.

ing of a word that has been dropped from usage or changed in meaning.[95] The obstacles presented by vocabulary are particularly acute when it comes to translating *hapax legomena* (HL)[96] or vocabulary that occurs only rarely. There were three main ways that the translators of the LXX resolved the difficulties presented by unknown lexemes.

Transliteration, Omission, Conjecture

At times they merely transliterated an unknown word into Greek characters[97] or did not translate the word. For example, OG Daniel leaves גוא untranslated all 10x that it appears in Daniel.[98] On other occasions they attempted to determine the meaning by some means of contextual guess such as exegetical and etymological renderings or contextual "changes."[99]

Exegetical renderings refer to the attempts of the translators to render a difficult term on the basis of their exegesis of the context. For example, in Genesis 1:2 the very difficult Hebrew expression ובהו תהו is rendered in the Greek by ἀόρατος καὶ ἀκατασκεύαστος *invisible and unformed*. The Hebrew expression occurs elsewhere in Jeremiah 4:23, but the meaning is uncertain. Understanding the intent of the translator in this particular case is not all that transparent either, but the rendering itself reflects the translator's exegesis of the context.[100]

Etymological renditions refer to cases where the translators guessed at the meaning of the word on the basis of its etymology.[101] For example, OG

---

95. See the article by J. Joosten, who discusses cases where the translators misunderstood the Hebrew due to semantic change and Aramaic influence ("On the LXX Translators' Knowledge of Hebrew," in *X Congress of the IOSCS*, ed. B. Taylor, SCS 51 [Atlanta: Scholars Press, 2001], pp. 165-79).

96. A *hapax legomenon* is a word that only occurs once in a text or literary unit.

97. Tov, "Transliterations."

98. See OG Dan. 3:6, 11, 15, 21, 23, 91(24), 92(25), 93(26); 4:7(10). See also E. Tov, "Did the Septuagint Translators Always Understand Their Hebrew Text?" in *De Septuaginta*, ed. A. Pietersma and C. Cox (Mississauga: Benben, 1984), pp. 53-70.

99. For a discussion see Tov, "Did the Septuagint Translators?"; Barr, "Guessing." Tov also mentions that in some cases the translators would employ a generic reading that seemed to fit from the context, rather than attempt a more elaborate translation using the methods discussed here.

100. For a full discussion of this verse see J. Dines, "Imagining Creation: The Septuagint Translation of Genesis 1:2," *The Heythrop Journal* 36 (1995): 439-50.

101. Tov distinguishes two types of etymological renditions ("Did the Septuagint Translators?" pp. 67-69). The other type of etymological rendering involves instances in which the translators recognized the root of the word in their *Vorlage* and employed a Greek equivalent from a word group that rendered the Semitic root elsewhere. Of course,

Daniel uses κληροδοσία *distribution by lot* to translate בחלקלקות *flatteries* in 11:21, 34 and בחלקות in 11:32. The reason for this is that the translator identified חלק as the root, but חלק *flatter* has a homonym חלק *portion*. κληροδοσία appears in only three other passages in the LXX (Ps. 77(78):55; Eccles. 7:12(11); 1 Macc. 10:89), and never for חלק *portion*, which is usually rendered by μερίζω *divide*, μερίς *portion*. In Daniel 11:21, 34 (32?) the translator incorrectly guessed that בחלקלקות was derived from חלק *share* and chose to translate with κληροδοσία.[102] The volume by X. Jacques is a very useful aid for identifying etymological roots because it groups Greeks words that are related by their etymology.[103]

Finally, the last type of contextual guess refers to times in which the translators seem to have read the consonantal text differently in order to produce their translation. That is, their reading is based on an adjustment of one or more letters in the consonantal text. For example, in Daniel 8:25 the MT has the difficult reading, ובאפס יד *without hand*, which OG renders with καὶ ποιήσει συναγωγὴν χειρὸς *and [then] he will make/cause a gathering by [his] hand*. However we construe the Greek, the reading seems to be derived from the translator's reading of באפס as a hiphil perfect of אסף (והאסיף *he will cause a gathering*).[104] The argument that the translator has reread the consonantal text is based on the fact that the addition of the auxiliary verb ποιέω was one way a translator could render causatives[105] and συνάγω frequently renders אסף. In effect, the translator read a ה for ב, transposed the letters פס, and read the changed letters as a hiphil perfect with ו consecutive. The motivation for this change was that the translator did not know the meaning of the *hapax legomenon* באפס. Now, it may be that a variant had already arisen in the text before the translator, but given the evidence it is more likely that the translator adjusted the text so that he could make sense out of it.[106]

---

not all of those instances constitute a guess because sometimes the translation conformed to Greek usage. The examples given below illustrate both ways that the translators employed etymology in their translations. See also Tov, *Text-Critical Use*, pp. 241-50.

102. Other instances where a cognate of κληροδοσία translates a cognate of חלק are Josh. 12:7; Ps. 15(16):5; Hos. 5:7; Isa. 53:12.

103. X. Jacques, *List of Septuagint Words Sharing Common Elements* (Rome: Biblical Institute, 1972).

104. A similar reading of the verb occurs in TH, but towards a very different interpretation. See R. Hanhart, "The Translation of the Septuagint in Light of Earlier Tradition and Subsequent Influences," in *Septuagint, Scrolls and Cognate Writings*, ed. G. J. Brooke and B. Lindars, SCS 33 (Atlanta: Scholars Press, 1992), esp. p. 364.

105. See Tov, "Representation of the Causative Aspects," pp. 422-23.

106. Tov, "Did the Septuagint Translators?" pp. 61-64.

Langue and Parole

Another distinction made by Saussure was that between *langue* and *parole* (there are no generally accepted translation equivalents in English). *Langue* refers to language as an abstract system, which is common to all speakers of a language community, while *parole* refers to the actual discourse of individuals within the community.[107] Both of these aspects of language play an important role in the study of TT. In the act of translation the original translator has to read the source text (which as a written document is an example of *parole*) and attempt to decode the meaning of that text on the basis of his/her knowledge of the grammar of the source language *(langue)*. The translator then has to encode the message of the source text in the receptor language *(parole)* on the basis of his/her knowledge of the grammar of that language *(langue)*. These are minimum requirements for what the translator does, though we cannot be absolutely sure how the neurological process takes place.[108]

TT analyzes language as it is employed in the receptor text, so it is an investigation of the *parole* of that particular unit of translation. The basis for the comparison is the source text, but TT is an analysis of the way in which the translator chose to render the source text in the target language. Another word to refer to the choices made by an author in speech or writing is *style*.[109] Even though the content of the translation is highly influenced by the source text, the translator still chooses particular words (sometimes based on phonology), syntax, and rhetorical devices in the creation of the translation.

While TT is a description of the *parole* in a particular translation unit, it is important to recognize that the translator's interpretation of the source text is based on his/her understanding of the *langue* of the source language as it is applied to that particular text. It is for this reason that we can say that the study of TT will expose the translator's discourse analysis of the parent text.[110] Another way of describing the process of translation and the perspective of the one engaged in the study of TT is to visualize it as we have below.

107. Lyons, *Semantics*, 1:239.

108. N. Chomsky (*Rules and Representations* [Oxford: Basil Blackwell, 1980], pp. 3-87, 185-216) has argued that the faculty for language is genetically encoded in the brain; but, even if this is true, we do not know how the process takes place. Lyons provides a useful overview in *Language and Linguistics*, pp. 248-57.

109. See S. Ullmann, *Language and Style* (Oxford: Basil Blackwell, 1964), pp. 101-242. For an excellent volume on style and discourse as it relates to biblical studies, see E. Nida et al., *Style and Discourse: With Special Reference to the Text of the Greek New Testament* (Cape Town: Bible Society, 1983). A full discourse analysis of the translation is beyond the parameters of TT because of its concern to compare the translation with its *Vorlage*.

110. Whether the translator renders words or phrases more or less in isolation from

Perspective of TT

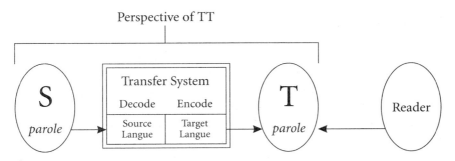

The S stands for the source text while the T stands for the target text or translation. The Transfer System is the translator. There are other factors that enter into the process of decoding the meaning of the source text, such as the translator's knowledge of vocabulary and cultural differences, but the present focus is the interplay of *langue* and *parole* for the translator who acts as the medium of transferring the source text into the target language. The diagram also makes clear that the analyst of TT stands above the source and target texts, able to view both simultaneously, and, therefore, is in a position to describe the means by which the translator (Transfer System) went about the task of translating the source text into the target language. Ideally, the analyst of TT would be omniscient regarding the language, time, and place in which both texts were produced and would have both texts in their original form. Unfortunately, that does not happen in contemporary translation work, let alone when someone analyzes the TT of an ancient biblical text.

It is obvious from the discussion thus far that we are far from the ideal position to do an analysis of the TT of a book in the LXX. However, despite the deficiencies in our knowledge regarding the production and copying of both the MT and LXX, the task is not impossible. We can never attain absolute certainty in our results, but we can achieve a high degree of probability.

TT Is an Analysis of Structure

The emphasis on *structuralism* in linguistics once again originates with Saussure. The thesis of structuralism is that every language has a unique rela-

---

the larger context or attempts to bear in mind the larger context as she/he treats the smaller units, she/he is grappling with the structure of the discourse. Furthermore, the fact that a translator makes a more or less word-for-word formally equivalent translation does not necessarily entail that she/he did not consider the larger context, though they did tend to work with smaller units. See Soisalon-Soininen, "Beobachtungen," p 431.

tional structure, and that the elements we identify when we analyze a particular sentence (sounds, words, meanings, etc.) derive both their essence and their existence from their relationships with other units in the same language system. "We cannot first identify the units and then, at a subsequent stage of the analysis, inquire about what combinatorial or other relations hold between them: we simultaneously identify both the units and their interrelations."[111] "The theoretically important point is that the structure of the language-system depends at every level upon the complementary principles of selection and combination."[112]

The selection and combination of different units also affect the semantic information of the message.[113] This is most obvious at the paradigmatic level. For example, the words *the big dog* do not convey the same meaning as *the brown dog* where color, and not size, is the point of emphasis even though the two phrases could be applied to the same particular canine. The role of syntagmatic relations in determining meaning can be illustrated by contrasting *the big man* (the combination *big man* may suggest either the man is fat or he is the person in charge) with *the big brother* (here the combination of *big* with *brother* suggests that the person is older or may function as some type of guardian). The word *big* is used in both instances, but it is the context that will determine what the use of *big* is intended to mean in either of these particular combinations of words. A more extensive discussion of the structural relations among the senses of words is given in the following chapter.

The connection between the structure of the language system and semantic information conveyed is critical for the analysis of TT because the structure of two different languages will inevitably reveal differences. In the process of translating the translator is immediately confronted with the clash between structure and meaning. That is, if the translator attempts to render the source text using the same surface structures in the target language *(formal equivalence)*, then there is liable to be some loss of meaning. Loss of meaning occurs because the surface structures of the target language do not convey meaning in the same way as do the surface structures of the source language. Conversely, the decision to render the meaning of the *Vorlage* will often require the choice of different surface structures in the target language

---

111. Lyons, *Semantics*, 1:231-32.

112. Lyons, *Semantics*, 1:241; Silva, *Biblical Words*, pp. 108-12. The same principles apply to the morphological and syntactical structure. Syntax will be discussed below. For an example of this approach applied to the morphology of the Hebrew verb, see Gleason, *Introduction*, 67-73.

113. Lyons, *Semantics*, 1:241-42; Nida, *Toward a Science*, pp. 99-101. For a good discussion of the theory of semantic fields, see Lehrer, *Semantic Fields*, pp. 15-43.

(dynamic equivalence).[114] In the LXX the translators were able to reproduce the formal structure of their Semitic *Vorlage* largely because of the freedom allowed in Greek word order. However, as the previous criticisms of the literal approach to the analysis of TT revealed, in the midst of the basically formal approach there is relevance in the variations that we do find. At this point it is best to offer some examples to illustrate the differences between the linguistic structure of Hebrew and Greek, and how they relate to TT.

One area in which significant differences in the structures of two languages will appear is syntax,[115] and one subject to study within syntax is the way in which clauses are connected to one another through the use of conjunctions. Conjunctions do not have referential meaning but function on the syntactic level to indicate the logical relationship between two or more clauses. For this reason they are referred to as functional or grammatical morphemes.[116] Since clause connectors indicate the relationship between clauses, their translation in any given instance depends on the connection between the clauses in which they appear. For example, ו in Hebrew may be translated among other things as *and, but,* and *that is* (epexegetical use), or it may serve to mark a change in the discourse. The καί in Greek serves similar functions. In theory, a translation would express in the appropriate style and syntax of the target language the logical relationship of the two clauses in the source language. The process of reproducing these logical relationships from one language into another presents certain challenges because no two languages use conjunctions in the same way. To continue the example of ו and καί, the extensive use of ו in Hebrew means that discourse is chiefly paratactic in style, whereas Greek tends to prefer elaborate subordinate clauses and par-

---

114. Nida, *Toward a Science,* pp. 159-76. For the most part we have to be concerned only with the surface (as opposed to deep) structure of grammar because the LXX translators reproduced so much of the formal structure of their source. However, occasions where the translators made additions to the text to make an element explicit that was only implicit in the source text or made transformations (e.g., changed an active verb to a passive) do reflect their understanding of deep structure. For explanations of deep structure (transformational) grammar, see J. Lyons, *Chomsky* (London: Fontana, 1970); A. Radford, *Transformational Syntax: A Student's Guide to Extended Standard Theory* (Cambridge: Cambridge University Press, 1981).

115. Syntactical criteria for the analysis of TT have been the focus of Soisalon-Soininen, Aejmelaeus, and Sollamo in their investigations of the Septuagint. Besides the works previously mentioned see the bibliography. A handy compendium of I. Soisalon-Soininen's work has been published as I. Soisalon-Soininen, *Studien zur Septuaginta-Syntax, AASF,* B, 237 (Helsinki: Suomalainen Tiedeakatemia, 1987).

116. G. Yule, *The Study of Language* (Cambridge: Cambridge University Press, 1985), p. 61; Ullmann, *Principles of Semantics,* p. 59.

ticipial constructions. However, despite the options available for the Greek translator the LXX more often than not renders the ‭ with καί, while δέ appears relatively seldom. In original Greek the situation is reversed.[117] As Aejmelaeus has so cogently argued, the significance of the translation of ‭ for TT is not so much the use of καί (since that was the formal equivalent), but the type and frequency of alternative renditions.[118] Different patterns of usage may also indicate different translators of scriptural units or later recensionists.[119] Depending on the consistency of TT, a particular usage may be valuable for textual criticism as well.

Other ways that syntactical differences between languages affect TT have to do primarily with the way in which the translator fills the required positions of the source language in the target text. Here we are talking about paradigmatic and syntagmatic relations on the syntactic level. For example, the clause *he barks* consists of a noun phrase (subject) *he* and a verb phrase (predicate) *barks*. We could replace the noun phrase with any number of different options such as *Lassie, The ferocious dog,* or *The ferocious one.* We could also expand the noun phrase by adding some kind of qualifier, such as the dog *on the porch,* or the dog *who is on the porch,* and so forth. It will be noticed that it is possible to add slots in various positions on the syntagmatic level, but that only certain classes of structures can fill particular positions. *Ferocious* and *on the porch* cannot fill one another's slots, while *on the porch* and *who is on the porch* are interchangeable but are composed of different structures.

The point of all this discussion for TT is that different languages, such as Hebrew and Greek, not only arrange their slots differently; they also can fill

117. This was noted to be the case in the OG and TH versions of Daniel by A. P. Wikgren, "A Comparative Study of the Theodotionic and Septuagint Translations of Daniel" (Ph.D. diss., University of Chicago, 1932), pp. 18, 25; see also R. Martin, "Some Syntactical Criteria of Translation Greek," *VT* 10 (1960): 295-310. Aejmelaeus ("Significance of Clause Connectors," pp. 368-71) finds that γάρ and οὖν are also comparatively infrequent in the LXX.

118. Aejmelaeus, "Significance of Clause Connectors," pp. 369-70. See particularly her criticism of McGregor, who described the statistical differences in how ‭ is rendered in the Pentateuch as meaningless.

119. This type of comparison is the basis of several investigations, such as those by Thackeray, Tov, and McGregor. See Thackeray, "Bisection" and "Renderings of the Infinitive Absolute in the LXX," *JTS* 9 (1908): 597-601; D. Barthélemy, "Les devanciers d'Aquila: première publication intégrale du texte des fragments du Dodécaprophéton," *VTSupp* 10 (Leiden: Brill, 1963); J. D. Shenkel, *Chronology and Recensional Development in the Greek Text of Kings,* HSM 1 (Cambridge, Mass.: Harvard University Press, 1968); Tov, "Three Dimensons"; W. Bodine, *The Greek Text of Judges,* HSM 23 (Chico, Calif.: Scholars Press, 1980); L. Greenspoon, *Textual Studies in the Book of Joshua,* HSM 28 (Chico, Calif.: Scholars Press, 1983); and L. J. McGregor, *The Greek Text of Ezekiel: An Examination of Its Homogeneity* (Atlanta: Scholars Press, 1985).

them differently.[120] When transferring a message from one language to another the translator first has to decode the syntactic structure of the source text and then has to choose appropriate structures in the target language to encode the translation.[121] A translator following a model of formal correspondence attempts to fill each slot in the target text with the same structure, and in the same order, as the source text. However, there are often other options available for the translator to employ. For example, in Daniel 1:5 the MT reads: מִפַּת־בַּג הַמֶּלֶךְ *from the table of the king*. OG substitutes an adjective in the attributive position for the definite noun in the genitive and translates with ἀπὸ τῆς βασιλικῆς τραπέζης *from the royal table*. The Greek language allowed the translator to choose a structure that can fill a different slot in order to convey the same meaning. Compare TH who translates formally with ἀπὸ τῆς τραπέζης βασιλέως *from the table of the king*.

Structural divergences and the ability to choose alternative renderings can result in various types of changes in the formal structure of the target text when compared to the source text. The example in the previous paragraph illustrated a change in word order as well as in word class (morphology). The addition or omission of articles, prepositions, conjunctions, and pronouns in a translation is also common due to differing linguistic structures.[122] What is required in one language is redundant in another.[123] The number of changes will be affected by the degree to which the translator attempts to adhere to the formal structure of the source text. Some of these changes may at times reflect a formal rendering of a text that was slightly different from MT, but extreme care and judicious arguments must guide any argument about a specific text.[124]

---

120. S. E. Porter, *Idioms of the Greek New Testament* (Sheffield: JSOT Press, 1992), pp. 286-97. For an examination of word order in biblical Hebrew see T. Muraoka, *Emphatic Words and Structures in Biblical Hebrew* (Jerusalem: Magnes, 1985), pp. 1-46; E. J. Revell, "The Conditioning of Word Order in Verbless Clauses in Biblical Hebrew," *JSS* 34 (1989): 1-24.

121. This is the emphasis of J. Heller's investigation ("Grenzen sprachlicher Entsprechung der LXX," *MIO* 5 [1969]: 234-48) in which he states, "Man muß also gleich . . . die Frage stellen, inwieweit die Abweichungen des LXX von ihrer Vorlage durch die sprachlichen Möchlichkeiten des Griechischen bedingt wurden."

122. See the analysis and application of case theory to the Greek case system in S. Wong, "What Case Is This Case? An Application of Semantic Case in Biblical Exegesis," *Jian Dao* 1 (1994): 75-107.

123. Nida, *Toward a Science,* pp. 226-38.

124. See the discussion of nonvariants in Tov, *Text-Critical Use*, pp. 217-28; cf. Aejmelaeus, "What Can We Know?"; J. Wevers, "The Use of the Versions for Text Criticism: The Septuagint," in *La Septuaginta en la Investigacion Contemporanea (V Congreso De La IOSCS)*, ed. N. Fernández Marcos (Madrid: Instituto Arias Montano, 1985).

We will explore the significance of the morphological and lexical structure of language for TT in further detail below, but our discussion has demonstrated that TT has to be concerned with the detailed analysis of structure. In the process of translating from one language into another the ancient translator had to resolve the tension of reproducing the meaning of the *Vorlage* in an acceptable form in the target language. The overwhelming preference in the LXX was to encode that meaning in the target language using structures similar to those in the source language, but this was not always practical or desirable. Different translators departed from formal equivalence for divergent reasons. For this reason, the analysis of TT in the LXX is based on the detailed study of the structure of a translation unit — word by word, phrase by phrase, clause by clause — by comparing and contrasting the way in which the translator made a particular rendition in a specific context with all other renditions of the same element.

Close attention to the structure assumes, as we have argued, that the translators worked *primarily* with small units of Scripture in an *ad hoc* kind of way. At the same time, the analysis of patterns and particular characteristics within the unit of translation should also flag those instances in which the translations have been particularly influenced by the circumstances of the translator. For example, we have already mentioned A. van der Kooij's demonstration that some of the departures from the *Vorlage* in Isaiah exhibit coherence within the OG text.

TT Takes the Source Language as Its Point of Departure

Considering what we have already written about the translation process, there should be little need to establish this last point. As we have emphasized, the aim of TT is to describe the way in which a translator rendered the source text; therefore, the point of comparison for the renderings in the target language is always going to be the parent text.[125] During the recent resurgence of studies in the field of TT this principle has been taken for granted.[126] However, there have been several works that have not followed this principle and

125. Soisalon-Soininen, "Methodologische Fragen," pp. 426-28; Aejmelaeus, "Significance of Clause Connectors," pp. 362-69.

126. Other studies worthy of note that have not yet been mentioned include C. Rabin, "The Ancient Versions and the Indefinite Subject," *Textus* 2 (1962): 60-76; D. Weissert, "Alexandrian Word-Analysis and Septuagint Translation Techniques," *Textus* 8 (1973): 31-44; J. A. L. Lee, "Equivocal and Stereotyped Renderings in the LXX," *RB* 87 (1980): 104-17.

must be used with great care.[127] There is little gained, as far as TT is concerned, if the investigator compares the use and frequency of a certain Greek construction in the LXX without investigating the *Vorlage*. Translating or *retroverting* the Greek back into its presumed Hebrew/Aramaic *Vorlage* can be difficult and always involves some speculation. The actual task of retroversion is greatly aided, however, by T. Muraoka's volume that gives all the Greek lexical equivalences in the LXX for every Hebrew and Aramaic term in the HB.[128] One can use this aid to help decide what might have been the reading in the *Vorlage* for the OG.

Emphasizing that TT analyzes the means by which the translator rendered the source text does not mean that the target language is ignored, because the significance of the renderings employed for a specific construction is better understood when they are compared to contemporary writings in the source language.[129] Such a comparison yields information concerning, on the one hand, the degree to which the translators conformed to contemporary usage of the target language, or, on the other hand, the influence of the source language.[130]

In conclusion, the description of the TT of a unit of translation requires the comparison of the translation equivalents of the unit with the elements of the source text from which they were derived. The comparison of the translation equivalents with their usage in contemporaneous texts of the target language will also illuminate the degree to which the translation adheres to the standard of usage in the target language.

---

127. This is particularly true of M. Johannessohn, *Der Gebrauch der Kasus in der Septuaginta* (Berlin: Weidmannsche, 1910) and *Der Gebrauch der Präpositionen in der Septuaginta* (Berlin: Weidmannsche, 1925). The same can be said of Rife's investigations, though at the time he was concerned with the question of whether the Gospels were translations of Semitic originals.

128. T. Muraoka, *Hebrew/Aramaic Index to the Septuagint* (Grand Rapids: Baker, 1998); see also T. Muraoka, *A Greek-Hebrew/Aramaic Index to I Esdras*, SCS 16 (Chico, Calif.: Scholars Press, 1984).

129. R. Sollamo, "Some 'Improper' Prepositions, such as ENWPION, ENANTION, ENANTI, etc., in the Septuagint and Early Koine Greek," *VT* 28 (1975): 473-75, and *Renderings of Hebrew Semiprepositions*, pp. 3-10.

130. Aejmelaeus ("Significance of Clause Connectors," p. 363) notes that the degree of difficulty involved in the source text is another factor to consider in the analysis of TT.

Summary

1. The agreement of a citation in the NT with the OG does not necessarily prove a relationship between the two readings. Due to the complex nature of the linguistic relationships that exist between the NT, OG, and MT, the aim of this chapter has been to provide a theoretical foundation for the analysis of TT based on linguistic principles. This was developed in four stages.

2. First, we provided a definition of TT and commented briefly on five aspects of the definition: *The purpose of the study of TT is to describe the way in which individual translators engaged in the task of translating a unit of Scripture for a community.*

3. Second, we outlined the methodology for analyzing TT that focuses on literalism. The five criteria for literalness in a translation are: consistent representation of terms in translation ("stereotyping"), segmentation and representation of the constituent elements of the Hebrew words, word order, quantitative representation, and availability and adequacy of lexical choices. Literalism focuses on those aspects of the translation that mirror the formal aspects of the source text; for this reason, a literal translation is frequently viewed more positively and assumed to be more faithful to the source text than is a free translation.

4. Though an analysis of literalism offers a natural starting point because the majority of the LXX books are "more or less" literal, we criticized it as a means for an analysis of TT at several points. Literalism is limited as a methodology for studying TT because it focuses on describing the literalness of a particular book in relation to other books. Furthermore, the fact that a translation reproduces a great deal of the formal features of the source text does not mean that the translator *intended* that the reader could retranslate back from the Greek to the Hebrew. Without a detailed comparison of the texts, statistics really do not help us to understand the way in which the translator approached the text.

5. Fourth, we laid the foundations for a proposed model of TT by giving five presuppositions for TT: *TT is Descriptive; TT is Primarily Synchronic; TT Accounts for* Langue *and* Parole; *TT is Structural;* and *TT Takes the Source Language as its Point of Departure.* The following chapter will outline a model for the study of TT.

CHAPTER THREE

A Model for TT

Having established some presuppositions and discussed their implications for the analysis of TT, we can begin the process of providing a guide for examining a text. We will do this in two steps. First, we will introduce a model for the analysis of TT that may be applied to many types of translations. Our purpose in this section is to introduce and discuss the four main components of the translation process. Many examples will be given, but not in every case. We have already provided examples for some of the categories in the previous chapters. Second, in the next chapter we will see how the transmission history of the LXX and the later recensions impacts on the use of the NT. This is necessary to complete our understanding of the nature of the textual witnesses with which we are working. We will focus a lot of attention in our discussion on the analysis of vocabulary because that is the major area of concern when determining the source of a quotation in the NT. Vocabulary is also the most complex area for evaluating TT. Through all of this it is incumbent upon us to remember that a greater appreciation for the LXX is only one piece, albeit an important one, toward understanding the NT writers' use of Scripture.

An Overview of TT Analysis

We recall from the previous chapter's diagram of the perspective of analyzing TT that the act of translation requires the use of a transfer system (a translator) to decode the message of the source text and encode that message in the target language. The translator has to first decode the individual structural elements of the source text, which are the morphology, lexicology, and syntax of the source language. The translator then encodes that message in the target language. However, the translator must make adjustments in the formal structure of the message being encoded due to the different linguistic structures of the two languages. The number of adjustments depends largely upon the inherent differences in the two languages and how closely the translator attempts to maintain a formal correspondence with the source text. There are also other reasons why adjustments are made in the case of the ancient versions. For example, the translator may have wanted to clarify something that was unclear or omit something that was redundant. Other changes were introduced unintentionally due to such problems as textual corruptions or errors by the translator. Finally, we have to deal with the actual translated element in the target text. What is the effect on the meaning of the structure which has passed through the transfer system? Is it basically synonymous, or has some alteration taken place? The perspective of TT enables us to analyze the elements in the source text and compare them to the translation in order to understand what adjustments were made in the transfer system by the translator. We could depict the process in this way:[1]

Element of Translation $\rightarrow$		Adjustment and Motivation $\rightarrow$	Effect on Meaning
Source Text		*Target Text*	*Comparison*
Morphology	Morphology	Unintentional	Synonymous
Lexicology	Lexicology	or	or
Syntax	Syntax	Intentional	Alteration

It goes without saying that, in order for the analyst of TT to understand what the translator has done in comparison to the presumed *Vorlage,* it is necessary to be able to retrovert or reconstruct reliably the *Vorlage* from which the translation was made. There are three basic steps to this process.[2] One can also employ the MT as a guide to reconstructing the *Vorlage* of the OG because generally there is a close relationship between the source of the OG/LXX and the MT.[3] The first step is to concentrate on the similarities between the two texts. In this way one can establish where the *Vorlage* from which OG was translated is the same as or very similar to the MT. After this, one can examine the differences that suggest that the Greek translator may

---

1. See also the discussion by H. M. Szpek and her diagram of the process in *Translation Technique in the Peshitta to Job, SBLDS* 137 (Atlanta: Scholars Press, 1992), pp. 13-60.

2. E. Tov, *The Text-Critical Use of the Septuagint in Biblical Research* (Jerusalem: Simor, 1981), p. 99. See his whole discussion on how to make reliable retroversions.

3. See the discussion of the definition of TT in the previous chapter.

have been translating a *Vorlage* that varied from the MT. Finally, one's goal is to determine — to the best of one's ability — the *Vorlage* that the translator read. In practice, all three of these steps require a great deal of care and attention to detail. For example, the close relationship between the two texts does not necessarily imply that the *Vorlage* of the OG/LXX book was equivalent to the MT. In reconstructing the *Vorlage* one has to account for additions, omissions, and textual corruptions in either the Greek or the Hebrew texts, and the examination of specific differences is aided by the analysis of the whole unit in question. In the end, a careful analysis will often enable one to distinguish between the way in which the *Vorlage* of the OG may have differed from the MT, on the one hand, and adjustments to a *Vorlage* similar to MT that were introduced by the translator, on the other.[4]

Element of Translation

The analysis of TT is based on the presupposition that we have to define what the translator has done before we can begin to answer how and why he or she did it. The distinction between the translator decoding the source text and then encoding the message in the target text recognizes that there is a distinction between the meaning (semantic structure) found in the source text and the formal surface structure chosen by the translator to render that meaning in the target text.[5] When a text is translated from one language into another there are a variety of words and/or expressions that may be used to translate a particular phrase or expression.

It is by means of this formal comparison of the two texts that differences are discovered that were introduced by the translator. Therefore, it is only after this initial comparison that the analyst can begin to formulate answers to the questions about the transfer system: that is, how the translator made changes (Adjustment), why the changes were made (Motivation), and finally the effect that these changes had on the meaning. The elements of translation with which we need to be concerned can be classified under three subcategories: Morphology, Syntax, and Lexicology. In the end, every rela-

---

4. Cf. the remarks of A. van der Kooij, *The Oracle of Tyre, VTSupp* 71 (Leiden: Brill, 1998), pp. 110-11.

5. See W. L. Chafe, *Meaning and the Structure of Language* (Chicago: University of Chicago Press, 1970), pp. 15-91. So also R. Sollamo, who refers to "vocabulary, morphology, and syntax" as the elements that may be investigated (*Renderings of Hebrew Semiprepositions in the Septuagint, AASF, DHL* 19 [Helsinki: Suomalainen Tiedeakatemia, 1979], p. 775).

tionship between two texts, both the similarities and differences, can be described as additions, omissions, or substitutions in the forms of the words, the choice of particular words, or the way in which the words are put together to form larger meaningful units of discourse.[6] We will now examine these subcategories in more detail.

Morphology

As a working definition a *morpheme* could be described as "a minimal unit of meaning or grammatical function."[7] For example, the phrase *the old players* consists of three words but five morphemes. *The* and *old* are both free morphemes because they can stand alone, but the former is regarded as a functional morpheme since it does not have meaning by itself. The word *players* has three morphemes. *Play* like *old* is a lexical (it has meaning) morpheme, and, like many other free morphemes, *play* can serve as the basic building block (stem) for other words. Words are constructed through the addition of bound morphemes such as *er* (meaning "person who does something") and *s* (indicating plural) to a stem.

The Semitic languages Hebrew and Aramaic have a morphological structure that differs from the Indo-European Greek language. Therefore, for the purposes of TT it is important to identify the morphemes in the source text and compare how the morphemes are represented in the translation,

---

6. P. Gentry ("The Place of Theodotion-Job in the Textual History of the Septuagint," in *Origen's Hexapla and Fragments,* ed. A. Salvesen, Texte und Studien zum antiken Judentum 58 [Tübingen: Mohr Siebeck, 1998], p. 200, n. 6), apparently in contradiction to the proposal of Szpek and myself, states: "Since the methodology must be determined by the nature of the materials, it is doubtful if one can describe a 'model' for analysis of translation technique in all texts." I find this remark puzzling and vague. What exactly does he mean when he suggests that the nature of the translation should dictate the method of analysis? More specifically, how is what I have proposed inadequate? If the translation has large pluses or minuses in comparison to the presumed *Vorlage,* then they are treated as additions or omissions. If the translation diverges from the presumed source because it may have been translating a different *Vorlage,* then this is a substitution based on a textual difference. The formal comparison and analysis of texts works as well for larger differences at the paragraph or chapter level as it does for smaller differences at the morphological, lexical, or clause structure.

7. G. Yule, *The Study of Language* (Cambridge: Cambridge University Press, 1985), p. 60. For a good introduction to morphology and biblical Hebrew see W. R. Garr, "The Linguistic Study of Morphology," in *Linguistics and Biblical Hebrew,* ed. W. Bodine (Winona Lake, Ind.: Eisenbrauns, 1992); or see the technical discussion of morphology in E. Nida, *Morphology: The Descriptive Analysis of Meaning* (Ann Arbor: University of Michigan Press, 1949).

while bearing in mind the differences in morphological structure between the two languages. The morphological elements that we might want to compare between Hebrew and Greek are how they represent definiteness, number, gender, person, word class, pronoun, suffix, tense, mood, and voice.[8]

Generally speaking, functional and bound morphemes tend to be particularly numerous and diverse in their usage in all languages, and so it is not surprising that they pose particular difficulties for the TT of the LXX.[9] For example, the fact that the bound morpheme ל has diverse functions in Hebrew (as a preposition used spatially, temporally; with the infinitive construct; marker of dative, apposition, idiom with יֵשׁ denoting possession)[10] means that a mere percentage indicating how often the morpheme is formally represented by a distinct preposition or article in the Greek text would be of little value. The function of the morpheme in each case has to be determined in order to compare how it is translated in all passages where it has a similar grammatical function. For example, in Exodus 2:4 the ל is bound to an infinitive construct to form לְדֵעָה *to know,* but the infinitive μαθεῖν *to learn* is all the OG requires for translation.[11] In contrast, in Jonah 1:13 לְהָשִׁיב *to return* is rendered in the OG by τοῦ ἐπιστρέψαι. In this case the article τοῦ is intended to formally render the ל, though it is unnecessary.

Very important morphological differences between Hebrew and Greek also exist in the nominal and verbal systems.[12] For example, aspect/tense and

---

8. Interchanges of active/passive, noun/verb, and noun/adjective in the source text and the translation are transformations involving the deep structure of grammar. For a discussion, see Nida, *Toward a Science of Translating* (Leiden: Brill, 1964), pp. 195-201, 228; for examples, see C. Rabin, "The Ancient Versions and the Indefinite Subject," *Textus* 2 (1962): 60-76. See the discussion of definiteness in Hebrew in J. Barr, "Determination and the Definite Article in Biblical Hebrew," *JSS* 34 (1989): 307-35.

9. Tov (*Text-Critical Use,* pp. 219-28) classifies many of these morphological differences as nonvariants for the purposes of textual criticism because it is so difficult to determine whether the addition or omission of these morphemes in the LXX reflects the actual reading of the *Vorlage.*

10. See B. Waltke and M. O'Connor, *An Introduction to Biblical Hebrew Syntax* (Winona Lake, Ind.: Eisenbrauns, 1990), pp. 602-10 for uses with infinitive construct and pp. 205-12 for uses as a preposition.

11. Compare TH, which has the pleonastic article τοῦ.

12. See the discussion by J. Wevers where he remarks on the differences in the verbal and nominal structure of Greek and Hebrew ("The Use of the Versions for Text Criticism: The Septuagint," in *La Septuaginta en la Investigacion Contemporanea (V Congreso de la IOSCS),* ed. N. Fernández Marcos [Madrid: Instituto Arias Montano, 1985]). E.g., Greek inflects nouns in five cases, three genders, and two numbers, whereas Hebrew has three numbers (dual), two genders, and no case system, though it does inflect for state. Works specifically treating the translation of verbs include J. Barr, "Translators' Handling of

mood are far more distinctive in the morphological structure of Greek than of Hebrew.[13] Therefore, when the Greek translators had to grammaticalize a verb in the translation, they had to impose features of tense and mood that were not part of the formal structure of their *Vorlage*. In addition, the system of verbal stems of Hebrew makes different distinctions in *Aktionsart* (the kind of action depicted by the verb) than does Greek.[14] These distinctions are partially compensated for in Greek through the grammaticalization of voice, but in certain cases (causatives, intensives) the translators could convey the meaning only through their lexical choices.[15] These examples indicate that TT has to be concerned with the way in which the morphological features of the source text were conveyed in the target text.

Verbs in Semantically Ambiguous Contexts," in *VI Congress of the IOSCS*, ed. C. Cox, SCS 23 (Atlanta: Scholars Press, 1988); I. Soisalon-Soininen, "Die Konstruction des Verbs bei einem neutrum Plural im griechischen Pentateuch," *VT* 29 (1979): 189-99; I. Soisalon-Soininen, *Die Infinitive in der Septuaginta* (Helsinki: Suomalainen Tiedeakatemia, 1965); R. Sollamo, "The LXX Renderings of the Infinitive Absolute Used with a Paronymous Finite Verb in the Pentateuch," in *La Septuaginta en la Investigacion Contemporanea (V Congreso de la IOSCS)*, ed. N. Fernández Marcos (Madrid: Instituto Arias Montano, 1985); A Aejmelaeus, "*Participium Coniunctum* as a Criterion of Translation Technique," *VT* 32 (1982): 385-93; T. V. Evans, *Verbal Syntax in the Greek Pentateuch* (Oxford: Oxford University Press, 2001). See also the detailed analysis of the translation of the verb in Theodotion Job by P. Gentry in *The Asterisked Materials in the Greek Job*, SCS 39 (Atlanta: Scholars Press, 1995), pp. 170-241.

13. The function of the Greek tense forms has been the subject of intense debate over the years. For a review of the discussion, see S. E. Porter, *Verbal Aspect in the Greek of the NT, With Reference to Tense and Mood* (New York: Peter Lang, 1989), pp. 1-109; B. M. Fanning, *Verbal Aspect in New Testament Greek* (Oxford: Clarendon, 1990), pp. 8-125. See Evans, *Verbal Syntax*, for an excellent summary and critique of the recent discussion of verbal aspect.

14. See the general discussion of the Hebrew verb in Waltke and O'Connor, *Introduction*, pp. 343-50, and the discussion of the stems, pp. 351-452.

15. Wevers, "Use of the Versions," p. 19. See also E. Tov, "The Representation of the Causative Aspects of the *Hiph'il* in the LXX. A Study in Translation Technique," *Bib* 63 (1982): 417-24. Tov analyzes how verbs occurring in the hiphil are represented in the LXX. He groups them into four categories: (1) verbs that bear no special features; (2) causative suffixes; (3) use of auxiliary verbs; and (4) reversal of the causative action.

The first category is the most frequent and represents causative forms that could be adequately represented by a Greek verb already expressing the semantic meaning of the causative. The second group comprises those verbs that were expressed through the use of the so-called Greek causative suffixes (-οω, -εω, -αω, -υω, -ιζω, -αζω, -ανω, -αινω, -υνω, -ευω). The auxiliary verb of the third category is usually ποιέω (with adjective/adverb/verb/noun) although other verbs are used as well (pp. 422-23). In the fourth category are a few examples of places where the causative action of the verb was reversed in the translation.

Syntax

Syntax is the study of the structure and ordering of morphemes and groups of morphemes (i.e., words) in meaningful combinations. We have already dealt with the nature of syntactic combinations and their relevance for TT in the discussion of structure in the previous chapter. Syntagmatic or paradigmatic concerns may contribute to differences at the word, phrase, clause, or sentence level of the translation. We need only add that the choice of Greek conjunctions can entail differences in word order (e.g., γάρ, δέ, οὖν) or require a particular grammaticalization of the verb (e.g., ἵνα, ὅπως + subjunctive).

Lexicology

Lexicology is concerned with the analysis of individual lexemes (words) as translation equivalents for the vocabulary of the source text. At the level of the formal comparison of the target text to the source text the analysis of vocabulary for TT is not strictly concerned with meaning. The reason we say this is because of occasions when the suitability of the meaning of a particular choice of word really did not enter into the decision-making process of the translator. For example, the translators often utilized an SE to translate a word in the *Vorlage* without regard to the semantic range of the SE as an adequate choice for those particular contexts.[16]

Paradigmatic Relationships As with morphology and syntax, the analysis of vocabulary for TT essentially involves a comparison of contrasting lexical structures. H. Gleason illustrates this principle when he contrasts how speakers of various languages classify the colors of the rainbow. While English classifies the colors in six categories *(purple, blue, green, yellow, orange, red)*, Shona uses four and Bassa only two.[17] Clearly there is no difference in the denotational field described; it is the languages that make different types of distinctions.[18] The fact that English (and by extension the English speaker)

---

16. It is for this reason Tov argues that Greek words became, more or less, "mere symbols representing Hebrew words" and that the description of the meaning of such words in the LXX could be dependent on the meaning of the Hebrew equivalent ("Three Dimensions of LXX Words," *RB* 83 [1976]: 535).

17. H. A. Gleason, *An Introduction to Descriptive Linguistics,* rev. ed. (London: Holt, Rinehart and Winston, 1961), p. 4.

18. Words are not, therefore, labels for concepts like exhibits in a museum (the "museum myth"). See J. Bennett, *Linguistic Behaviour* (Cambridge: Cambridge University Press, 1976), pp. 5-10; J. Lyons, *Structural Semantics* (Oxford: Basil Blackwell, 1963), pp. 30-33.

makes more distinctions between the colors does not make it "better" nor more "advanced." Every language has the capacity to refer to all aspects of human experience, they just do so differently.[19] This example also helps to demonstrate that the meaning of each color term in each language is to a certain extent determined by its relation to the other terms on the color continuum.[20] The same principle of structural relations applies to the use of most vocabulary.

Linguists refer to the analysis of a conceptual field, such as color in the preceding paragraph, as an example of a "semantic field." The analysis of semantic fields involves the collection and investigation of the relationship in the set of words that belong to a domain (subject area).[21] For example, we could investigate the words that belong to the domain of *color,* or the subdomain of terms that constitute the domain *red* (pink, scarlet, wine, red). The advantage of this type of analysis is that it emphasizes and contrasts the paradigmatic choices that are available in a particular domain.[22]

The significance of the paradigmatic relationships (or sense relations) between words in differing languages becomes obvious as soon as one undertakes the task of translating, or, as in our case, the analysis of TT. As J. Lyons states,

> It is not so much that one language draws a greater or less number of semantic distinctions than another which prevents the matching of their vocabularies one-to-one (although the normal bilingual dictionaries encour-

19. J. Lyons states, "the grammatical and lexical structure of different languages will tend to reflect the specific interests and attitudes of the culture in which they operate. What it does not mean, however, is that every grammatical and lexical distinction must be correlated with some important difference in the patterns of thought of the society using the language" (*Semantics* [Cambridge: Cambridge University Press, 1977], 1:250; cf. E. Nida, *Language Structure and Translation* (Stanford: Stanford University Press, 1975), pp. 184-91; Nida, *Toward a Science,* pp. 50-56.

20. Lyons, *Structural Semantics,* pp. 38-39. Although the study of B. Berlin and P. Kay indicates that the majority of speakers in any language identify a common focus for color terms, this does not nullify the basic fact that speakers of different languages draw distinctions on the color continuum differently. See B. Berlin and P. Kay, *Basic Colour Terms: Their Universality and Evolution* (Los Angeles: University of California Press, 1969).

21. See Lyons, *Semantics,* 1:250-61; A. Lehrer, *Semantic Fields and Lexical Structures* (London: North-Holland, 1974), pp. 1-17; Nida, *Toward a Science,* pp. 47-50; E. Nida, *Componential Analysis of Meaning* (Paris: Mouton, 1975), pp. 174-91.

22. For an example of a lexicon based on semantic domains, see the ambitious work edited by J. P. Louw and E. A. Nida, *Greek-English Lexicon of the New Testament* (New York: United Bible Societies, 1988).

age this view). It is rather that these distinctions are made in completely different places.[23]

Assuming that the translator understood the meaning of a given word in its *Vorlage*,[24] the analysis of TT attempts to understand how the translator matched the structural relations of the vocabulary of the receptor language to that of the source text. At one and the same time, the analyst has to keep one eye on the paradigmatic relations among the words in the source text and the other eye on the paradigmatic relations that exist in the target language among the possible translation equivalents for the words in the *Vorlage*.[25] The interaction of these opposing forces had significant consequences on the vocabulary of the LXX. It is why we have some Semitic words that are rendered with half a dozen or more equivalents; and in other cases the same translator employed an SE for the majority or even all of the occurrences of a different lexeme, even if the semantic range of the translation equivalent did not match that of the source lexeme. On still other occasions the translators employed the technique of lexical leveling.

Albert Pietersma has argued that the analysis of the lexical meanings of the vocabulary of the Septuagint is further complicated by the nature of the translation: that is, it should be understood by using the model of an interlinear translation.[26] Since the purpose of the Greek translation was to bring the reader to the Hebrew text, the tendency was to employ stereotyped equivalents for vocabulary, which resulted in instances where the semantic range of the chosen Greek equivalent did not fit the context. The inevitable consequences of accommodating Greek words to the lexical structure of the Hebrew was that varying degrees of semantic change occurred in some of the vocabulary. For example, in the NT the meaning of διαθήκη is *covenant* and

---

23. Lyons, *Structural Semantics*, pp. 37-38; S. Ullmann, *The Principles of Semantics* (Glasgow: Jackson, Son & Co., 1951), pp. 54-62.

24. For example, there were instances where cultural differences, the use of rare words, or diachronic changes in the language caused the translators of the LXX considerable difficulty. There were also instances where the translator was confused about the meaning of words due to polysemy (different senses of the same lexeme) or homonymy (different lexemes that share the same spelling). The distinction between a simple figurative extension of meaning and polysemy, on the one hand, and between polysemy and homonymy, on the other, is often difficult to discern. See Ullmann, *Principles*, pp. 114-37; M. Silva, *Biblical Words and Their Meaning* (Grand Rapids: Zondervan, 1983), pp. 113-14.

25. See the discussion in G. Dorival, M. Harl, and O. Munnich, *La Bible grecque des Septante* (Paris: Éditions du Cerf, 1988), pp. 243-53.

26. See A. Pietersma's discussion of the translation of vocabulary in "The Psalms" in *A New English Translation of the Septuagint* (New York: Oxford, 2000), p. xiv.

THE USE OF THE SEPTUAGINT IN NEW TESTAMENT RESEARCH

δόξα has narrowed to *glory* because they were employed as SEs in the LXX. In some cases new words (neologisms) were created or words were simply adopted into the Greek language and written in Greek letters (loanwords) like σάββατον *sabbath* from שַׁבָּת.

The use of multiple equivalents, SE, and lexical leveling in the LXX reflects the same tension that we experience when we encounter the problem of translating the related set of meanings of different lexemes and the differing meanings of the same lexeme from one language into another. The challenges that the translation of the Semitic vocabulary presented to the Greek translators (not to mention the times they did not know the meaning of the text) also teach us that the examination of vocabulary has to be very detailed. With regard to the technique of using SE or lexical leveling, we should also emphasize once again that it is the departure from an otherwise uniform approach (the "marked" use) that is instructive to our understanding of the TT in a translation unit.

Syntagmatic Relationships While most studies of vocabulary for TT have concentrated on paradigmatic relations, as evidenced by the degree of the use of SE by the translator, the role of syntagmatic relations has been virtually neglected. This theory emphasizes the meaningful relationships that exist between particular combinations of words in a syntagm. For example, W. Porzig points to the relationship between biting and teeth; barking and dog; blonde and hair.[27] The most significant aspect of the syntagmatic relationship between words is that it limits or defines the paradigmatic choices in any given context. Syntagmatic relations between words are also referred to as the study of their collocations.[28] For example, the words strong and powerful may be used to describe a person, but strong would not be used in collocation with "car," though powerful could. Likewise, we refer to tea being strong but not powerful.[29]

We could say that paradigmatic relations focus on the vertical dimension of words whereas syntagmatic relations focus on the horizontal dimension. That is, the vertical dimension ($\downarrow$) considers how words might be interchanged to fill a particular slot, while the horizontal dimension ($\rightarrow$) concentrates on the context limits or restricts the choice of a particular word.

---

27. W. Porzig, *Das Wunder der Sprache* (Bern: Francke, 1950), p. 68.

28. "Collocations refers to the combination of words that have a certain mutual expectancy" (H. Jackson, *Words and Their Meanings* [New York: Longman, 1988], p. 96).

29. Example from M. A. K. Halliday, "Lexis as a Linguistic Level," in *In Memory of J. R. Firth*, ed. C. E. Bazell et al. (London: Longmans, 1966), pp. 150-51.

Paradigmatic	vs.	Syntagmatic

angry   stomped
The sore man stormed toward the . . .   The woman has blond hair.
upset   hurried

The understanding of syntagmatic relationships has obvious implications for TT. In many cases the choice of translation equivalents for the source text will be defined or limited by the collocational restrictions of the vocabulary in the target language. However, at the same time, the target language will make adjustments and introduce changes because of the different lexical structures and also because of cultural differences.[30] One of the most significant ways that syntagmatic relationships may affect TT, however, is when the translator is forced to choose between particular translation equivalents. For example, if the translator tends to employ lexical leveling for the vocabulary in the source text in a particular semantic domain, then there is a problem when two words that have been rendered by the same lexeme suddenly appear in the same context. Does the translator again employ the same word for both or use an alternative for one of the words? If the translator chooses an alternative, are there any indications why the alternative was employed for the one word, but not the other? Is one rendering more favored than the other? An examination of the TT of the vocabulary will help to answer that question.[31] This issue is discussed below under the category of *Adjustment.*

Another main way that syntagmatic relationships affect TT is the occasions in which one language uses a syntagm while the other language may require only a single lexeme to render roughly the same meaning. For example, OG Daniel 11:27 renders כזב ידברו *they shall exchange lies* with ψευδολογήσουσιν *they shall speak falsely.* OG Daniel employs this technique quite frequently. Other examples are 2:13, where OG translates דתא נפקת *a decree went out* with ἐδογματίσθη *it was decreed,* and 1:4, where ומביני מדע וטובי מראה . . . וידעי דעת *good of appearance . . . and knowers of knowledge and discerners with insight* is translated by καὶ εὐειδεῖς . . . καὶ γραμματικοὺς καὶ σοφοὺς *good looking . . . and educated and wise.*

Other syntagmatic features in Hebrew that should be considered when analyzing TT are the construct genitive relation and infinitive absolutes mod-

---

30. Lyons, *Semantics,* 1:265.

31. This question is treated in more detail in my article "Lexical Inconsistency: Towards a Methodology for the Analysis of the Vocabulary in the Septuagint," in *IX Congress of the IOSCS,* ed. B. Taylor, SCS 45 (Atlanta: Scholars Press, 1997), pp. 81-98.

ifying another verb. Syntagmatic features in Greek that require attention are verbs that are followed by a particular case, infinitive or object clauses; and prepositions because they require a certain case.

Adjustment

Adjustment refers to the types of changes that have been made in the formal structure of the source text as it passed through the transfer system. It is here that we are describing what the translator has actually done in the translation, because the analysis of TT is concerned with describing how the translator has rendered the various elements of the source text into the target text. Adjustments in the translation can be generally classified as additions, omissions, or substitutions at the morphological, syntactic, or lexical level.

Morphological Adjustments

In our previous discussion of morphology we noted that there are numerous differences in the functional morphemes of Hebrew and Greek as well between their nominal and verbal systems. The analysis of TT should investigate how the morphological elements of the source text have been rendered in the target text. For example, how does the translator treat various verb forms such as the perfect, imperfect, infinitives, and the different stems? Is the construct genitive normally rendered with the genitive case? How does the translator treat definite nouns? Are they always rendered with an article in the translation? If not, is there any pattern to those instances in which the translator does not employ the article?

One must always take care in the analysis of the way in which the translator has rendered the elements of the source text, but this is particularly true in the case of bound morphemes in Hebrew. The reason for this is that it is difficult to know whether the difference between the OG/LXX and the MT is due to the translator or whether it stems from a textual difference (real or perceived) that was in the *Vorlage* of the Greek translator. For example, the addition or omission of an article or καὶ in the LXX when compared to the MT may indicate the addition or omission of a corresponding ה or ו in the *Vorlage* from which the translator was working, but it may not. Sometimes it is just not possible to determine whether some morphological and grammatical differences are real variants or nonvariants.[32] However, if the analysis of

32. The term "nonvariants" is used to refer to differences in the translation com-

TT is done carefully, and if it considers the various possibilities for adjustments in the LXX while being able to show the pattern of what the translator has done elsewhere, then a reasonable case can be made concerning whether a difference in the LXX reflects an alternative *Vorlage* or is due to the translator.

Syntactical Adjustments

Syntactical adjustments can occur at the phrase, clause, sentence, or paragraph level. Adjustments at the sentence or paragraph level usually involve additions or omissions in the target text when compared to the presumed *Vorlage*. For example, the LXX has an addition in Proverbs 5:3 compared to the MT μὴ πρόσεχε φαύλῃ γυναικί *Do not listen to a worthless woman*. The preference for Greek to employ hypotactic constructions as opposed to the parataxis in the Hebrew resulted in changes in the sentence structure as well, though the tendency of the LXX translators was to follow the syntax of the Hebrew.

Lexical Adjustments

In the previous discussion of the synchronic nature of TT, we have already encountered some types of lexical adjustments that the translators of the LXX made, such as lexical leveling, omission, transliteration, and contextual translations. At other times, primarily due to lexical inadequacy, the translator may have adopted a loan translation, used a word in an innovative way, or even created a new word for the translation. Apart from these conditions there are still numerous lexical adjustments expected in a translation because of the differing lexical structures of two languages as well as the sheer volume of data with which we are working when we examine vocabulary.

Typically, analysis of vocabulary for TT in Septuagint studies has resulted in an examination of the way in which a few selected terms from MT have been rendered in the translation.[33] Hopefully, we have made the point

---

pared to MT that do not reflect or cannot be demonstrated to reflect an actual variant in the *Vorlage* compared to MT. Besides the article and ֏/καὶ, differences in number, pronouns, prepositions, and active vs. passive are problematic when attempting to determine whether the difference in the translation reflects a true variant reading. See Tov, *Text-Critical Use,* pp. 217-27; M. Goshen-Gottstein, "Theory and Practice of Textual Criticism," *Textus* 3 (1963): 130-58.

33. For an example, see D. O. Wenthe, "The Old Greek Translation of Daniel 1–6," Ph. D. dissertation, University of Notre Dame, 1991. Gentry *(Asterisked Materials in the Greek Job)* is much more thorough in that he examines each lexeme in LXX Job and the number of lexemes that the Greek word employs to translate MT Job. However, Gentry

by now that such an analysis is inadequate at best and misleading at worst. Understanding the adjustments made at the lexical level between the translation and the source text requires a comparison of the way in which the vocabulary in a semantic domain of the Greek overlaps with and is employed to translate the vocabulary of a semantic domain in the Hebrew.

There are two main approaches to examining lexical relations: componential analysis and sense relations.[34] In the case of TT where the specific concern is to compare the lexical relations between two languages, the approach of sense (paradigmatic) relations should prove to be more useful. There are two basic types of sense relations: relations based on similarity and relations based on oppositeness.

Relations Based on Similarity These are the most important sense relations for the analysis of vocabulary because the majority of cases where alternative translation equivalents are employed in the translation of a lexeme are based on similarity. There are two types of relations based on similarity: overlapping and inclusive. Overlapping relations are those to which we usually assign the term synonymy.[35] Synonymy recognizes that two or more words can be substituted for one another in a given context in order to produce the same meaning.[36] Overlapping relations may be diagrammed in the following way:

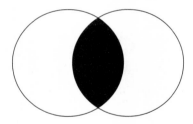

does not investigate the lexical relationships shared by different lexemes and how they overlap in their translation of the vocabulary of MT Job.

34. Lyons, *Semantics*, 1:333.

35. Nida, *Componential Analysis*, pp. 16-17; E. Nida, *Exploring Semantic Structures* (Munich: Fink, 1975), pp. 31-32; Jackson, *Words and Their Meanings*, pp. 65-74; Lyons, *Structural Semantics*, pp. 74-78. W. E. Collinson ("Comparative Synomics: Some Principles and Illustrations," *Transactions of the Philosophical Society* [1939]: 54-77) distinguishes nine different types of synonymy.

36. See the discussion of types of *sameness* in R. Harris, "Synonymy and Linguistic Analysis," in *Language and Style*, ed. S. Ullmann (Oxford: Basil Blackwell, 1973), pp. 11-12. We accept Lyons's assertion that "synonymy must be bound with context"; therefore, two words do not have to be synonymous in all contexts to be regarded as synonymous in any one context.

For example, the relationship between terms for speech is quite complex in both Hebrew (הודע, קרא, הגיד, אמר) and Greek (λέγω, ἀναγγέλλω, καλέω, βοάω). We could easily add to the list of terms since both languages and the relationships become even more complex when we consider that most appear in multiple verbal forms.

Inclusive relations (hyponymy) explores the connections between words by arranging them in hierarchies, that is, the meaning of some words is included within the meaning of others. For example, *red, pink,* and *rose* (co-hyponyms) are all included within the meaning of *red.* By the same token *red* is a co-hyponym with other colors such as *brown, yellow, green* and *blue,* which are all hyponyms of the superordinate *color.*[37] We could diagram these relationships in this way:

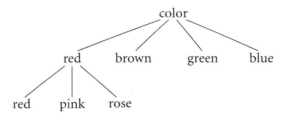

The higher one goes up the hierarchy, the more general is the terminology, while the lower one goes in the hierarchy, the more specific is the terminology. The sense relationships could be diagrammed differently by the addition of different sense components in the hierarchical structure (e.g., different colors or primary vs. secondary colors). The point is that during the course of translation there are times when the translator may choose either a more general or a more specific term in the hierarchical structure as a translation equivalent. For example, how does the translator treat kinship and gender terms? Are terms such as ἄνθρωπος *man* (generically) and ἀνήρ *male, husband* employed differently? What about divine names? A notorious example of the use of a more specific term is the rendering ἡ παρθένος *the virgin* in OG Isaiah 7:14 for *the young woman* הָעַלְמָה in the MT.

Relations Based on Opposition (Antonymy) The significance of *antonymy* for TT is that the translator may choose to express the meaning of the *Vorlage* through a translation equivalent or syntagm that is opposite in meaning to an equivalent in the target text, regardless of what he finds in the *Vorlage.* For ex-

---

37. See the discussion of hierarchical structuring in Nida, *Toward a Science,* pp. 73-82; Lyons, *Structural Semantics,* pp. 69-72; Lehrer, *Semantic Fields,* pp. 20-24.

THE USE OF THE SEPTUAGINT IN NEW TESTAMENT RESEARCH

ample, a translator might have chosen to employ πονηρός as the equivalent for חטא (the SE in the LXX is ἁμαρτία) in a particular context in order to express a contrast with ἀγαθός. In fact, this does not happen in the entire LXX, but it is possible that the choice of a translator could be influenced by similar conditions. It is also possible that a translator could transform a negative statement and express it positively or vice versa.

Figurative Language and Idioms

Changes due to the use of figurative language (simile, metaphor, metonymy, synecdoche) and idiomatic expressions pose a difficulty not only for translators but also for our classification. The reason for this is that figures of speech and idioms bring lexical items together in a way that is unique to each language.[38] For example, North American English speakers would recognize that referring to someone being "up the creek" is a shortened version of "up the creek without a paddle," but non-English speakers would never know apart from contextual clues that this phrase refers to someone who is in difficulty. A biblical example is the use of ידע *know* someone in the HB to refer to sexual relations, as in Genesis 4:1 וְהָאָדָם יָדַע אֶת־חַוָּה אִשְׁתּוֹ *Now the man knew his wife, Eve*. This is translated with a formally equivalent clause in the OG Ἀδὰμ δὲ ἔγνω Εὕαν τὴν γυναῖκα αὐτοῦ *Now Adam knew his wife, Eve*. Some English translations employ the formal equivalent as well, possibly because the expression has gained some currency in English through the influence of the Authorized Version. However, retaining the sense of the original might be better achieved through a rendering such as "had (sexual) relations with" or "made love with."

In the LXX one finds that the translators normally employ formal equivalents for figurative language. However, one does need to be aware of such uses and how to classify them. Idiomatic phrases and figures of speech can usually be treated as single semantic units because the meaning of the whole is not derived from the individual meanings of the parts (e.g., *hit the ceiling, in the doghouse, up the creek*).[39] However, given the problems that such expressions can create, there are times when these should be treated separately rather than trying to examine them as lexical or syntactic adjustments.

---

38. The use of figurative expressions in the Scriptures is explored in G. Caird, *The Language and Imagery of the Bible* (Philadelphia: Westminster, 1980).

39. See especially, Chafe, *Meaning and Structure*, pp. 44-50; cf. Nida, *Componential Analysis*, pp. 113-15; Louw and Nida, *Greek-English Lexicon*, p. 7.

Motivation

The reasons that may have led to an adjustment in the translation are considered under the category Motivation.[40] When we consider the question, "Why did the translator introduce an adjustment (or change) to the text?" there are two subcategories: intentional changes and unintentional changes.

Intentional Changes (Ambiguity, Redundancy, Harmonization, Language Difference, Phonology, Ideology)

Intentional changes are those that were deliberately introduced by the translator, though there are various reasons why a translator introduces a change. For example, translators sometimes substituted the subject for a personal pronoun or added the subject to make it explicit when the Hebrew had employed only the verb to make the subject explicit. A similar type of clarification would be the addition of a qualifier to make something more specific. A case in point is Exodus 18:20 where OG adds τοῦ θεοῦ *of God* to τὰ προστάγματα *the ordinances* when MT has הַחֻקִּים *the statutes*. The opposite tendency also occurred whereby the Greek translators would sometimes employ a pronoun for a noun or omit elements from the *Vorlage* that were redundant. Hebrew, for example, tends to repeat possessive suffixes for each item when linked, whereas Greek tends to simplify and employ only one. Although the Greek translators followed their source texts in the majority of cases, there are many instances in which they did not repeat the use of the pronoun.[41]

Harmonization occurs when the translator employs a Greek rendering of a phrase or larger syntactical unit from one passage as the equivalent in another passage. The net result to the Greek reader is that the passages have the same wording even though the texts of their respective *Vorlagen* had differences. A translator may harmonize to another passage in the same translation unit or to a passage found elsewhere in the LXX. For example, one would expect harmonizations in the parallel texts of Psalms 13 (14) = 52 (53) and Psalms 17 (18) = 2 Reigns 22, or between the parallels in books such as Samuel and Kings or Jeremiah 52 and 4 Reigns 24–25.

Language difference refers to adjustments that were introduced by the translator due to the differences between the *parole* of the source and target

---

40. See Szpek, *Translation Technique*, pp. 40-49 for her discussion of the reasons why translators introduced changes.

41. See the full treatment of the use of pronouns in the OG Pentateuch in R. Sollamo, *Repetition of the Possessive Pronouns in the Septuagint*, SCS 40 (Atlanta: Scholars Press, 1995).

languages. For example, on the one hand there is no Greek equivalent for the possession idiom יֵשׁ לְ *there is to X = he has,* and so it is rendered in a variety of ways. On the other hand, the use of the verb ἔχω *I have* in Greek, which is sometimes employed for the possession idiom of Hebrew, also indicates an adjustment on the part of the Greek translator because there is no equivalent verb in Hebrew.[42]

Phonological considerations that motivate a translation equivalent may be derived from either the source text or the receptor language. The former type have often been referred to rather inaccurately as homophones, that is, the use of Greek words to render a similar sounding word in the Semitic text.[43] J. de Waard suggests that the classification "phonological translation" be employed in its place.[44]

Though phonological translations were employed in the LXX, James Barr has warned that translations based on phonetic resemblance were "a very minor factor in vocabulary choice."[45] Yet the fact that phonetic considerations played a role in instances where the translator had two or more possible equivalents cannot be ignored. In order to demonstrate that it was highly probable that the translator was motivated by phonetic similarity in these cases, one must be able to justify it on the basis of the translation technique. For example, if an uncommon word was selected over the normal equivalent to translate a word in a given instance, then one could reasonably argue that it is phonetically motivated. In Daniel 3:4 OG has ὁ κῆρυξ ἐκήρυχε for קָרֵא וְכָרוֹזָא *the herald proclaimed.* The phonological motivation for the choice of

---

42. See I. Soisalon-Soininen, "Der Gebrauch des Verbes ῎EXEIN in der Septuaginta," *VT* 28 (1978): 92-99.

43. G. B. Caird, "Homoeophony in the Septuagint," in *Essays in Honour of W. D. Davies,* ed. R. Hammerton-Kelly and R. Scroggs (Leiden: Brill, 1976), pp. 74-88; C. Fritsch, "Homophony in the Septuagint," in *Sixth World Congress of Jewish Studies,* ed. A. Shinan (Jerusalem: Jerusalem Academic Press, 1977), pp. 115-20; J. Barr, "Doubts about Homoeophony in the Septuagint," *Textus* 12 (1985): 1-2.

44. J. De Waard ("'Homophony' in the Septuagint," *Bib* 62 [1981]: 555) classifies five major types of phonological translations: I A. neither lexical nor grammatical translation has been affected; I B. only grammatical translation has been affected; II A. a shift of components of meaning has taken place without a grammatical change; II B. a shift of components has taken place with grammatical change; III. one component of meaning has been retained and one deleted, or one component of meaning has been retained and one added; IV. a specific rendering has been given instead of a generic one; and V. a synecdoche is the result of phonological translation. H. St. J. Thackeray (*A Grammar of the Old Testament in Greek,* vol. 1 [Cambridge: Cambridge University Press, 1909], pp. 36-38) refers to translations using Greek words of similar sound to the Hebrew.

45. Barr, "Doubts," p. 77.

the verb κήρυσσω is borne out by the fact that this is the only place where it occurs in OG Daniel. TH translates קרא with the usual LXX equivalent βοάω.

Phonological motivation may also derive from the receptor language: that is, the translator may choose a word because it has sounds that are similar to those of a word or words in the immediate context (e.g., rhyming, alliteration). Here again we have to be cautious about making excessive claims for phenomena that may be explained in other ways. However, there is no *a priori* reason to exclude this motivation. For example, in Daniel 12:10 MT has והרשיעו רשעים *the wicked shall act wickedly,* which, like the example above, also invites similar sounding phonemes in the translation because of the alliteration in the MT. TH obliges by translating with ἀνομήσωσιν ἄνομοι *the lawless shall act lawlessly.* OG also retains the play on sound, but with different equivalents, ἁμάρτωσιν οἱ ἁμαρτωλοί *the sinners shall sin.*[46] Contrary to Barr, such examples seem to be quite plentiful in the LXX.

In many cases the translators introduced adjustments to the translation based on their own ideology. This is often referred to, as we have seen earlier, as *Tendenz.* Sometimes the scholarly discussions about ideology or *Tendenz* as a motivation can be confusing, however, because scholars are using terms in different ways. The problem in this particular area is that all translation requires interpretation. Thus, if we were to go to an extreme, we could classify all translation as influenced by the translator's own beliefs and cultural context. In discussions about TT in the LXX this does not actually happen, but there are times when a translation is characterized as an example of *Tendenz,* when such a description is misleading. For instance, there are those who would describe a translation based on dynamic equivalence as opposed to formal equivalence as an example of *Tendenz.* In both of these approaches, though, the translator is attempting to render the meaning of the source text.[47] The formal approach merely attempts to adhere more strictly to a one-to-one relationship at the morphological and lexical level; so, it is unhelpful to equate a dynamic approach with *Tendenz.* In our view, a rendering that exhibits *Tendenz* is one that represents a departure from the original meaning of the source text based on the ideology of the translator. For example, A. van der Kooij has presented a careful analysis and comparison of the Hebrew and Greek texts of Isaiah 23 and concludes that the OG reflects a reapplication to the circumstances of the translator. It is important to note that van der Kooij offers a close reading of the OG text in its own right

---

46. T. Muraoka ("Literary Device in the Septuagint," *Textus* 8 [1973]: 20-30) argues that the LXX translators utilized alliteration in Job 1:1, 8; 2:3; 3:16; Num. 12:12.

47. See the discussion of *formal* vs. *dynamic/functional* equivalence in chapter 2.

and demonstrates that it has its own internal coherence even as it departs from MT.[48]

In evaluating TT one must also be sure that departures from the meaning of the source text are due to the intention of the translator. Sometimes a translation that appears to be the result of *Tendenz* may be a contextual translation because the translator misunderstood the meaning of the source text. One must be particularly wary of attributing *Tendenz* to a LXX translator when an unusual Semitic construction or rare vocabulary is found in MT.

Unintentional Changes (Linguistic Interference, Versional Influence, Textual Corruption)

The main source of unintentional changes in the work of translation is textual corruption. In fact, for most books of the LXX, we can confidently assert that textual corruption is the main reason for textual changes, period. Textual corruption can stem from a variety of reasons. It ranges from problems reading the source text due to the physical condition of the manuscript, to errors of sight whereby the translator accidentally omits words *(parablepsis)* or confuses letters *(transposition,* confusing letters that are similar in form/orthography). Rather than supply a list of examples here, we suggest that a reader who is not acquainted with this area should consult a volume devoted to textual criticism.[49]

Linguistic interference occurs when knowledge of a language cognate to the language of the source text leads to a misunderstanding of the *Vorlage.* Linguistic interference was bound to happen to the Greek translators because Hebrew and Aramaic are cognate languages and Aramaic was far more dominant as a spoken and written language than Hebrew was through the Second Temple period. Thus, there were many times that the translators rendered vocabulary based on what terms meant in Aramaic rather than in Hebrew.[50]

There are also occasions in which translations reflect the influence of other versions. Since the OG was the first translation of the HB, the Greek translation of the Jewish Scriptures tends to be more of an influence on other versions and translations of the HB. The original translation of the Scriptures did take place within, and was intended for, the Hellenistic-Jewish commu-

48. van der Kooij, *Oracle of Tyre,* pp. 48-109.

49. Tov, *Text-Critical Use;* E. Tov, *Textual Criticism of the Hebrew Bible* (Minneapolis: Fortress, 1992); P. K. McCarter, *Textual Criticism: Recovering the Text of the Hebrew Bible* (Philadelphia: Fortress, 1986).

50. For examples, see J. Joosten, "On the LXX Translators' Knowledge of Hebrew," in *X Congress of the IOSCS,* ed. B. Taylor, *SCS* 51 (Atlanta: Scholars Press, 2001), pp. 165-79.

nity, however, and so there are examples of translations in the LXX that reflect interpretative traditions that are preserved in Jewish sources. The pesherite texts in the *DSS* provide the best evidence for such influence, but the available comparative material is quite small. Most other Jewish written sources have a later origin (Talmud and Mishnah) and, therefore, cannot be assumed to be a source for an OG reading. However, since the Greek recensions (Symmachus, Aquila, Origen's Hexapla, Lucian, and some readings designated as Theodotion) emerged in the early centuries of the common era there is more likelihood that some of their readings have been influenced by other sources.

Effect on Meaning

The analysis of TT is primarily concerned with the way in which the translator has rendered the *Vorlage* into the target language; therefore, the focus is upon how the elements of the source text have been rendered in the target language, what kind of adjustments were made in the process of translation, and why. However, the culmination of the act of translating is the creation of a new version in a new language. From the perspective of the individual analyzing TT, comparing the translation to the source text enables one to discern instances in which the translator has altered the meaning of the *Vorlage* due to the TT and the adjustments that were made. Some of these changes can result in clarity or confusion for readers, but there can also be times when the meaning is very different or even the antithesis of the sense of the source text. Most readers of the new version do not realize that the meaning is affected in translation, however, because they are not able to read the language of the *Vorlage*. Otherwise, we would have no need for translations in the first place.

The significance for our study of the changes in meaning that can occur through translation is that once the Greek Jewish translation of a book was created it took on its own life in the Greek-speaking Jewish community and eventually in the Early Church. The Greek Jewish Scriptures, which included translations of the Hebrew Scriptures as well as books composed originally in Greek, became for all intents and purposes the Bible of the Early Church. They were employed for worship and quoted and referred to as authoritative. The use of the Greek Jewish Scriptures by the Early Church was by no means exclusive, but its impact was significant. Therefore, if we have established that the Greek translation of the Jewish Scriptures imparts a different meaning to its readers when it is compared to the same passages in the MT, and that the Greek Jewish Scriptures enjoyed significant use in the Christian community, then it is reasonable to hypothesize that the NT writings exhibit an influence from the Greek Jewish Scriptures that is distinct from that of the Hebrew Scriptures. As the Bible of the Early Church, the Jewish Scriptures, written and transmitted in Greek, were an integral part of the faith community during the development and formation of the theology expressed in the NT.

Summary

1. In the present chapter we outlined a model of TT. There are four basic aspects to the model: element of translation, adjustment, motivation, and effect on meaning.

2. The analysis of TT begins by comparing the similarities and differences between the structural elements in the source and receptor texts. Those elements have been defined as morphology, lexicology, and syntax. Comparing the similarities and differences among the structural elements in the source and target texts focuses the analysis on the distinctions in the formal surface structures of the two texts.

3. The morphological, lexical, and syntactic structures of Hebrew (and Aramaic) and Greek are very different; thus, we expect to find differences in how the Greek will render the meaning of its *Vorlage* even when it is attempting to provide a formally equivalent translation.

4. Lexical relationships offer the greatest challenge for analyzing TT due to their number and complex structural relations. Most studies of vocabulary for TT have concentrated on the paradigmatic relationships between words (the vertical dimension), while we have suggested that syntagmatic relations (the horizontal dimension) must be considered as well. Syntagmatic relations affect the paradigmatic choices in any given context. The study of syntagmatic relations is particularly important for understanding situations where the translator was forced to choose between particular translation equivalents.

5. Adjustment refers to the types of changes that have been made in the formal structure of the source text when it is rendered into the target language.

6. Motivation, the third stage of our process, refers to the reason why changes were made in the target text when compared to the source text. Some of the changes are inevitable due to the differing linguistic structures of two languages, while others are introduced by the translator. The types of changes can be categorized as intentional or unintentional.

7. The final stage of analyzing TT has to do with the effect on meaning that is produced by the translation. How much has the meaning of the

text changed in the process of translation? This question is particularly pertinent to our study because the Greek translations of the Hebrew Scriptures took on their own life in the Greek-speaking Jewish community and eventually in the Early Church. The Greek Jewish Scriptures became for all intents and purposes the Bible of the Early Church; therefore, it is reasonable to expect that the NT writers and the texts they produced exhibit an influence from the Greek texts of the Jewish Scriptures that is distinct from what they might have believed and written if they had only the Hebrew Scriptures.

CHAPTER 4

The Origin of the Septuagint and Its History

I n the preceding chapters we have discussed the nature of the translation of the Greek Jewish Scriptures and a methodology for the analysis of TT. Up to this point, we have focused on the question of discerning the difference between the MT and OG and the way in which the Hebrew Scriptures were translated into Greek. Unfortunately, with regard to use of the Jewish Scriptures in the NT writings it is not simply a matter of determining whether a NT writer has cited Greek or Hebrew in a quotation. For a variety of reasons that we will explore in this chapter, the analysis of the citation of texts in the NT requires a nuanced approach.

We will begin by taking a step back to outline briefly the origins of the Septuagint. We will then consider the subsequent history of the transmission of the LXX, particularly with regard to the way in which this affects our understanding of the use of the LXX in the NT. The discussion of the transmission history of the LXX will begin with four sample passages from the NT that will help illustrate the complex issues surrounding the identification of the sources that may have been employed by the NT writers. The initial remarks on our sample passages will become more intelligible as we discuss the transmission history of the LXX and the factors that complicate our understanding of the way in which the texts were used by the NT writers. In particular, we will learn the way in which the growth of recensions of the LXX affects our understanding of the Scriptures. We will conclude by outlining the process for analyzing a NT citation based on the material that we have covered.

The Origins of the Septuagint

The fact that the NT was written in Greek provides a good reason to presume, though it does not necessarily entail, that the Greek Jewish Scriptures were a primary influence on its contents. However, we will provide sufficient evidence to clarify the direct and indisputable connection between the two in this chapter and the next. As mentioned earlier, the name Septuagint originally referred to the translation of the Pentateuch into Greek, but the tradition that the seventy or seventy-two elders translated the Bible was eventually applied to the whole Greek Jewish Scriptures.[1] Debate about the origins of the translation usually begins with the *Letter of Aristeas,* which claims to have been written by Aristeas during the reign of Ptolemy II (285-246 B.C.E.). However, it is more likely that the *Letter of Aristeas* dates from some time after 160 B.C.E.,[2] though according to the words of Aristobulus (181-145 B.C.E.), which are preserved by Eusebius, the actual enterprise of translating began during Ptolemy's reign.[3] The grandson of Ben Sira also knows of the translation of other Scriptures (ca. 132 B.C.E.),[4] so the task must have begun earlier than his time. The beginning of the project can probably be safely dated ca. 250, although Nina Collins has attempted to date the year of the translation of the Pentateuch to 281 B.C.E.[5]

The *Letter of Aristeas* claims to give an account of the writer's visit to the High Priest in Jerusalem at the request of Demetrius, the Royal Librarian, to obtain translators to provide a translation of the books of the Jewish Law (28).[6] The amount of space devoted to this task is actually quite short. The ac-

---

1. See M. Müller, *The First Bible of the Church: A Plea for the Septuagint,* JSOTSS 206 (Sheffield: JSOT Press, 1996), pp. 68-78, who discusses the statements of various Early Church Fathers. A thorough discussion of the name *Septuagint* and the *Letter of Aristeas* is also provided by Albert Sundberg, "The Septuagint: The Bible of Hellenistic Judaism," in *The Canon Debate: On the Origins and Formation of the Bible,* ed. L. M. McDonald and J. A. Sanders (Peabody: Hendrickson, 2002), pp. 158-68.

2. See R. Sollamo, "The Letter of Aristeas and the Origin of the Septuagint," in *X Congress of the IOSCS,* ed. B. Taylor, SCS 51 (Atlanta: Scholars Press, 2001), pp. 329-42.

3. S. Jellicoe, *The Septuagint and Modern Study* (Oxford: Clarendon, 1968), pp. 47-52; Müller, *First Bible,* p. 47; E. Schürer, *The History of the Jewish People in the Age of Jesus Christ (175 B.C.–A.D. 135),* rev. G. Vermes et al. (Edinburgh: T. & T. Clark, 1973-87), 3.1.684.

4. See the discussion of the canon in the next chapter.

5. N. Collins, "281 BCE: The Year of the Translation of the Pentateuch into Greek Under Ptolemy II," in *Septuagint, Scrolls and Cognate Writings,* ed. G. J. Brooke and B. Lindars, SCS 33 (Atlanta: Scholars Press, 1992).

6. The paragraph references and English translations are taken from the version by Shutt.

count is interrupted with a variety of digressions and a long section consisting of the king's questions to the translators and their responses (187-294). There were to be six translators from each tribe and they were to bring a copy of the law with them from Jerusalem (46-51, hence seventy-two). The translators were "men of the highest merit and of excellent education due to the distinction of their parentage; they had not only mastered the Jewish literature, but had made a serious study of that of the Greeks as well" (121). Under the supervision of Demetrius, and with ample provision for their needs, the translators were taken to a secluded place where "they set to completing their several tasks, reaching agreement among themselves on each by comparing versions" (302). The conclusion was that "in seventy-two days the business of translation was completed, just as if such a result was achieved by some deliberate design" (307). The version was then read before the Jewish community who applauded the labor of the translators, and then a curse was made against anyone who should try to change or alter the form of the text (311). Only after the translation had won such universal acclamation was it read to the king.

While the letter claims a Palestinian origin for the LXX by the choice of translators and the long section in which the king questions the translators, the language of the Greek Pentateuch is consistent with what is known of the Greek language that was common in third-century Egypt.[7] The insistence on the Palestinian origins of the LXX through the choice of translators and the origins of the copy of the law in Jerusalem, coupled with the stress on the comparable status of the LXX to the Hebrew text by the pronouncements in the letter not to alter the form of the text, indicates that the letter was written as a defense for the LXX translation. S. P. Brock notes that it is difficult to know whether the defense is a response to Palestinian Jews who questioned the validity of the translation or whether it was designed to encourage Egyptian Jews about the authoritative character of the text.[8] Regardless of the specific reason for the apologetic nature of the letter, its origin was in Egypt, and it was written to establish the authority of the Greek translation. As we will discover, it is clear that the claims for the divine nature of the translation were not persuasive within the Jewish community because the process of revising the text toward the Hebrew began prior to the common era.

In time, the authority of the Greek translation, which was later defended by Philo, compared to the Hebrew Scriptures became even more

---

7. J. Wevers, "An Apologia for Septuagint Studies," *BIOSCS* 18 (1985): 18.
8. S. P. Brock, "The Phenomenon of the Septuagint," *OTS* 17 (1972): 21-27.

contentious because of the advent of the Christian Church. Christians tended to adopt the Greek translation as their Jewish Scriptures, and the division between the Christian and Jewish communities widened because the meaning of the Greek differed from that of the Hebrew in places. A prime example of the important differences between the Hebrew source text and the Greek translation is the Matthean quotation of Isaiah 7:14 ἡ παρθένος *the virgin* in 1:23. The NT quotation can be derived only from the Greek. Eventually, in order to protect its claim for the authority of the Greek translation of the Scriptures, the Early Church argued that they were divinely inspired like the Hebrew Scriptures.[9] The *Letter of Aristeas* and Jewish writers like Philo, who defended the authority of the Greek Jewish Scriptures, set precedents for the Christian case. It was the great biblical scholar Jerome (348-420) who defended the authority of the Jewish Scriptures in their original Hebrew language and whose views were echoed by reformers like Martin Luther, who prepared the way for the later dominance of the Hebrew canon for the Protestant Church. Ironically, though Jerome defended the authority of the Hebrew Scriptures, his Latin translation (the Vulgate) became the official Scriptures of the Roman Catholic Church at the council of Trent in 1546.

Explanations for the Origins of the LXX

One of the theories of the origin of the LXX — which is now dismissed — is the view of P. Kahle, who argued that the LXX is best understood as a Greek targum. This theory understands the Greek Scriptures as consisting of a variety of Jewish commentaries on the Hebrew Scriptures that developed more or less independently from one another within the Jewish community. Kahle based his theory on the fact that there are a variety of Greek texts and translations of the HB, which indicated to him that there was no original authoritative OG text.[10] His views have received very little support, and the views of Paul Lagarde hold sway in all research on the LXX. Lagarde held that all extant manuscripts of the LXX offer a mixed text of the original Greek translation of each particular book and are the result of an eclectic process.

Despite the claim of the *Letter of Aristeas* (11-12) that the translation of the Pentateuch was initiated at the request of the Egyptian King Ptolomy II,

9. See Müller, *First Bible*, pp. 68-78 for a presentation of the evidence for the endorsement of the Greek Jewish Scriptures in the patristic writers.
10. P. Kahle, *The Cairo Geniza* (Oxford: Blackwell, 1959), pp. 211-28.

there have been two other main explanations for the origin of the LXX.[11] The first theory, which is associated with H. St. J. Thackeray, is that the translation of the Hebrew Scriptures into Greek was made to meet the liturgical needs of the Alexandrian Greek Jews.[12] The advantage of this view is that it offers a reasonable *Sitz im Leben* for the translation. The Jewish community in Egypt, separated from the language and culture of Palestine, eventually would have required a translation for its worship, which was central to its life. Thus, the Greek translation emerged to meet the liturgical needs of the community. Elias Bickerman has objected to the liturgical view by arguing that the Alexandrian Jewish community would hardly have needed a translation of the entire Pentateuch to meet its needs, and that the reading of the Scripture in the synagogue cannot be attested in the third century B.C.E.[13] These are valid criticisms and suggest that more attention should be paid to Brock's theory that the educational needs of the community were the primary motivation for the creation of the LXX.[14] With each passing year the distance from Palestine would have grown greater; thus, the desire of the Jewish community to preserve its religious heritage would have become more important. Given these circumstances, the leaders would have had to educate the Alexandrian Jewish community in its laws and customs by means of the Greek language. The weakness of this view, as Brock himself notes, is that there is a "complete lack of any evidence about Jewish education in Egypt in this period."[15]

Recently, the educational theory has been reformulated based on the nature of the OG translations. Albert Pietersma, building on the argument of Brock that the methodology of the LXX translators served to bring the reader to the source text, has argued that the best way to understand the Greek translations is by using the interlinear model. Pietersma is not suggesting that there ever existed an actual interlinear text of the Hebrew and the Greek Scriptures or that this model explains all of the LXX books; none-

---

11. See Jellicoe, *Septuagint and Modern Study,* pp. 63-64, 70-73 for Gaster's theory that the LXX had a Palestinian origin and for a summary of the transcription theory of Wutz. See also the discussion of these theories by N. Fernández Marcos, *The Septuagint in Context* (Leiden: Brill, 2001), pp. 53-65.

12. H. St. J. Thackeray, *The Septuagint and Jewish Worship* (Oxford: Oxford University Press, 1920). Jellicoe (*Septuagint and Modern Study,* pp. 64-70) has an excellent summary of Thackeray's views.

13. E. J. Bickerman, "The Septuagint as a Translation," *Proceedings of the American Academy of Jewish Research* 28 (1959): 7-8.

14. Brock, "Phenomenon," p. 16.

15. Brock, "Phenomenon," p. 16.

theless, he argues that the basic approach of formal equivalence employed by the translators creates a vertical relationship between the Greek translations and their Hebrew source texts. This vertical relationship is exemplified by the fact that the Greek translators tended to translate smaller units, phrase for phrase or even word for word at times, and that they were inclined to employ stereotypical equivalents in their translation of vocabulary, which created problems at the lexical level for determining meaning. We have discussed these issues previously in the chapters on translation technique. The point of these phenomena for Pietersma is that they demonstrate the subservient nature of the Greek translated texts to the Hebrew texts; the Greek translations served to help the Jewish-Greek reader understand the Hebrew source text. Thus, the proposed educational setting for the development of the LXX would best explain the fact that there is an interlinear relationship between the LXX and the HB.[16] However, since all of the LXX books do not share the same degree of formal equivalence to the Hebrew, it is unlikely that the proposed educational setting explains the translation of all the LXX books. Presumably, there may have been a variety of needs that resulted in the ongoing translation of the Scriptures into Greek. Certainly, the evidence of competing ventures and recensional activity prior to the common era suggests that the Greek-speaking Jewish community wanted their Scriptures in their own language.

The Remaking of the LXX Text

Whether or not one accepts that the educational needs of the Jewish community provided the original motivation for the inception of the LXX, around a century later the *Letter of Aristeas* was written to defend its authority. Certainly the process of revising the OG began before the common era, and throughout the first centuries of the Early Church there was a significant amount of revising what had already been translated and new initiatives as well. Brock identifies the increasing concern to protect the verbal inspiration of Scripture in the Hellenistic period as the initial catalyst for revising the OG and creating a more literal and acceptable version.[17] The result of this scribal activity during the NT period was a plethora of texts that could be used and compared to each

---

16. A. Pietersma, "A New Paradigm for Addressing Old Questions: The Relevance of the Interlinear Model for the Study of the Septuagint," in *Bible and Computer*, ed. J. Cook (Leiden: Brill, 2002), pp. 337-64.

17. Brock, "Phenomenon," pp. 18-22.

other. Eventually the existence of such a variety of revisions and translations would provide fodder for the creation of many textual variants.

Besides the impact of the scribal activity on the NT there were other related factors that must be considered when we examine the NT and its use of the Greek Jewish Scriptures. The purpose of the remainder of this chapter is to explain the way in which these various elements impact on our understanding of the NT. We will begin with four sample passages from the NT and discuss the way in which they have used the sources.

1. 1 Cor. 15:54

NT   κατεπόθη ὁ θάνατος εἰς νῖκος.
                Death has been swallowed up in victory.

OG Isa. 25:8   κατέπιεν ὁ θάνατος ἰσχύσας
                Death swallowed them up, having prevailed.

TH Isa. 25:8 (attribution in Q)
                κατεπόθη ὁ θάνατος εἰς νῖκος.
                Death has been swallowed up in victory.

MT Isa. 25:8(7)   בִּלַּע הַמָּוֶת לָנֶצַח
                He will swallow up death forever.

In this instance the reading in 1 Corinthians 15:54 that has the majority of support in the NT manuscripts is the one that agrees with the TH translation in Isaiah 25:8.[18] Nothing about this citation suggests that it is dependent upon the Hebrew text either. So, at the very least, Paul knew of a tradition in which this was the reading in a Greek manuscript for Isaiah 25:8, and he cited it as authoritative Scripture. It cannot be known whether or not Paul was aware of the OG text or any other variant reading and chose the TH version because it fit better with what he wanted to declare.

2. 1 Cor. 15:45

NT   ἐγένετο ὁ πρῶτος ἄνθρωπος Ἀδὰμ εἰς ψυχὴν ζῶσαν
                and the first man, Adam, became a living being

OG Gen. 2:7   ἐγένετο ὁ ἄνθρωπος εἰς ψυχὴν ζῶσαν
                and the man became a living being

18. C. Stanley (*Paul and the Language of Scripture: Citation Technique in the Pauline Epistles and Contemporary Literature* [Cambridge: Cambridge University Press, 1992], pp. 210-11) and D. A. Koch (*Die Schrift als Zeuge des Evangeliums: Untersuchungen zur Verwendung und zum Verständnis der Schrift bei Paulus* [Tübingen: Mohr, 1986], pp. 61-63) both discuss that the evidence for the TH reading is somewhat divided; it is most likely that Paul has followed some reading in the LXX tradition.

Sym TH Gen. 2:7 (attributed to Philoponus)
    ἐγένετο ὁ Ἀδὰμ ἄνθρωπος εἰς ψυχὴν ζῶσαν
    and the man, Adam, became a living being
MT Gen. 2:7   וַיְהִי הָאָדָם לְנֶפֶשׁ חַיָּה
    and the man became a living being

It is possible that Paul based his citation of Genesis 2:7 on a Greek manuscript that included Ἀδὰμ, which inspired his contrast of the *first man* Adam with Christ.[19] However, the attribution of this reading to Sym and TH is actually part of a longer citation by the church father Philoponus. Using the Church Fathers for textual criticism is a delicate task at the best of times because we do not know whether they are quoting directly or citing from memory, and there are times when their texts have been corrupted in transmission. It is for these reasons that the evidence from the Church Fathers is used primarily as a supporting witness for text-critical decisions. In this instance there are no other LXX witnesses that support the insertion of Ἀδὰμ, while at the same time it is easy to see the way in which Philoponus might have inadvertently added Ἀδὰμ in his long citation under the influence of 1 Corinthians 15:45. The majority of the NT manuscripts also support the reading in 15:45 as it appears above.[20] Thus, the evidence is not strong enough to argue that Paul's citation is based on a LXX manuscript that read like Philoponus's. It is more likely that Paul has reinterpreted Genesis 2:7 in light of the contrast he wishes to make between Adam and Christ.[21] Paul elaborates on this distinction between Adam and Christ in Romans 5:12-21.

3. Heb. 1:6

  NT   καὶ προσκυνησάτωσαν αὐτῷ πάντες ἄγγελοι θεοῦ
        And worship him all angels of God.

  OG Deut. 32:43 καὶ προσκυνησάτωσαν αὐτῷ πάντες υἱοὶ θεοῦ
        And worship him all sons of God (or *all you gods*).

  MT Deut. 32:43 There is no equivalent in the Hebrew for the reading in the OG.

19. This is the view of Stanley, *Paul*, pp. 208-9. It is true that Paul could "have found the words ὁ Ἀδὰμ ἄνθρωπος in his *Vorlage*" and then created the figure of the last Adam around it, but the presence of Ἀδὰμ in a manuscript is not necessary for the theological concept in Romans that distinguishes between the first and the last Adam, as Stanley argues.

20. Most notably B and the first corrector of p46, along with a few other witnesses, omit πρῶτος.

21. Cf. Koch, *Schrift als Zeuge des Evangeliums*, p. 135.

Although this passage does not involve a variant reading from one of the recensions, it is an excellent example of the complicated relationship that exists among the texts of the NT, MT, and OG. The first matter to deal with is the difference between the MT and OG. Why is there no equivalent for the OG in the MT? Looking at the passages in parallel alignment will help us to understand the problem.

MT Deut. 32:43	OG Deut. 32:43
1	εὐφράνθητε οὐρανοὶ ἅμα αὐτῷ
2	καὶ προσκυνησάτωσαν αὐτῷ
3	πάντες υἱοὶ θεοῦ
˜ הַרְנִינוּ גוֹיִם עַמּוֹ	εὐφράνθητε ἔθνη μετὰ τοῦ λαοῦ αὐτοῦ
5	καὶ ἐνισχυσάτωσαν αὐτῷ πάντες ἄγγελοι θεοῦ
6 כִּי דַם־עֲבָדָיו יִקּוֹם	ὅτι τὸ αἷμα τῶν υἱῶν αὐτοῦ ἐκδικᾶται

MT Deut. 32:43	OG Deut. 32:43
1	*Praise, O Heavens, together with him,*
2	*and worship him,*
3	*all sons of God.*[22]
4 *Praise, O Nations, his people,*	*Praise, O Nations, with his people,*
5	*and strengthen him, all angels of God,*
6 *for he vindicates the blood*	*for he vindicates the blood of his children.*
of his servants.	

Referring to the OG text of Deuteronomy 32:43 we see that there are two lines beginning with the word εὐφράνθητε *Praise,* but there is no equivalent in MT for the whole first line (numbered 1-2 above). Instead, verse 43 in MT begins with the line הַרְנִינוּ גוֹיִם עַמּוֹ *Praise, O Nations, his people.* The OG also has another addition in the verse (numbered 5 above). The net result is that the MT has only one clause invoking praise (line 4) whereas the OG has two (lines 1 and 4). If there were not two additions, most scholars would probably readily agree that the initial one is most likely an error in the trans-

---

22. Presumably, υἱοὶ θεοῦ is a translation of something like בני האלהים *sons of god* in its source text (cf. Gen. 6:2). The Hebrew word בֵּן *son* (as well as the Aramaic equivalent בר) was used in construct with another noun to indicate that an individual or group belonged to a class of beings. See P. Joüon, *A Grammar of Biblical Hebrew,* trans. and rev. T. Muraoka (Rome: Editrice Pontificio Istituto Biblico, 1991), p. 129j. Thus, בני האלהים *sons of god* equals the class of divine beings or gods, which is the basis for the translation in the NRSV. We use *sons of God* because υἱοὶ θεοῦ was not a Greek idiom that was equivalent to the Hebrew expression. The Greek reflects formal equivalence.

mission of the MT. Due to parablepsis the scribe for the MT passed from a first occurrence of הַרְנִינוּ (rendered by εὐφράνθητε) in line 1 to the second in line 4 and omitted a whole clause (our lines 1 to 3), which is preserved in the OG. However, the nature of the addition as well as the presence of the second clause in line 5 may suggest to some that the longer reading in the OG is the result of a double translation or explanatory addition to what was originally only one clause as we have in the MT. It seems to me that this view may be rooted in an uncritical assumption that the Hebrew text is inherently more trustworthy than a translation or just plain bias towards the MT. These comments are not intended to denigrate the MT, because it is an important witness to the biblical text, but the MT is not equivalent to the OT or HB. The allegiance that has been shown toward the MT by scholars despite the evidence of the other witnesses is similar in many ways to those who regard the King James version as the only trustworthy English translation. It is always possible that the Greek translator made additions to a text like the MT, but the question is whether that is likely and what is the best explanation for the available evidence? After all, if the two clauses that are represented in the OG were based on a Hebrew *Vorlage,* the OG would witness to two parallel clauses advocating praise to God and parallelism is a characteristic of Hebrew. Purely, from the contents and style of the texts, then, there is no good reason to prefer the MT over the OG. Assuming that we can determine an original text in this instance, what reading should we prefer?

It becomes all the more unlikely that the Greek translator arbitrarily added material to his translation when we consider that there are not similar examples of the translator adding clauses elsewhere in the book. Furthermore, the presence of the second addition (line 5) and the similarities of vocabulary in the OG between our lines 1-3 and 4-5 suggest that it is more likely that something has been omitted in the Hebrew text. Though it would be difficult to solve the differences between the MT and OG in this particular verse to everyone's satisfaction, the similarity between πάντες υἱοὶ θεοῦ *all you sons of God* or *all you Gods* and πάντες ἄγγελοι θεοῦ *all angels of God* in the OG may offer further evidence that the MT has omitted elements though a series of textual errors rather than indicating that the OG reflects a double translation.

The fact that Hebrews 1:6 has καὶ προσκυνησάτωσαν αὐτῷ πάντες ἄγγελοι θεοῦ *And worship him all angels of God* might mean that ἄγγελοι *angels* was present in some Greek manuscript of Deuteronomy that the writer of Hebrews used or that there was a Hebrew manuscript with the word מלאכים *angels.* At the same time, we note that the text of Hebrews 1:6 also does not clearly support the longer OG text in Deuteronomy 32:43 either. In OG 32:43

we read καὶ <u>ἐνισχυσάτωσαν</u> αὐτῷ πάντες ἄγγελοι θεοῦ *And* <u>strengthen</u> *him all angels of God* while Hebrews 1:6 has the verb προσκυνησάτωσαν *worship,* which appears in the first clause of OG Deuteronomy 32:43. How do we explain the use of the different verb on the part of the writer of Hebrews? There are several possible answers and ways to approach a solution to this question.

Prior to the discovery of the *DSS,* one line of approach was to suggest that the quotation actually represents a conflation of a couple of different passages. We have already seen that the combination of passages does happen in the NT writings elsewhere. It is possible that this happened in Hebrews 1:6 because the text of LXX Psalm 96(97):7 reads προσκυνήσατε αὐτῷ πάντες οἱ ἄγγελοι αὐτοῦ *Worship him all his angels.* Therefore, it could be argued that the Scripture cited by the writer of Hebrews is a combination of Psalm 96:7 and Deuteronomy 32:43 from the LXX. The attraction of this suggestion is that it does combine an imperative form of the verb *worship* with *angels.*

Though LXX Psalm 96(97):7 may have played a role in shaping Hebrews 1:6, it seems unnecessary to posit its use when all of the elements for the quotation are present in OG Deuteronomy 32:43. Why should we presume the combination of two separate texts when we require the use of only one? Beginning in v. 4 of chapter one the writer of Hebrews contrasts the Son, meaning Christ, and the angels, by emphasizing the superiority of the Son through a series of citations from Scripture. The quotation from Deuteronomy 32:43 underscores the subordinate position of the angels in comparison to the Son because the angels *worship* him. Given the theological purposes of the writer in this context it is reasonable to conclude that the author was aware of a manuscript of Deuteronomy 32:43 similar or identical to the longer form of the OG and combined the two similar clauses to produce the one that we have in Hebrews 1:6. In fact, the parallelism of the two phrases *all you gods* or *all you sons of God* and *all you angels of God* invites the substitution, particularly since there is scriptural support for making an identification of *angels* with the *sons of God* (see MT Job 1:6; 2:1; Ps. 8:6(5)).[23]

The other possible answer to the question of the source for the quotation in Hebrews 1:6 is that it represents a direct quotation from a different *Vorlage.* However, the likelihood that there was such a text is reasonable because we find the text of OG Deuteronomy 32:43 repeated almost verbatim in the Odes of Solomon 2:43. What makes the text of Odes 2:43 so interesting is that it agrees almost verbatim with Hebrews 1:6: καὶ προσκυνησάτωσαν αὐτῷ πάντες οἱ ἄγγελοι θεοῦ *And worship him all the angels of God.*

---

23. In each of these cases where MT reads *god(s)* (ה)אלהים the OG translators have employed ἀγγέλους *angels.*

Odes 2:43
εὐφράνθητε οὐρανοὶ ἅμα αὐτῷ
καὶ προσκυνησάτωσαν αὐτῷ
πάντες οἱ ἄγγελοι θεοῦ
εὐφράνθητε ἔθνη μετὰ τοῦ λαοῦ αὐτοῦ
καὶ ἐνισχυσάτωσαν αὐτῷ
πάντες υἱοὶ θεοῦ
ὅτι τὸ αἷμα τῶν υἱῶν αὐτοῦ
ἐκδικᾶται

Deut. 32:43
εὐφράνθητε οὐρανοί ἅμα αὐτῷ
καὶ προσκυνησάτωσαν αὐτῷ
πάντες υἱοὶ θεοῦ
εὐφράνθητε ἔθνη μετὰ τοῦ λαοῦ αὐτοῦ
καὶ ἐνισχυσάτωσαν αὐτῷ
πάντες ἄγγελοι θεοῦ
ὅτι τὸ αἷμα τῶν υἱῶν αὐτοῦ
ἐκδικᾶται

Odes 2:43
Praise, O Heavens, together with him,
*and **worship him,***
all the angels of God.
Praise, O Nations, with his people,
*and **strengthen him,***
all sons of God,
for he vindicates the blood of his
  children.

Deut. 32:43
Praise, O Heavens, together with him,
*and **worship him,***
all sons of God.
Praise, O Nations, with his people,
*and **strengthen him,***
all angels of God,
for he vindicates the blood of his
  children.

The major difference between Odes 2:43 and OG Deuteronomy 32:43 is that the clauses in which *angels* (ἄγγελοι, plus the definite article οἱ *the*) and *sons* (υἱοὶ) appear are reversed. However, there are two clauses invoking praise just like the OG. Thus, in Odes 2:43 there is almost an exact parallel to Hebrews 1:6: *And worship him all angels of God* καὶ προσκυνησάτωσαν αὐτῷ πάντες ἄγγελοι θεοῦ. Though the Odes of Solomon are a Christian work written ca. 100,[24] the parallel between Odes 2:43 and OG Deuteronomy 32:43 indicates that the Odes are dependent on a source similar to the OG version. At the same time, the distinctive agreement *And worship him all angels of God* between Odes 2:43 and Hebrews 1:6 might mean that Hebrews 1:6 is based upon Odes 2:43.

Finally, we may note that among the *DSS* there are a number of fragments of several different texts of Deuteronomy from cave four. Though *4QDeut^c* and *4QDeut^h* both have texts that support readings in the LXX tradition of Deuteronomy, neither of the fragments preserves Deuteronomy 32:43. The passage is contained in *4QDeut^q*,[25] however, which reads:

24. J. H. Charlesworth, "The Odes of Solomon," in *The Old Testament Pseudepigrapha* (Garden City, N.Y.: Doubleday, 1983), pp. 726-27.

25. For the texts, see E. Ulrich et al., *Qumran Cave 4: IX: Deuteronomy, Joshua, Judges, Kings. DJD* XIV (Oxford: Clarendon: 1986). See p. 114 for *4QDeut^a*.

1	הרנינו שמים עמו	*Praise, O Heavens, his people!*
2	והשתחוו לו כל אלהים	*Worship him, every god,*
3	כי דם בניו יקום	*for he vindicates the blood of his children.*
4	ונקם ישיב לצריו	*He will bring vengeance to his enemies,*
5	ולמשנאיו ישלם	*and he will repay his enemies*
6	ויכפר אדמת עמו	*and cleanse the land of his people.*

The reading in *4QDeut*ᑫ is interesting because of the way that it is both similar to and different from the text in the OG and MT. First, we note that like
the MT it only has one clause that invokes praise to God. Second, והשתחוו
לו כל אלהים. *And worship him every god* (or *all gods/divine beings*) is almost
identical to OG's καὶ προσκυνησάτωσαν αὐτῷ πάντες υἱοὶ θεοῦ *And worship
him all sons of God*. The difference is that if we retrovert the reading of the
OG back into Hebrew we would get והשתחוו לו כל בני אלהים, i.e. the OG
has υἱοὶ *sons*, which reflects the fact that OG read the typical Semitic idiom
בני אלהים *sons of god* in its *Vorlage*. Third, the inclusion of עמו *his people* in
our line one of *4QDeut*ᑫ reflects the second clause in the OG where it is the
nations who are to offer praise to God's people. This clause with its exhortation for the angels to strengthen him is not otherwise represented in the
Qumran fragment. Fourth, though we did not include the whole of Deuteronomy 32:43 in our translation of the OG and MT, the clause ישלם
ולמשנאיו *and he will repay his enemies* (line 5 above) is another omission in
the MT that is represented in the OG. There are a couple of other differences
when these texts are compared, but we can limit our discussion to the present observations.

Despite the obvious agreement between *4QDeut*ᑫ and the OG in the exhortation *And worship him every god/all you gods*, there is not a direct dependence of the one upon the other. *4QDeut*ᑫ agrees with OG in preserving one
additional clause, but the omissions of εὐφράνθητε ἔθνη *Praise, O Nations*,
which is preserved in the MT, and καὶ ἐνισχυσάτωσαν αὐτῷ πάντες ἄγγελοι
θεοῦ *and strengthen him all angels of God*, which is supported in part by Hebrews 1:6 and Odes 2:43, mean that the opening invocation to praise in
*4QDeut*ᑫ is most likely the result of textual corruption from a text that was
originally longer like that preserved in the OG. This conclusion is confirmed
by the presence of עמו *his people* in *4QDeut*ᑫ. Therefore, both MT and
*4QDeut*ᑫ witness to variant readings that have suffered corruption from an
originally longer text of this verse, but their errors are independent from one
another. It is easier to visualize this by placing the opening lines of the
*4QDeut*ᑫ, MT and OG in parallel alignment.

4QDeut^q	MT	OG
1 הרנינו שמים עמו		εὐφράνθητε οὐρανοί ἅμα αὐτῷ
2 והשתחוו לו		καὶ προσκυνησάτωσαν αὐτῷ
3 כל אלהים		πάντες υἱοὶ θεοῦ
4	הַרְנִינוּ גוֹיִם עַמּוֹ	εὐφράνθητε ἔθνη μετὰ τοῦ λαοῦ αὐτου
5		καὶ ἐνισχυσάτωσαν αὐτῷ πάντες ἄγγελοι θεοῦ
6 כי דם בניו יקום	כִּי דַם־עֲבָדָיו יִקּוֹם	ὅτι τὸ αἷμα τῶν υἱῶν αὐτοῦ ἐκδικᾶται

4QDeut^q	MT	OG
1 *Praise, O Heavens,* his ***people,***		*Praise, O Heavens, together with him,*
2 *and worship him,*		*and worship him,*
3 *every god,*		*all sons of God.*
4	*Praise, O Nations, his people,*	*Praise, O Nations, with his **people,***
5		*and strengthen him, all angels of God,*
6 *for he vindicates the blood of his **children.***	*for he vindicates the blood of his **servants.***	*for he vindicates the blood of his **children.***

The differences between these texts is striking, and, when considered along with Odes 2:43 and Hebrews 1:6, they provide an excellent example of the plurality of texts that existed in the period when the NT emerged. It is also interesting to note that although modern translations offer various renditions of Deuteronomy 32:43 and refer to the LXX and Qumran for support, none of them include two invocations to praise in the manner that is witnessed to by the OG.[26] For example, a footnote in the NIV informs the reader that the Septuagint adds *and let all the angels worship him.*[27] The NRSV, which follows *4QDeut^q*, actually has several footnotes, though the reader would never be able to piece together the differences between the texts, and one of the notes is misleading.[28] The NRSV correctly notes that the MT lacks *worship him, all you gods!* and that a manuscript from Qumran (*4QDeut^q*) and the Greek (it does not specify what Greek text) have *children* rather than *ser-*

26. It is also doubtful whether one could actually understand how the translators of the modern versions justify their particular renderings without an analysis of the ancient texts.

27. *New International Version* (Grand Rapids: Zondervan, 1973).

28. *New Revised Standard Version* (Oxford: University Press, 1989).

vants as in the MT. However, it also suggests that the manuscript from Qumran and the Greek read *heavens* against *nations* in the MT. This is misleading because the OG does not use *heavens* in collocation with the phrase *with his people*. These are parts of two separate clauses in the OG. This brief foray into the modern translations is the type of evidence that confirms our earlier suggestion that there is a bias against the OG because it is a translation, especially when our analysis has shown that the longer version in the OG preserves the most original text that we can reconstruct.

To conclude our discussion of this complex passage, it is most probable that the author of Hebrews cited a source like that witnessed to in Odes 2:43 verbatim, though he may have creatively modified a text like OG Deuteronomy 32:43. Regardless, the net result is that the passages in Odes 2:43 and Hebrews 1:6 are both related to the longer reading preserved in the OG that is not in the MT or *4QDeut^q*. Thus, if we were to presume that the OG is in some way the "original" text, or at least that it represents the earliest witness to the original text that we presently have, then we can observe that *4QDeut^q*, MT, and Odes 2:43/Hebrews 1:6 represent three separate and distinct ways that the text was transmitted and they all would have been read as Scripture.

4. 1 Pet. 1:24-25

NT 1 Pet. 1:24-25	OG Isa. 40:6-7	1QIsa^a 40:6-7	MT Isa. 40:6-8
πᾶσα σὰρξ	πᾶσα σὰρξ	כול הבשר	כָּל־הַבָּשָׂר
ὡς χόρτος	χόρτος	חציר	חָצִיר
καὶ πᾶσα	καὶ πᾶσα	וכול	וְכָל־
δόξα αὐτῆς	δόξα ἀνθρώπου	חסדיו	חַסְדּוֹ
ὡς ἄνθος χόρτου	ὡς ἄνθος χόρτου	כציץ השדה	כְּצִיץ הַשָּׂדֶה
ἐξηράνθη ὁ χόρτος	ἐξηράνθη ὁ χόρτος	יבש חציר	יָבֵשׁ חָצִיר
καὶ τὸ ἄνθος ἐξέπεσεν	καὶ τὸ ἄνθος ἐξέπεσε	נבל ציץ	נָבֵל צִיץ
			כִּי רוּחַ יְהוָה
			נָשְׁבָה בּוֹ
			אָכֵן חָצִיר הָעָם
			יָבֵשׁ חָצִיר
			נָבֵל צִיץ
τὸ δὲ ῥῆμα	τὸ δὲ ῥῆμα	ודבר	וּדְבַר־
κυρίου	τοῦ θεοῦ ἡμῶν	אלוהינו	אֱלֹהֵינוּ
μένει	μένει	יקום	יָקוּם
εἰς τὸν αἰῶνα.	εἰς τὸν αἰῶνα.	לעולם	לְעוֹלָם

NT 1 Pet. 1:24-25	OG Isa. 40:6-7	1QIsa*ᵃ* 40:6-7	MT Isa. 40:6-8
All flesh	All people	All people	All people
is like grass,	are grass,	are grass;	are grass;
and all	and all	their	their
its glory	the glory of	constancy	constancy[29]
	humanity.		
like the flower	like the flower	is like the flower	is like the flower
of grass.	of grass.	of the field.	of the field.
The grass withers,	The grass withers,	The grass withers,	The grass withers,
and the flower	and the flower	the flower fades,	the flower fades,
falls,	falls,		
			when the breath
			of the Lord
			blows upon it;
			surely the people
			are grass.
			The grass withers,
			the flower fades;
but the word	but the word	but the word	but the word
of the Lord	of our God	of our God	of our God
endures	endures	will stand	will stand
forever.	forever.	forever.	forever.

Our first observation is that the reading in 1 Peter has only a few minor variants and is fairly similar to the OG, which is closer to the shorter reading in the Qumran manuscript 1QIsa*ᵃ* than to that in the MT.[30] There are other variants in the LXX manuscripts, but we will concentrate on the shorter reading. Looking at the second apparatus in the Göttingen edition, we find that with minor variations the addition of ὅτι πνεῦμα κυρίου ἔπνευσεν εἰς αὐτὸν ἀληθῶς χόρτος ὁ λαὸς ἐξηράνθη ὁ χόρτος ἐξέπεσε τὸ ἄνθος *because the breath of the Lord blows upon it; surely the people are grass. The grass withers, the flower fades* is attributed to Sym and TH. Aq is also named as having the addition along with Sym and TH in one manuscript (86), while in another

29. The Hebrew noun is חסד, which is normally glossed as "goodness," "loving kindness," or "steadfast love." The latter refers particularly to God's kindness toward humanity. Also, the MT has the singular suffix while 1QIsa*ᵃ* has the plural.

30. There are corrections by a second hand in 1QIsa*ᵃ* to bring the text into conformity with what we read in the MT, but the original scribe had the shorter reading. The text of this passage in 1QIsa*ᵃ* is described more completely in T. H. Lim, *Holy Scripture in the Qumran Commentaries and Pauline Letters* (Oxford: Clarendon, 1997), pp. 144-46.

the attribution to Aq is shorter (omitting ὅτι . . . αὐτόν) and has πράσον for χόρτος. The addition of these words, which is marked with an asterisk in some manuscripts, brings the LXX texts into closer conformity with the MT. Due to the later dominance of the proto-MT form of Isaiah, during the course of the transmission of the texts the words were added so that the Greek text would more closely mirror the Hebrew.

Prior to the discovery of the *DSS* we could easily draw the conclusion that the shorter OG reading was due to parablepsis by the translator because יבש חציר נבל ציץ *the grass withers, the flower fades* occurs twice in the MT. Presumably the person copying the manuscript began by writing this phrase, and then when he looked back at the passage, his eyes went from the first place where the phrase occurred to the second. With the evidence of *1QIsaᵃ*, however, it is more likely that the OG translation was based on a Hebrew manuscript of Isaiah that contained the shorter reading, though the shorter reading was due to an error of parablepsis by a scribe copying the Hebrew text.

The other variant between the OG and MT/1QIsaᵃ that is interesting to note is that the OG has δόξα ἀνθρώπου *the glory of humanity* for חסדו *their (its) constancy*. Due to the appearance of δόξα *glory* in the OG and 1 Peter, the editors of BHS have suggested that the *Vorlage* for the OG was different (1 Peter really has no bearing on the issue if the quotation relies on the OG). There is some validity to this suggestion because this passage would be the only occurrence in which δόξα renders חסד (appears over 250x) in the entire LXX. However, the MT and *1QIsaᵃ* agree in their reading. So, either the OG engaged in some *Tendenz* at this point or the translator read a different word even though the *Vorlage* actually had חסדו.

The other curiosity about δόξα ἀνθρώπου in the OG is that 1 Peter 1:24 has δόξα αὐτῆς *its glory*. In other words, the choice of *glory* depends on the OG, but the use of the pronoun would go back to a singular suffix as in the MT. How is this best explained? Given the fact that there is virtually no textual support for the inclusion of ἀνθρώπου in 1 Peter, either the author of 1 Peter had access to both the Hebrew and Greek Scriptures or there was an LXX manuscript that had the pronoun αὐτῆς instead of ἀνθρώπου. Without more textual evidence it is impossible to know which of these choices is more likely.

The Relationships between the Texts

The texts that we have examined above illustrate the complicated nature of the relationships between the manuscripts of the MT, LXX, and NT. When working with quotations of Scripture in the NT the question usually is not as simplistic as, "Is this based on a Hebrew or Greek text?" Rather, the question is, "Which text or texts might this reading reflect?" In some cases a quotation from the Scriptures appears to be directly from the OG or a translation from the Hebrew Scriptures. Likewise, many allusions or references in the NT to events or people in the Scriptures are general in nature, and there is nothing significant about the type of text that the author is employing. Other times, however, quotations do not correspond directly with our existing OG or MT. In some of these cases we have witnesses to an alternative Greek text that was probably the basis for the quotation, such as in 1 Corinthians 15:54. In others the explanation may lie in an alternative Semitic text such as we now have available in the *DSS,* and is exemplified by the citation of Isaiah 40:6-8 in 1 Peter 1:24-25. Still other citations like Hebrews 1:6 demonstrate evidence of an alternative Greek textual tradition, but their foundation in a Semitic source is less clear.

The citation of the form of the above texts in the NT in contrast to what is preserved in the HB also demonstrates their theological significance. For now it is sufficient to note that particularly in the cases of 1 Corinthians 15:54 and Hebrews 1:6 the writers were dependent upon the Greek texts to make their point. The subject of the theological use of the LXX will be the focus of the next chapter.

A text such as 1 Peter 1:24-25 also serves to remind us that our understanding of the use of the LXX in the NT is part of the broader picture of the way in which the Jewish Scriptures were employed in the NT. It is clear from the use of the Greek Jewish Scriptures by the Early Church that they were influential contributors to the development of the theological thought of the NT writers.

Though we have secured the knowledge that the textual relationships between the NT and the Jewish Scriptures were very complicated, we have yet to provide an adequate basis for understanding why they were so complex and a way in which to interpret the data. The purpose of the remainder of this chapter is to establish a framework for understanding the nature of the Greek Jewish Scriptures and their use by the NT writers within the larger context of the Scriptures that were available for use in the first century. Specifically, we will examine four factors that bear on determining the sources or textual witnesses used by the NT writers: textual corruption, textual fluidity, method of citation, and the impact of the recensions on the transmission of the text.

Textual Corruption

Our society has become accustomed to the notion of a standard text because of the invention of the printing press. The printing press allowed for mass duplication of a written document and ensured that each copy would be exactly the same. Nowadays, personal computers and word processing programs allow for far more flexibility in the creation of a document, but once it is completed we have the capability to produce countless duplicates of this original. Prior to the invention of the printing press, however, documents were copied by hand, and error was natural to the process of copying ancient manuscripts. The environmental conditions, writing utensils, and the fact that documents were written in continuous script all contributed to the multiplication of errors.

There are various levels at which textual corruption plays a role in ancient manuscripts, particularly when the subject is the use of the LXX texts in the NT. The most basic level is within the transmission history of the text itself. Therefore, our first task is to determine the best critical text given the manuscript evidence. Much of this work has been done for the NT, and we have an excellent critical text available in NA[27]. In addition to providing a critical text, the apparatus of NA[27] also provides the most important textual variants. As we shall see below, however, the task of textual criticism is much more difficult for the LXX. Through the efforts of the editors for the Göttingen series we have critical texts for a number of the books of the LXX, but there are many books that still remain to be completed.

The task of providing critical editions for the LXX is more difficult than in the case of the NT as well. There are three reasons for this. The first is that we have fewer manuscripts to compare for a given book in the LXX than we do for a book in the NT. For the NT there are over five thousand complete or partial manuscripts, while for the LXX the number is far less. For example, there are only three main witnesses to the text of the OG version of the book of Daniel.[31] The second reason why critical texts for the LXX are more difficult to create is the date of the manuscripts. Apart from the relatively few Greek manuscripts that have been discovered among the *DSS*, our witnesses to the LXX are mostly from the third century c.e. and later. Two to three hundred years is a long time for errors to accumulate during the copying of manuscripts! Third, most of the books of the LXX are translations of the books of the HB. Although we can determine with reasonable certainty that many variants were the type of inner-Greek corruptions that one expects to occur during the process of copying texts, many decisions about what were

31. As Septuagint scholars well know, other than scattered patristic references and what can be surmised from NT citations, papyrus 967 was the first — and to date only — pre-Hexaplaric witness to the OG text of Daniel. The other two manuscripts are 88, which dates from the ninth to eleventh centuries c.e., and the Syh (Syro-Hexapla), which is a copy of an extremely literal translation of Origen's Hexapla into Syriac that was completed by Paul of Tella in 615-617 c.e.

the most likely readings of the OG are based on the relationship between the reading of the OG text and that of the MT.[32] Thus, there is a reciprocal relationship between the OG and HB, and all the witnesses to the texts in both of these traditions have suffered corruption. Despite these circumstances NT research is often concerned with determining whether the NT writer is employing as its source a text from the OG (or at least a witness in the LXX tradition) rather than the HB (or a Semitic witness). Obviously, answers are often not nearly as plentiful as questions, particularly when we factor in the effects of textual fluidity.

Textual Fluidity

In an earlier chapter we discussed the analysis of TT, which is necessary if one wants to compare the OG/LXX and its presumed *Vorlage* with the MT. However, even when we can determine with reasonable certainty the Hebrew *Vorlage* for a given reading in the OG, it is not a straightforward procedure to compare the OG to the Hebrew text. The reason for this is that the translation of the Hebrew Scriptures into Greek took place prior to the time when the text of the HB became standardized. Although there is no consensus concerning this issue, there is general agreement that the text of the HB was not standardized until sometime well after the end of the first century of the common era, and it may have been as late as the fifth century. By *standardization,* we mean the selection of one text form, from among many variant text forms, to represent the authoritative text. Once the text was standardized the copies of the text would have been very similar. We know, for example, from the evidence of the LXX and the *DSS* that some books of the Hebrew Bible existed in more than one literary form (see below). After the decision was made to standardize the text, one form of the Hebrew text became dominant while the other literary editions disappeared because they were not the form of the text that had been standardized. Standardization is not to be confused with the process of canonization, which has to do with the selection of particular books as authoritative Scripture by particular communities,[33] but the canon-

---

32. For the use of the LXX for text-criticism of the HB, see J. Wevers, "The Use of the Versions for Text Criticism: The Septuagint," in *La Septuaginta en la Investigacion Contemporanea (V Congreso De La IOSCS)*, ed. N. Fernández Marcos (Madrid: Instituto Arias Montano, 1985); A. Aejmelaeus, "What Can We Know About the Hebrew *Vorlage* of the Septuagint?" *ZAW* 99 (1981): 58-89; E. Tov, *The Text-Critical Use of the Septuagint in Biblical Research* (Jerusalem: Simor, 1981).

33. Although our discussions will treat the issue of canon, it is far too complex a subject to cover adequately within the parameters of this volume. It is sufficient at this

ization of particular books as inspired Scripture presumably helped precipitate the standardization of a particular form of the canonical books.

We know that there was no standard text of the HB before the second century C.E. because of the textual evidence of the LXX, the Samaritan Pentateuch, and the *DSS*. For example, the OG versions of Jeremiah and Job are considerably shorter than their counterparts in the MT. The books of Exodus, Samuel, and Daniel also have significant differences in content in places in the OG versions as compared to the MT.[34] At one time some scholars would have ignored these differences when commenting on the text of the HB, but it has become impossible to do so. The weight of the evidence is too great to be ignored.

As we discussed earlier, there are instances, for example, Proverbs, in which the differences between the Greek and Hebrew texts would seem to stem from the activity of the translator. That does not seem to be the case in the other books we have mentioned, however. In addition, for the book of Jeremiah there is now manuscript evidence from the *DSS* that supports the fact that there was a shorter Hebrew text of Jeremiah.[35] Moreover, although a majority of the manuscripts discovered at Qumran exhibit a proto-MT text, there are a significant number that do not.[36] To a certain degree the popularity and dominance of the proto-MT form in Palestine is also evidenced by the

---

point to acknowledge that the Jewish canon was not closed prior to the end of the first century. The implications of this will be explored more in the following chapter. For detailed discussions, see the recent volume edited by Lee McDonald and James Sanders, *The Canon Debate: On the Origins and Formation of the Bible* (Peabody: Hendrickson, 2002). See also A. C. Sundberg, *The Old Testament of the Early Church* (Cambridge, Mass.: Harvard University Press, 1964); J. Barr, *Holy Scripture: Canon, Authority, Criticism* (Philadelphia: Fortress, 1983); J. Barton, *Oracles of God* (Oxford: Oxford University Press, 1986).

34. For detailed discussions of the literary contents of the Septuagint texts of these books in comparison to the MT, see P. Gentry, *The Asterisked Materials in the Greek Job*, SCS 39 (Atlanta: Scholars Press, 1995); E. Tov, *The Septuagint Translation of Jeremiah and Baruch* (Missoula, Mont.: Scholars Press, 1976); E. Tov, "The Literary History of the Book of Jeremiah in the Light of Its Textual History," in *Empirical Models for Biblical Criticism*, ed. J. H. Tigay (Philadelphia: University of Pennsylvania Press, 1985); E. Ulrich, *The Qumran Text of Samuel and Josephus*, HSM 19 (Chico, Calif.: Scholars Press, 1978); A. Aejmelaeus, "Septuagintal Translation Techniques — A Solution to the Problem of the Tabernacle Account," in *Septuagint, Scrolls and Cognate Writings*, ed. G. J. Brooke and B. Lindars, SCS 33 (Atlanta: Scholars Press, 1992); D. O. Wenthe, "The Old Greek Translation of Daniel 1–6," Ph.D. dissertation, University of Notre Dame, 1991.

35. See J. G. Janzen, *Studies in the Text of Jeremiah*, HSM 6 (Cambridge, Mass.: Harvard University Press, 1973).

36. E. Tov (*Textual Criticism of the Hebrew Bible* [Minneapolis: Fortress, 1992], p. 115) suggests that 60 percent of the biblical manuscripts at Qumran are proto-MT.

fact that those texts associated with the *kaige* tradition tend to translate a *Vorlage* that is close to what is preserved in the MT, but our evidence for readings in most of the biblical books is limited.[37] The trend of textual diversity among the LXX, MT and *DSS* is also exhibited in the Samaritan Pentateuch.[38]

The existence of such a variety of forms of the text of the Hebrew Scriptures during the Second Temple period teaches us that there was no single authoritative text for some of the books that were regarded as Scripture at that time. For some books there is little evidence of textual diversity, but that may be only the result of chance. There might have been a very different textual tradition for the book of Ruth, for example, but it has not been preserved for us. The fact is we just do not know the extent of the textual diversity that existed because our knowledge is based on the textual evidence that we have discovered. Based on the texts that we do possess, however, there were multiple literary editions of some books of the Hebrew Bible in the period when the NT was being written.

Out of the multiple forms of the Hebrew texts for the individual books of Scripture the rabbis chose particular texts that later became standardized into what we now refer to as the MT. Why did they choose to standardize the longer form of Jeremiah or a particular version of Daniel? Who knows? For some books the answer to the question why a particular form was preserved may only be a matter of chance or survival. For others it is probably related to the fact that the specific text chosen and preserved was the one in use by the dominant group or "winners" in the religious and political arena, while the text of the marginalized group or "losers" became extinct.

The fact that there was no standardized text prior to the second century helps us to understand better the nature of the OG translation of a particular book in the HB. Since there was no standardized text, the OG translation of a particular book provides a snapshot of a particular text form of the Hebrew book that existed at that time. Therefore, in addition to accounting for the various changes and errors that may have occurred through the process of translation from Hebrew into Greek and the subsequent inner-Greek errors that accumulated in the translated text during its subsequent transmission and copying, we also realize that the OG text that we reconstruct is a witness to a particular Hebrew *Vorlage,* **but it is not the Hebrew text that has been**

---

37. Daniel is the only book for which we have a complete translation of "Theodotion," and we have already mentioned our position that Daniel is not part of the *kaige* recension as presently defined. However, the TH translation of Daniel certainly reflects a translation that is formally equivalent to a *Vorlage* that is very similar to the MT.

38. Tov provides a description of the Samaritan Pentateuch and the way in which it diverges from MT (*Textual Criticism,* pp. 80-100).

preserved for us in the MT. Thus, the comparison and evaluation of particular variant readings between the texts of the OG and the MT must keep in view the overall character of the relationship between the unit of translation and the presumed *Vorlage* to which it is being compared. The later dominance of the text form in the MT should not mislead us when we examine the relationship of the texts that existed prior to the end of the first century.[39] Though it has been common in biblical scholarship to give priority to the MT as the main witness to the HB, that position is no longer tenable. For example, Emanuel Tov, one of the preeminent authorities on the text of the HB, used to advocate that "textual criticism aims at the literary composition which has been accepted as binding (authoritative) by Jewish tradition. . . . This implies that the textual criticism of the Hebrew Bible aims at the literary compositions as contained in [the MT], to the exclusion of later (midrashic) compilations . . . and earlier and possibly parallel compositions."[40] In his most recent article on the subject, however, Tov has reversed his opinion in this matter and argues that MT should no longer hold this position since it is only one textual witness. "We suggest that we should single out no stage as the presumed Ur-Text . . . all these early stages were equally authoritative."[41] This helps explain why in some cases a NT citation of or an allusion to a passage in the HB may seem to reflect a different form of the text. Most likely it does.

Citation of the Texts

We have already discussed in chapter one the difficulties of comparing citations in the NT to possible sources due to the freedom exercised by the writers with respect to the use of the Scriptures. By and large the NT writers seem to have employed written sources for their quotations, though they may occasionally have relied on memory. It is possible that the NT authors also had some blocks of Scripture that acted as a type of reference manual, but they

39. The diversity and pluriformity of texts for books of the HB also raises questions about the goals of textual criticism for the HB. Is it possible to reconstruct an original text of books such as Jeremiah, Job, and Daniel when there were multiple literary editions? See E. Ulrich, "The Canonical Process, Textual Criticism, and Latter Stages in the Composition of the Bible," in *Sha'Arei Talmon*, ed. M. Fishbane, E. Tov, and W. W. Fields (Winona Lake, Ind.: Eisenbrauns, 1992), pp. 267-91; E. Ulrich, "Pluriformity in the Biblical Text, Text Groups, and Questions of Canon," in *The Madrid Qumran Congress*, ed. J. T. Barrera and L. V. Montaner, vol. 1 (Leiden: Brill, 1992).

40. See Tov, *Textual Criticism*, pp. 164-80.

41. E. Tov, "The Status of the Masoretic Text in Modern Text Editions of the Hebrew Bible," in *The Canon Debate: On the Origins and Formation of the Bible*, ed. L. M. McDonald and J. A. Sanders (Peabody: Hendrickson, 2002), p. 248.

also acted as *authors,* changing the text in ways due to context or their own theological purposes. The impetus for their creative application of the Scriptures was their conviction about the way that God had fulfilled the expectations of the covenant people through Christ "according to the Scriptures."

A good example of creative freedom in handling the Scriptures is attributed to Jesus in Matthew 11:10 (Luke 7:27), which seems to combine Malachi 3:1 and Isaiah 40:3 and states: Ἰδοὺ ἐγὼ ἀποστέλλω τὸν ἄγγελόν μου πρὸ προσώπου σου, ὃς κατασκευάσει τὴν ὁδόν σου ἔμπροσθέν σου *See, I send my messenger before you, who will prepare your way before you.* The facts are that the NT citation is not equivalent to the vocabulary of the OG, and that there are also departures from the MT — but those are not our concern at this particular point.[42] The freedom with respect to the sources is seen in the Matthean Jesus combining two different texts and applying them to John the Baptist (the messenger), and this application is based on the interpretation that Jesus is the Lord of whom the prophets were speaking. The reinterpretation results in two changes to the texts: both the MT and OG in Malachi 3:1 have *before me,* and both Malachi 3:1 and Isaiah 40:3 have *the way* in the OG and MT, while Matthew 11:10 has *before you* and *your way.* Therefore, in addition to the corrupt nature of the texts with which we are working, due in no small part to the textual fluidity of the time, we also have to contend with the changes introduced by the NT writers in their citation of the texts.

New Recensions and Translations

As if the multiplicity of texts of the HB, all of which were susceptible to textual corruption, were not enough, the transmission history of the LXX includes a number of recensions that were made to the Greek text. One of the main reasons for the production of Greek versions at the beginning of the common era was probably the existence of multiple Semitic forms of some biblical books. Another reason for the rise of multiple Greek versions of the Hebrew Scriptures in the early centuries of the common era was the theological discussions between Jews and Christians.[43] However, revision of the translations and/or new translations of books probably were initiated even before the beginning of the common era. This is known because some of the books in the LXX, such as Ruth, Canticles, and Lamentations, exhibit a close relationship with the translational approach in other books that are attributed to TH or the *kaige*

---

42. Among other differences, Matt. 11:10 adds ἔμπροσθέν σου *before you* at the end.

43. See S. P. Brock, "Phenomenon" and "Aspects of Translation Technique in Antiquity," *Greek, Roman, and Byzantine Studies* 20 (1979): 69-87; cf. Bickerman, "Septuagint."

tradition. There is also the *Letter of Aristeas,* which seems to have been written to defend the authority of the OG against competing ventures. So, it would seem that the process of revising the OG and the production of new translations may have begun even before the whole of the Hebrew Scriptures had been translated into Greek.[44] Below we will discuss the most important revisions of the OG and the new translations of the Hebrew Scriptures.

Origen and the Hexapla

The primary source of knowledge of the work of the versions by Theodotion, Aquila, and Symmachus is readings preserved from the Hexapla, which was composed by Origen (ca. 230-240 C.E.). Origen (b. 185) traveled extensively in Rome, Palestine, and Alexandria, which afforded him unique opportunities to study the Scriptures, and in 234 he moved to Caesarea where he established a school and eventually began work on his monumental text known as the Hexapla. In six parallel columns Origen set out: (1) the Hebrew text as he knew it; (2) a Greek transliteration of the Hebrew; (3) Aquila; (4) Symmachus; (5) the LXX; and (6) Theodotion. Origen employed Aristarchian symbols to indicate the relationship between the LXX and the Hebrew text. Greek words that had no counterpart in his Hebrew text were placed between an obelus and a metobelus, while Hebrew words that had no counterpart in the LXX were inserted in the text from another version, usually from the "Theodotion" text, and marked by an asterisk and a metobelus.[45] The largest preserved portions of the Hexapla are the Milan fragments of the Psalms, though they lack the first Hebrew column.[46]

---

44. It is possible to speak of a trend or a continuum toward more formal translations, but it is not possible to provide an absolute chronology of the translation of the Hebrew Scriptures into Greek. The most that we can determine is a relative chronology of translations. For example, O. Munnich ("La Septante des Psaumes et la Groupe *Kaige,*" *VT* 33 [1983]: 75-89) and S. Olofsson ("The Kaige Group and the Septuagint Book of Psalms," in *IX Congress of the IOSCS,* ed. B. Taylor, *SCS* 45 [Atlanta: Scholars Press, 1996]) have argued that the Psalms were employed by the later translators in the *kaige* tradition.

45. A more complete description of the use of the symbols and their appearance is provided by H. B. Swete, *An Introduction to the Old Testament in Greek,* rev. R. R. Ottley (Cambridge: Cambridge University Press, 1914), pp. 69-72. There is a separate apparatus in the Göttingen volumes that indicates the Hexaplaric readings.

46. See G. Mercati, *Psalterii Hexapli Reliquiae. Pars Prima: Codex Rescriptus Bybliothecae Ambrosianae O 39 Sup. Phototypice Expressus et Transcriptus* (Vatican City: Biblioteca Apostolica Vaticana, 1958). For a discussion of the Milan codex, see the articles on the Hexapla in A. Salvesen, *Origen's Hexapla and Fragments,* Texte und Studien zum antiken Judentum 58 (Tübingen: Mohr Siebeck, 1998).

The exact nature and extent of the Hexapla remain something of a mystery, however, primarily because of the scarcity of our manuscript evidence. For example, not only is the Hebrew column not preserved in the Milan fragments, but the Aristarchian symbols are not used either. Furthermore, Eusebius, who is an important source of information for the Early Church, never mentions the presence of the Aristarchian symbols in the Hexapla; and even Origen does not explicitly state that he employed them there. For these reasons it has been argued that the fifth column did not include the symbols, but that they must have been used in a separate recension that has not survived.[47] However, the symbols are well attested in the Syrohexapla, which was a very literal translation of the fifth column into Syriac by Paul the Bishop of Tella in 611.[48]

Complicating the task of understanding Origen's endeavor are the ancient testimony and terminology used to describe it. At one time it was common belief that in addition to the Hexapla there was a Tetrapla (a four-columned work) by Origen. Neither Eusebius[49] nor Jerome ever used this term, however, and H. M. Orlinsky has argued that Epiphanius is responsible for creating this scholarly fiction.[50] Generally speaking, Epiphanius is not regarded as a reliable source, and it may be that his confusing references to a Hexapla and Tetrapla helped create some inconsistencies in the testimony about Origen's labor; but there are notes in Greek manuscripts and colophons in the Syrohexapla that refer to a Tetrapla.[51] At the same time, there are other manuscripts that reflect a Hexaplaric text; but, like the Milan fragments, they are also without Origen's signs. Part of the solution to the confusing testimony may lie in the fact that Tetrapla means "fourfold" rather than "four-columned," and so some references to the Tetrapla may have meant the

47. Jellicoe, *Septuagint and Modern Study,* p. 124.

48. A. Vööbus, *The Hexapla and the Syro-Hexapla* (Wetteren: Cultura, 1971). The best-known manuscript of the Syrohexapla is Codex Ambrosianus, which contains most of the writing Prophets and the Writings.

49. Whether Eusebius uses the term Tetrapla depends on the reading of a variant. The text in *Die griechischen christlichen Schriftsteller der ersten Jahrhunderte* reads Τετρασσοις with the best Greek witnesses, while Swete (*Introduction,* p. 65) reads with the variant Τετραπλοις.

50. See H. M. Orlinsky, "Origen's Tetrapla — a Scholarly Fiction?" in *Proceedings of the First World Congress of Jewish Studies,* vol. 1 (Jerusalem: Magnes and Hebrew University, 1952), pp. 173-82. The text of Epiphanius in question is *De Mensuris et Ponderibus* 19. Cited in Swete, *Introduction,* p. 65.

51. For the evidence of the colophons, see R. G. Jenkins, "Colophons of the Syrohexapla and the Textgeschichte of the Recensions of Origen," in *VII Congress of the IOSCS,* ed. C. Cox, SCS 31 (Atlanta: Scholars Press, 1991), pp. 261-77.

four Greek versions: OG, Aquila, Theodotion, and Symmachus. Thus, there are conflicting accounts of testimonies and textual evidence. We could interpret the omission of the Aristarchian symbols in some manuscripts as evidence that the Hexapla never contained them, but we could just as easily conclude that they were omitted by Christian copyists in the course of time because they were not aware of their significance. Thus, there is no satisfactory explanation to account for all the data. At this point, it seems prudent to recognize that there was textual diversity in the Origenic tradition, without offering a definitive answer to the question of whether or not there existed some form of a separate and distinct Tetrapla.[52]

According to Eusebius's account (*HE* 6.16.1-3), Origen discovered three other versions in addition to Theodotion, Aquila, and Symmachus. It is probable that these anonymous versions, referred to as Quinta, Sexta, and Septima, did not encompass the whole of the Hebrew Scriptures.[53] The best attested of the three versions is Quinta, which G. Mercati has shown to be represented in the sixth column of the Hexapla for the Psalter rather than Theodotion.[54] For reasons such as this there are questions about the contents of the sixth column of the Hexapla,[55] which naturally raise further questions about what the original Hexapla might have looked like and its purpose.

Although questions remain concerning the content of the Hexapla, generally there have been two reasons given for Origen's engagement in the task.[56] In his *Commentary on Matthew* (Matthew 19:18) Origen states that his intention was to *heal* (ἰάσασθαι) the text of the Septuagint.[57] Here the emphasis is on the text-critical value of the Hexapla. In the *Letter to Africanus*,

---

52. For a thorough presentation of the evidence, see S. Sippilä, "The Tetrapla — Is It All Greek to Us?" *SJOT* 10 (1996): 169-82. Sippilä concludes that it is possible to support the traditional view, but he believes that the "Tetrapla is only a synonym for the Hexapla" (p. 182).

53. See Jellicoe, *Septuagint and Modern Study*, pp. 118-24 for a more detailed discussion.

54. Mercati, *Psalterii Hexapli Reliquiae. Pars Prima*, pp. xix-xxxv.

55. D. Barthélemy ("Les devanciers d'Aquila: première publication intégrale du texte des fragments du Dodécaprophéton," *VTSupp* 10 [Leiden: Brill, 1963], p. 269) argues that TH is represented in the seventh column of the Minor Prophets. Schmitt ("Stammt der sogenannte θ′ Text bei Daniel wirklich von Theodotion?" *MSU* 9 [1966]: 281-392) has demonstrated that *Theodotion* in Daniel is not the same as the TH attested for the remainder of the sixth column.

56. For a full discussion, see A. Kamasar, *Jerome, Greek Scholarship, and the Hebrew Bible* (Oxford: Clarendon, 1993), pp. 10-25.

57. For the full text see *Die griechischen christlichen Schriftsteller der ersten Jahrhunderte*, vol. 40. Also in Swete, *Introduction*, p. 60.

however, Origen indicates that his purpose was to provide a means for Christians and Jews, who were debating each other over the Scriptures, to know whether or not they had particular passages in common.[58] Thus, the motive for the Hexapla would be apologetics. In the view of N. R. M. de Lange, both of these motives were equally important.[59]

Despite Origen's best intentions to "heal" the Septuagint text, his efforts were largely a failure. The failure was inevitable because Origen assumed that the OG was based on the Hebrew text that existed during his life in the third century, whereas it was around this time that the text of the HB was in the process of becoming canonized. The Pentateuch had been translated at least five hundred years earlier, and when we consider our earlier discussions about textual diversity and books with double literary traditions, it is easy to recognize that Origen's assumption could never lead to restoring the OG. By adding the words that were missing from his OG in comparison to his Hebrew text, Origen would naturally employ the Greek version that was closest to the Hebrew that he had, which would differ from book to book. In the end, Origen created a mixed text. The problem was exacerbated during the course of transmission by the errors of copyists, who either did not bother to reproduce the Aristarchian symbols or did so inaccurately.[60]

Theodotion

The sixth column of Origen's Hexapla has been attributed to the work of "Theodotion" of Ephesus, who, according to early testimony, lived in the mid-second century. The most reliable reference to Theodotion is by Irenaeus in his treatise *Against Heresies* (3.24), in which he refers to Theodotion as an Ephesian and a Jewish proselyte. Since Irenaeus mentions Theodotion prior to Aquila, scholars have assumed that Theodotion preceded Aquila.[61] Although another reference to Theodotion by Epiphanius is unreliable for the

---

58. For the text and a discussion, see N. R. M. de Lange, *La Lettre à Africanus sur l'histoire de Suzanne* (Paris: Editions du Cerf, 1983).

59. de Lange, *La Lettre à Africanus,* pp. 497-98; cf. J. Schaper, "The Origin and Purpose of the Fifth Column," in *Origen's Hexapla and Fragments,* ed. A. Salvesen, Texte und Studien zum antiken Judentum 58 (Tübingen: Mohr Siebeck, 1998), pp. 3-15.

60. See I. Soisalon-Soininen, *Der Charakter der asterisierten Zusätze in der Septuaginta,* AASF, B, 114 (Helsinki: Suomalainen Tiedeakatemia, 1959).

61. Contrary to the order of the appearance of Aquila, Theodotion, Symmachus, in the Hexapla. See Jellicoe, *Septuagint and Modern Study,* pp. 83-94, and the discussion by J. A. Montgomery, *A Critical and Exegetical Commentary on the Book of Daniel* (New York: Charles Scribner's Sons, 1927), p. 47.

purpose of dating,[62] it appears to be further early confirmation that such a figure did exist.[63] However, A. Salvesen has examined Epiphanius's testimony about Aquila, Symmachus, and Theodotion and notes the use of stereotyped descriptions of each. She concludes that Epiphanius was attempting to discredit the three, and his "account should be treated with caution." Furthermore, Salvesen states, "It is interesting that Theodotion . . . is not subjected to the same vilification as Aquila and Symmachus. This may be because there was no such translator, and Epiphanius therefore had only a hazy notion of his biography."[64]

Despite the early claims for the existence of Theodotion, there are difficulties in determining the exact nature and extent of the work associated with him. For example, there are quotations of Theodotion's version, particularly from Daniel, that are found in the NT. This has led some to conclude that the historical Theodotion added to the work of an earlier writer, whom scholars at one time designated Ur-Theodotion. The problem of Ur-Theodotion is that the NT documents that reveal dependence on TH were written prior to the period when the historical Theodotion is believed to have lived.[65] A very good summary and early discussion of the problem of Ur-Theodotion is provided in an article by J. Gwynn.[66] Gwynn dates the historical Theodotion prior to Aquila, ca. 180, and explains the Theodotionic citations in the NT as minor revisions to a prior Greek version that was held in high authority by the Church and predated the OG preserved from the fifth column of the Hexapla.[67] Since

62. Montgomery, *Daniel*, pp. 46-50; Swete, *Introduction*, pp. 42-43. Epiphanius (*De mens. et pond.* 17) places Theodotion under Commodus (ca. 180). This is obviously contradicted by Irenaeus's reference in *Against Heresies*, which was written in 180-189.

63. If this Theodotion was in any way responsible for any revision/translation work in the LXX, he would have done this work between 130 and 180. Montgomery *(Daniel)* suggests an early dating, whereas Jellicoe (*Septuagint and Modern Study*, p. 92) places him "towards the end of the second century A.D."

64. See Salvesen, *Texte und Studien*, pp. 287-89. See also Barthélemy, "Devanciers d'Aquila," pp. 146-47, and the discussion of Jerome's uncertain identification of Theodotion: "And Theodotion, at any rate, was an unbeliever subsequent to the advent of Christ, although some assert that he was an Ebionite, which is another variety of Jew."

65. For a survey of the evidence of citations and allusions to OG and TH Daniel in NT and patristic authors, see P. Grelot, "Les versions grecques de Daniel," *Bib* 47 (1966): 381-402; F. C. Burkitt, *The Old Latin and The Itala* (Cambridge: Cambridge University Press, 1896).

66. J. Gwynn, "Theodotion," in *A Dictionary of Christian Biography*, ed. W. Smith and H. Wace (London: John Murrow, 1887), 4:970-79.

67. Gwynn, "Theodotion," p. 976. On this basis Gwynn could explain the early citations of the Chisian LXX, as well as why the Church would accept a revision by a Jewish proselyte.

the work of D. Barthélemy, scholars have devoted more time to discussing the recensional characteristics of *kaige*-Theodotion, and it has become increasingly difficult to clarify the extent of Theodotion's participation in the recension that bears his name.[68]

As we discussed in our introduction, some have attempted to propose more characteristics for *kaige,* and in this approach *kaige*-Theodotion or the *kaige* recension is conceived of as a unified work. However, it has been shown that the TH column in books such as Daniel and Job cannot be connected with *kaige,*[69] and that the sixth column of the Psalter and the Minor Prophets is not the work of TH either.[70] Therefore, with respect to the historicity of "Theodotion," the most we can conclude is that there might have been someone by that name who lived sometime during the second century C.E. who did some work translating and updating existing works. However, the readings that are attributed to TH do exhibit a similarity in their approach to translating, and it can also be affirmed that the readings marked as TH appear to originate from fairly literal (or formal) translations (or in some books revisions of the so-called Septuagint) of the Hebrew Scriptures that were very similar to what later became the standardized Hebrew text, which we now know as the MT. Thus, these Hebrew Scriptures are usually designated as proto-MT. At the same time, the readings marked as TH are not so homogenous that we can conclude that they originate from the same individual or group that attempted to standardize translation equivalents. The available data do not support a more definitive description of these texts. In order to advance our understanding of the nature and extent of *kaige,* it is essential that a more rigorous methodology be employed to investigate TH readings in books in which a critical text has been established. Only a more refined methodology will provide the means to determine which texts, if any, may be so closely related as to justify the conclusion that they originate from the same individual or school of translators.[71]

68. Besides Montgomery *(Daniel)* and Jellicoe *(Septuagint and Modern Study),* J. D. Shenkel *(Chronology and Recensional Development in the Greek Text of Kings, HSM* 1 [Cambridge, Mass.: Harvard University Press, 1968], p. 17); K. G. O'Connell *(The Theodotionic Revision of the Book of Exodus, HSM* 3 [Cambridge, Mass.: Harvard University Press, 1972], p. 5); and Tov *(Textual Criticism,* p. 145) allow for the later use or revision of the recension by "Theodotion," whereas Barthélemy ("Devanciers d'Aquila") rejects his involvement altogether.

69. A. Schmitt had already argued that TH in Daniel is not equivalent to the TH in the remainder of the sixth column of the Hexapla. He restates his position in "Die griechischen Danieltexte (θ und ὁ) und das Theodotionproblem," *BZ* 36 (1992): 1-15.

70. See the discussion of the Hexapla above.

71. See T. McLay, "It's a Question of Influence: The Old Greek and Theodotion Texts

Aquila

Besides "Theodotion" there are two other famous Jewish translations of the LXX. Aquila (ca. 130 C.E.), a Jewish proselyte from Pontus who was possibly a disciple of Rabbi Akiba, produced an extremely literal translation of the Hebrew. He has been identified with Onqelos, who according to the Talmud was responsible for the targum of the Pentateuch. Aquila's attempts to maintain a one-to-one correspondence between the Hebrew and Greek words were so far-reaching that the version cannot be understood without knowing the Hebrew from which it was translated. Besides providing word-for-word (and morpheme-for-morpheme) equivalents in the Greek, Aquila also followed the word order of the Hebrew.[72] There is an index to Aquila that was begun by J. Reider and completed by N. Turner.[73] Unfortunately, reviews of the volume have pointed out numerous errors, and so it must be used with extreme caution.

Symmachus

The other Jewish version preserved in the Hexapla was completed by Symmachus toward the end of the second century C.E. According to Epiphanius, Symmachus was a Samaritan who became a Jewish proselyte, though Eusebius and Jerome identify him as an Ebionite Jewish Christian. He provided a translation that was more in the style of everyday Greek while still rendering the Hebrew text faithfully, but he retained within it some haggadic elements for his Jewish audience.[74] Salvesen concludes that Symmachus knew Aquila's version, but she is more cautious about distinguishing TH and OG in his work.[75] She also notes that Jerome shows more evidence of influence from Symmachus in the Vulgate translation than readings from either Theodotion or Aquila.[76]

---

of Daniel," in *Origen's Hexapla and Fragments*, ed. A. Salvesen, Texte und Studien zum antiken Judentum 58 (Tübingen: Mohr Siebeck, 1998), pp. 231-54.

72. For a more detailed discussion, see Jellicoe, *Septuagint and Modern Study,* pp. 76-83, or Fernández Marcos, *Septuagint in Context,* pp. 109-21.

73. J. Reider and N. Turner, *An Index to Aquila, VTSupp* 12 (Leiden: Brill, 1966).

74. For a thorough discussion of the person and translation of Symmachus, see A. Salvesen, *Symmachus in the Pentateuch, JSSM* 15 (Manchester: University of Manchester Press, 1991), pp. 283-97, or Fernández Marcos, *Septuagint in Context,* pp. 123-39.

75. Salvesen, *Symmachus,* p. 262.

76. Salvesen, *Symmachus,* p. 279.

Lucian and Hesychius

Besides the monumental work of Origen, Jerome mentions two other recensions of the OG: one by Hesychius for use in Egypt and the other by Lucian for Antioch (ca. 311). However, there is no textual evidence to confirm the existence of the Hesychian recension, and any description of it would be purely speculative.[77] Although there is more known about the Lucianic (or *Antiochene*) text, it can be isolated only in certain books such as the prophets, Judges, and the books of Samuel and Kings. Besides certain manuscripts (primarily boc₂e₂), the recension has been isolated in the quotations by Theodoretus of Cyrus and St. John Chrysostom.[78] The Lucianic recension is characterized by additions to conform it to the MT and by grammatical corrections and changes in style to smooth the Greek. As was the case with the translation attributed to "Theodotion," A. Rahlfs was able to distinguish readings in Lucian's recension that reflect earlier sources than the historical Lucian. Most of the research on this problem has focused on 1-4 Reigns (Samuel and Kings). Barthélemy argued that the manuscripts boc₂ e₂ actually represent the OG in 1-4 Reigns, while Cross believes that the Lucianic manuscripts provide evidence of a proto-Lucianic text that was revised toward a Hebrew text similar to 1QSamᵃ. Tov, in a later article, supported Barthélemy's position by suggesting that a proto-Lucianic revision is unnecessary, though he did argue that the Lucianic readings witnessed also to a second layer of Lucianic revision.[79]

In summary, the plethora of texts and revisions of the OG that cropped up during the first centuries of the common era complicate our field of in-

---

77. S. Jellicoe is more favorable in "The Hesychian Recension Reconsidered," *JBL* 82 (1963): 409-18; but contrast E. Tov, who does not even mention Hesychius in his summary ("The Septuagint," in *Mikra: Text, Translation, Reading and Interpretation of the Hebrew Bible in Ancient Judaism and Early Christianity*, ed. M. J. Mulder and H. Sysling (Philadelphia: Fortress, 1988).

78. The majority of work on the Antiochene recension is being done by scholars based in Madrid. See N. Fernández Marcos, "Some Reflections on the Antiochian Text of the Septuagint," in *Studien zur Septuaginta — Robert Hanhart zu ehren*, ed. D. Fraenkel, U. Quast, and J. Wevers (Göttingen: Vandenhoeck & Ruprecht, 1990); N. Fernández Marcos, "The Textual Context of the Hexapla: Lucianic Texts and Vetus Latina," in *Origen's Hexapla and Fragments*, Texte und Studien zum antiken Judentum 58 (Tübingen: Mohr Siebeck, 1998). See also the article by Bernard Taylor ("The Lucianic Text of 1 Reigns: Three Texts Compared and Contrasted," *BIOSCS* 29 [1996]: 53-66), who also has done work on the Lucianic text.

79. E. Tov, "Lucian and Proto-Lucian: Toward a New Solution of the Problem," *RB* 79 (1972): 101-13.

quiry even further. We have seen that the *DSS*, and to a lesser extent the Samaritan Pentateuch, offer evidence of alternative literary editions or textual pluriformity of some of the books of the Hebrew Bible. We also know that some time after the initial translation of the Pentateuch into Greek in Alexandria work began on translating other Scriptures, and many of these books exhibit significant differences from the MT. Moreover, probably before this process was complete there were competing ventures in the form of alternative translations and/or revisions to the OG, which can be deduced from the *Letter of Aristeas*. This activity before the common era to change and/or improve the OG text is evident in texts like the Greek Minor Prophets' Scroll and the TH version of Daniel; therefore, the process of revising the OG was well under way when the NT was written. It was not much later (probably after most, if not all, of the NT was written) that Aquila, Symmachus, possibly Theodotion, and a few others whose names and identities remain obscure (known by designations like Quinta, Sexta, Septima) made their own contributions. Origen attempted to bring the results of the work of these scholars together and relate them to the OG and to what he believed to be the HB, and to a certain extent he did. Another recension of the OG from early in the fourth century is identified with Lucian in Antioch, Syria.

Unfortunately, our knowledge of all of these versions is scanty, confined by and large to marginal notes in LXX manuscripts and citations by the Early Church Fathers. It is also difficult to explain the textual pluriformity of the Hebrew Scriptures that is witnessed to by the Greek Jewish Scriptures and by the *DSS* when compared to the MT. Without reviewing the theories of F. M. Cross, S. Talmon, E. Tov, and E. Ulrich about the origin and development of the Hebrew Scriptures[80] — because that would be chasing a rabbit that offers far too little sustenance for the effort required given our present purposes — we can affirm from the data that there was a lot of recensional activity in Palestine and the neighboring regions in the first centuries of the common era. Our largest pool of data apart from marginal notes and citations is for the work attributed to Theodotion in the book of Daniel and in some passages and sections in 1-4 Reigns, Proverbs, Job, Isaiah, Jeremiah, and Ezekiel.[81] However, even if TH Daniel and TH Job were connected with the Theodotion of these other books we would still have only a fraction of Theodotion's translation of the Scriptures.

80. See n. 24 in the introduction.
81. See Schmitt, "Stammt der sogennante," p. 112 for the fragments of Theodotion's text that have been preserved in these books. We could expand the list to include Ruth, Canticles, and Lamentations, which in their present Greek form reflect formal translations similar to those associated with Theodotion *(kaige)*.

It is no wonder that we often have to employ cautious language in the way that we frame our conclusions about the text that a NT writer was citing. The multiple text forms in both the Greek and Hebrew Jewish Scriptures that existed in the first century, the freedom with which the authors employed them, and the subsequent transmission of the text during a period of further recensional activity on the Greek Jewish Scriptures demand that our first question of a NT citation be, "Which text (or texts) might this reading reflect?" At the same time, our knowledge and awareness of these difficulties provide us with the means to evaluate the texts critically.

Analyzing a Citation

As we have demonstrated, answering the question, "Which text (or texts) might this reading reflect?" can be a complicated issue. In order to examine a NT citation we must consider the known biblical and nonbiblical writings in the Greek and Semitic (Hebrew and Aramaic) sources and their textual witnesses, including possibly the ancient versions and Church Fathers. In order to facilitate the analysis of a citation, a series of steps for determining the textual basis for a citation in the NT are given below.

1. Compare the NT text to the OG.

If they are different:	If they are the same:
Proceed to step 2.	On the basis of TT determine whether the agreement is distinctive within the Greek text or whether the NT writer could have translated a Semitic text (step 3).

2. Compare the text to the known evidence from other Greek texts and sources such as the versions.

If they are different:	If they are the same:
Proceed to step 3.	On the basis of TT determine whether the agreement is distinctive within the Greek texts or whether the NT writer could have translated a Semitic text.

3. Compare the text to the MT. Form an initial opinion as to whether the NT text is based on a Semitic *Vorlage* like the MT.

4. Compare the text to other Semitic sources. If there are alternative readings in any of these sources, analyze them to discern if they are related to the NT citation.

If they are not:	If they are:
Proceed to step 5.	Determine whether the NT citation is based on a *Vorlage* similar to this text.

5. Examine the NT citation to determine whether any of the differences from all the texts surveyed may be explained by adjustments that the NT writer has introduced due to the context. These may range from minor grammatical alterations to larger changes such as adding or omitting words for theological reasons.
6. Ensure that all possible sources for the citation have been examined. Is it possible that the citation reflects influence from a related biblical or nonbiblical text?
7. Are there any remaining questions or issues that cannot be resolved on the basis of the available textual evidence?

The procedure that has been outlined above addresses all of the issues that have been raised in this volume with respect to determining the origin of a quotation due to the problems of the textual evidence, the methods of citation, and the role that TT can play in the analysis of the texts. Although any allusions in a biblical text are by their nature more subtle and, therefore, more challenging when it comes to demonstrating that they are related to a Greek or Hebrew version, the same process may reveal that a NT passage is based on a particular scriptural tradition. In the following chapter we will offer more examples of citations and allusions in the NT that depend on the Greek Jewish Scriptures and discuss in greater detail the consequences of these insights for NT research.

Summary

1. The term Septuagint (LXX) originally referred to the translation of the Pentateuch into Greek but eventually became applied to the whole Greek Bible. The *Letter of Aristeas*, which dates from some time after 160 B.C.E., places the origin of the translation during the reign of Ptolemy II (285-246 B.C.E.).
2. The insistence of the *Letter of Aristeas* on the Palestinian origins for the

translation and on its comparable status to the Hebrew text indicates that the letter was written as an apology. It is difficult to know whether the apology is a response to Palestinian Jewry who questioned the validity of the translation or whether it was designed to convince Egyptian Jews of the authoritative character of the text.

3. Several explanations have been offered for the origins of the LXX, but Pietersma's theory that the educational needs of the community were the primary motivation for the creation of the LXX would seem to provide the most plausible solution for its origin.

4. A comparison of four NT passages with extant texts from the HB, OG, and *DSS* revealed that determining the influence and use of the Greek Jewish Scriptures by the NT writers requires careful comparison and examination of all the textual witnesses. The fact that a citation does not seem to stem from our present-day MT does not necessarily mean that it stems from the OG/LXX. Several factors were identified that bear on determining the sources or textual witnesses used by the NT writers: textual corruption, textual fluidity, method of citation, and the impact of the recensions on the transmission of the text.

5. The fact that there was no standardized text of the HB prior to the second century helps us to better understand the nature of the OG translation of a particular book, which provides a snapshot of a particular text form of the Hebrew text that existed at the time of the translation. Therefore, in addition to the task of textual criticism on both the HB and the OG, we also realize that the OG text that we reconstruct is a witness to a particular Hebrew *Vorlage*, not to the Hebrew text that has been preserved for us in the MT.

6. The multiple text forms and textual fluidity that are the bane of the textual critic's existence are complicated even further by the production of recensions to the OG. The works of *kaige*-Theodotion, Aquila, Symmachus, and others contribute still more variant readings that are only partially preserved, and not with any consistency. Though our knowledge of these recensions is scanty, at least it is superior to our understanding of the people who created them!

7. Origen, through his creation of the Hexapla, is primarily responsible for the preservation of many readings in the LXX tradition, but his labor has made the present-day task of reconstructing the OG more difficult. The lack of precision in the attributions, questions about the nature and content of Origen's Hexapla, and the inevitable corruption of the texts during the process of their copying supply the contemporary textual critic with a jigsaw puzzle that is more than a few pieces short.

8. Though from our perspective there is a quagmire of texts, manuscripts, and variant readings for the books of the LXX, the Greek Jewish Scriptures provided the basis for much of the NT writers' learning of the Scriptures as they contemplated the implications of Jesus being the fulfillment of Israel's expectations. The result of that theological thought and experience is expressed ultimately through their writings.

9. Discerning the way in which the Jewish Scriptures, particularly those written in Greek, were employed by the NT writers is complicated even more by the freedom with which the latter referred to the Scriptures. In spite of the obstacles to understanding the use of the Greek Jewish Scriptures in the NT, significant knowledge about the subject can be attained, though attaining it presents a formidable challenge.

10. A seven-step process for analyzing a citation was provided that incorporates all of the material and issues presented in this volume.

CHAPTER 5

The Impact of the LXX on the NT

In the previous chapters we have examined the complex relationships that exist between the biblical texts and the reasons why it is no easy task to determine how the Greek Jewish Scriptures were employed by the NT writers. Not only were there multiple forms of at least some of the books of the HB, but the OG text was being revised and new translations were being created as well. Focusing the discussion on quotations has enabled us to illustrate and explain these issues.

The purpose of this chapter is to investigate more fully the influence of the Greek Jewish Scriptures on the NT. In particular, it is our purpose to demonstrate that the Greek Jewish Scriptures had a significant impact on the theology of the NT writers and that this should be accounted for in NT research. Perhaps due to the dominant role of Protestant theologians in the past two centuries, our inheritance from Luther (and Jerome) is to approach NT theology by presupposing that the NT writers' concepts developed from the Hebrew Scriptures.[1] For example, a treatment of the "kingdom of God" will invariably begin by dealing with Hebrew terms such as מלכות *reign.* Can this methodology be justified given what we know of the use of the Scriptures by

1. A. C. Sundberg (*The Old Testament of the Early Church* [Cambridge, Mass.: Harvard University Press, 1964], esp. pp. 8-11) provides a thorough investigation of the development of the Hebrew canon and explains the ways in which Luther influenced the formation of the Protestant canon. See also L. McDonald, *The Formation of the Christian Biblical Canon,* rev. ed. (Peabody: Hendrickson, 2001). An example of the lack of a distinctive treatment is provided by Rowan Greer (J. L. Kugel and R. A. Greer, *Early Biblical Interpretation* [Philadelphia: Westminster, 1986], pp. 109, 155), who acknowledges that the Scriptures used by the NT writers were Greek but continuously refers to the "Hebrew scriptures."

the NT writers? It is not that I believe a change in methodology will introduce some earth-shattering consequences into NT research. However, it is still worth asking how our treatment of NT theology would be modified if we were to presuppose that the Jewish Scriptures in Greek provided the principal cultural, liturgical, theological, and literary context for the NT writers as they reflected on the way in which Jesus had fulfilled the expectations of God's covenant people according to the Scriptures.

It is impossible within the confines of the present work to do more than offer some examples and suggestions of the way in which a greater appreciation for the LXX will enhance our understanding of the theological milieu from which the NT emerged. We will begin by discussing in a little more detail the evidence that the Jewish canon was not fixed in the first century c.e. before examining the implications of the use of the LXX writings in the NT.

Scripture in the Early Church

It is clear that the LXX tradition witnesses to a larger body of Scripture than what eventually became fixed in the HB. These extra books are now commonly known as the Apocrypha to Protestants and the deutero-canonical books to Catholics. We have also noted that the content of some of the books included in the LXX varies considerably from the corresponding books in the HB. Daniel, for example, is preserved both in the OG and in a "Theodotion" version, but there are considerable differences between them. At the same time, the TH version of Daniel is very similar to the version in the MT, but it includes the deutero-canonical Additions. Thus, there are three literary versions of Daniel!

One explanation for these differences prior to the discovery of the *DSS* was that in addition to the Hebrew canon of the MT there was also an Alexandrian canon established by Hellenistic Jews. In the light of the discovery of the *DSS*, A. C. Sundberg investigated the "Alexandrian hypothesis" and found it lacked foundation,[2] but he made two important points that bear on our research. First, he established that the NT documents exhibit a wider knowledge and use of writings than those contained in the LXX. For example, there is the well-known citation of 1 Enoch 1:9 in Jude 14, and the reference to the Martyrdom of Isaiah in Hebrews 11:37, and to Jannes and Jambres in 2 Timothy 3:8. In the previous chapter we also investigated Hebrews 1:6, which shares some relationship, directly or indirectly, with Odes 2:43. The extensive acquaintance

2. Sundberg, *Old Testament*, pp. 3-60.

with and usage of the Apocrypha and Pseudepigrapha in the NT are further evidenced when we examine the marginal references to the literature in NA[3] and the Early Church Fathers.[4] Thus, Sundberg correctly concluded that the "Alexandrian hypothesis" does not account for these additional data. Second, Sundberg demonstrated that there was no unanimity regarding what books were considered authoritative in the Early Church.[5] Certainly, there was a great deal of agreement over many books, but there were also differences.

On the basis of Josephus or the early lists of books by some of the Church Fathers some scholars have argued that for all intents and purposes there was a first-century Hebrew tripartite canon equivalent to the present-day canon of twenty-four books. So, for example, Josephus mentions twenty-two books: the five books of Moses, thirteen by the prophets, and four more (by prophets) comprising hymns and practical advice. (The text of Josephus's words is provided below.) From the outset we can observe that twenty-two books is not the same as twenty-four books, and it is also a puzzle how one might tally thirteen prophetic books; nevertheless, the attempt has been made. In order to make these numbers coincide, R. Beckwith interprets them as follows: the five books of Moses refer to the Pentateuch; the thirteen volumes of the prophets are Joshua, Judges, Samuel (1 and 2 count as one), Kings (1 and 2), Isaiah, Jeremiah-Lamentations, Ezekiel, the twelve Minor Prophets, Daniel, Esther, Ezra-Nehemiah, Job, and Chronicles; and the final four are suggested to be Psalms, Proverbs, Song of Songs, and Ecclesiastes.[6] Unfortunately, this view cannot bear the weight of critical scrutiny. On what basis are the books of Job, Ezra-Nehemiah, Esther, and Daniel counted among the prophets? Why should Jeremiah and Lamentations be counted as one book? Rather than dwelling on these questions, however, we will examine the intention of the comments by Josephus in his treatise, *Against Apion* 1:37-40. Josephus states:

> 1.37 Accordingly . . . then, seeing that the writing (of the records) is not the personal prerogative of everyone, nor is there actual disagreement among

3. See also Hans Hübner's volume on the Pauline literature (*Vetus Testamentum in Novo*, vol. 2: *Corpus Paulinum* [Göttingen: Vandenhoeck & Ruprecht, 1997]).

4. See the list of references in A. C. Sundberg, "The Septuagint: The Bible of Hellenistic Judaism," in *The Canon Debate: On the Origins and Formation of the Bible*, ed. L. M. McDonald and J. A. Sanders (Peabody: Hendrickson, 2002), p. 194.

5. Sundberg (*Old Testament*, pp. 56-61) has a useful discussion and a table that demonstrates the differences in the lists of authoritative books according to various writers and councils.

6. R. Beckwith, "Formation of the Hebrew Bible," in *Mikra: Text, Translation, Reading and Interpretation of the Hebrew Bible in Ancient Judaism and Early Christianity*, ed. M. J. Mulder and H. Sysling (Philadelphia: Fortress, 1988), pp. 50-51.

any of the things written, but the prophets alone learned the highest and oldest matters by the inspiration of the God, and by themselves plainly recorded events as they occurred, 38 so among us there are not myriads of discordant and competing volumes, but only twenty-two volumes containing the record of all time, which are rightly trusted. 39 Now of these, five are those of Moses, which comprise both the laws and the tradition from human origins until his passing. . . . 40 From Moses' passing until the Artaxerxes who was king of the Persians after Xerxes, the prophets after Moses wrote up what happened in their times (or, as they saw things) in thirteen volumes. The remaining four (volumes) comprise hymns toward God and advice for living among humanity.[7]

In his detailed examination of this passage S. Mason has shown that Josephus's testimony about the twenty-two books cannot be used as evidence to support the view that there was a tripartite or even a bipartite Hebrew canon. In their context Josephus's words are intended to contrast the uniformity and accuracy of the Jewish historical records compared to those of the Greeks that are flawed by contradictions (see *Against Apion* 1:15-18) in their "myriads of discordant and competing volumes." Writing was a matter of "personal prerogative" for the Greeks, whereas the "prophets alone" could write Judean history. Their record keeping was shown to be superior in that they captured the diversity and antiquity of their history in these twenty-two books.[8] The actual identification of the thirteen volumes written by the "other prophets" after Moses and the four remaining volumes is uncertain, however. Without Josephus plainly stating what these books were, our only resort is conjecture, which explains the tendency to identify these volumes with the present-day Hebrew canon. However, any such attempt has to be seen as conjecture. Furthermore, besides the special pleading involved in arranging the Hebrew books to match Josephus's numbers, the inaccuracy of this conjecture is revealed when it is tested by Josephus's use of Scripture elsewhere. For example, in his *Antiquities of the Jews,* where he offers his own digest version of the history of the Jewish people, Josephus employs the Greek Scriptures of 1 Esdras, the Additions to Esther, and 1 Maccabees. One could easily argue that these books should be counted among the twenty-two books in *Against Apion*.

7. The translation is according to S. Mason, "Josephus and His Twenty-Two Book Canon," in *The Canon Debate: On the Origins and Formation of the Bible,* ed. L. M. McDonald and J. A. Sanders (Peabody: Hendrickson, 2002), p. 113.

8. Mason, "Josephus," p. 114. Mason does argue that whatever books Josephus had in mind that collection was complete.

The earliest known possible list of specific books comprising the Jewish canon is that of Melito (ca. 170), who omits Esther and Lamentations and refers to Esdras rather than Ezra-Nehemiah. Slightly later is Origen's list, which includes 1 and 2 Esdras and the Epistle of Jeremiah, while excluding Ezra-Nehemiah. Some scholars would prefer to explain away all the differences in these early lists in an effort to maintain a first-century Hebrew canon of twenty-four books. For example, E. E. Ellis suggests that the omission of Esther from Melito's list was either by "accident or design," and he argues that Lamentations was included with Jeremiah. Though he admits in a footnote that Esther was possibly, if not probably, deliberately omitted from the list,[9] he continues in his argument as though Esther's omission by one group really does not affect the question of what was actually considered the canon of the HB. He then argues that the "Letter" referred to by Origen in his list "Jeremiah-Lamentations-Letter" is a scribal gloss.[10] He outlines his position in three points: (1) Jerome, Epiphanius, and rabbinic tradition exclude Baruch and the Letter of Jeremiah from the Hebrew canon; (2) other fourth-century lists that combine Baruch or the Letter of Jeremiah with the book of Jeremiah were influenced by the content of the Greek and Latin Bibles in current use; and (3) fixing the text of Origen to the current usage could account for the addition of the Letter to Jeremiah–Lamentations. In rebuttal, we would reply that Ellis's first argument begs the question because at issue is what Origen, not Jerome or anyone else, regarded as Scripture. The third argument actually depends on the second, yet the view that Origen's statement is a gloss introduced by a later scribe based on fourth-century usage is nothing more than special pleading without manuscript support. Furthermore, the inclusion of Baruch and the Letter of Jeremiah in Greek and Latin codices in the fourth century would have been based on some earlier precedent, which Ellis also fails to explain.

Similarly, Beckwith has argued that the number of books in the HB was fixed during the period of the Early Church.[11] Like Ellis, Beckwith ignores the differences in the early lists, such as the fact that Origen includes the Epistle of Jeremiah, because Origen's list contains the books that are now part of the Hebrew canon. However, if the list refers to all the authoritative books, then the Epistle of Jeremiah would also belong. Both Ellis and Beckwith have to explain that 1 and 2 Esdras in Origen's list refer "in all likelihood" to Ezra-

9. See E. E. Ellis, *The Old Testament in Early Christianity: Canon and Interpretation in the Light of Modern Research*, WUNT 54 (Tübingen: Mohr, 1991), p. 11, n. 34.

10. Ellis, *Old Testament*, pp. 14-15.

11. R. Beckwith, *The Old Testament Canon of the New Testament Church* (Grand Rapids: Eerdmans, 1985).

Nehemiah in the HB rather than the books in the LXX of that name. In another contradiction, Ellis admits that Origen did defend the Greek additions to Daniel as canonical, but he argues that this "does not represent a different judgment about *the books* that belong in the canon" (emphasis his) since it is about the content of a book.[12] If this were true, then we would point out that the relationship of the Letter of Jeremiah (or Baruch) to the book of Jeremiah is the same as that of the additions of Daniel to the book of Daniel. Or is there a difference only because Ellis has decided that to be the case? Moreover, does not Origen's argument for the additions to Daniel undermine the supposed uniform nature of the canon of the HB for which Ellis is arguing? Finally, we would ask, "If the canon of the HB were all that clear in the second and third centuries, then why are there differences in books that are included and omitted in these lists, and why is there so much need to explain what the ancients actually must have meant?"

The fuzzy picture of what might have been regarded as the Jewish canon in the second and even third century is not made any clearer in the NT. The NT refers to the Jewish Scriptures in a variety of ways, but "the Law and the Prophets" is the common designation. The frequent references to the "Law and the Prophets" in such places as Matthew 5:17; 7:12; Luke 16:16 clearly suggest that there were two groupings of Scriptures in the Early Church, though that does not mean that the specific form and contents of both of these groupings, particularly the Prophets, had been definitely fixed.

The most inclusive reference to the Jewish Scriptures in the NT is Luke 24:44, which refers to "the Law of Moses, the Prophets, and the Psalms." Due to the elastic use of "Prophets" in the NT and by Josephus, it would hardly be justified to conclude from this passage that the number and order of the prophetic books in the Hebrew canon had been determined. Even if it had, we would still lack evidence regarding which books made up the Writings.[13] Wishful thinking fails as a criterion to justify interpreting the Psalms as an all-inclusive reference to the books now included in the Writings. Rather, the additional reference to the Psalms in Luke 24:44 echoes earlier statements that make comments about the Scriptures. For example, Jesus ben Sira refers to "the study of the law" and "the wisdom of all the ancients" (Sir. 39:1), while 4QMMT refers to "the book of Moses, the books of the prophets, and of David." In another early reference to the Scriptures Philo speaks of "laws and oracles delivered through the mouths of the prophets, and psalms and anything

12. Ellis, *Old Testament,* p. 16.

13. See J. Barton, *Oracles of God* (Oxford: Oxford University Press, 1986), pp. 35-48 for a discussion of the NT evidence and the use of the term "Prophets."

else" (*Contemplations* 25).[14] Clearly, "the wisdom of all the ancients," "of David," and "psalms and anything else" are vague references to writings that were deemed to be Scripture, and are similar to the comments expressed by Josephus. Luke 24:44 refers to the Psalms as one of those books that were regarded as Scripture.

Thus, there were other writings in addition to the Law and the Prophets (though one should not identify Prophets in this context with that specific group of books designated as such in the HB) that were regarded as Scripture, such as the Psalms, but the boundaries had not yet been clearly drawn. This is not to suggest that all of the books that later formed the canon of the HB were not regarded as authoritative Scripture during the NT period. Based on their inclusion in the various lists and their continued transmission by scribes, it is safe to say that most enjoyed universal recognition as Scripture. The evidence just does not support the position that the number and order of the books were fixed at that time; furthermore, other books certainly received the same recognition as Scripture. There are also other uncertainties regarding the content of the books that will be illuminated by our discussion of the LXX below.

Any conclusion concerning which books were regarded as authoritative for the NT writers, then, has to account for the internal evidence from the NT Scriptures. As we have seen above, this usage extended well beyond the books that became recognized in the HB. Differences in the number and order of the books that were regarded as Scripture in the Early Church continued into the following centuries.[15] The NT use of a broad range of writings as authoritative, which extends beyond the limits of the books that became fixed in the Jewish canon, is in complete accord with the textual situation that existed in the first century, which we have discussed in previous chapters. There were multiple editions of some books and a variety of versions and revisions of different books. All this is to say that the Jewish Scriptures were in a fair degree of flux during the NT period. However, the forces that would eventually lead to the standardization of the Hebrew text and the fixing of the authoritative books in the Jewish tradition must also have been in place because the canon was fixed some time during the early centuries of the Church.

---

14. For a more complete discussion of these statements and the NT references to the Scriptures, see C. A. Evans, "The Scriptures of Jesus and His Earliest Followers," in *The Canon Debate: On the Origins and Formation of the Bible,* ed. L. M. McDonald and J. A. Sanders (Peabody: Hendrickson, 2002), pp. 185-195.

15. In addition to Sundberg, see the helpful work by M. Müller, who deals at length with the testimony of the Early Church Fathers and their use of the Scriptures (*The First Bible of the Church: A Plea for the Septuagint,* JSOTSS 206 [Sheffield: JSOT Press, 1996], pp. 68-97).

The use of the Greek Jewish Scriptures by the NT writers is itself a lethal argument against the view that there was any type of fixed "canon" of Jewish Scriptures in the first century c.e. Even if we were to grant that such a canon existed, NT writers clearly would not have regarded it as the only scriptural authority. The fact that the OG/LXX text was cited in the NT, in contrast to the Hebrew Scriptures, demonstrates that the Greek Jewish Scriptures as witnessed to by the LXX were deemed to be Scripture for the Early Church; therefore, these texts were regarded as normative for life, belief, and practice. The Early Church's use of the Greek texts as Scripture mirrors the same authority that the Greek Scriptures received from the Hellenistic Jewish community. The *Letter of Aristeas,* which was written to defend the authority of the LXX translation for the Alexandrian Jewish community, clearly establishes that the Greek translation of the Pentateuch was Scripture for the Greek-speaking Jews.[16] The external evidence of our Greek codices, which contain the apocryphal/deutero-canonical writings, is a simple testimony to the authority that the Greek Scriptures exercised in the life of the Early Church.

The Use of the LXX in the NT

If we are correct in arguing that the use of the Greek Scriptures in the NT proves that they were regarded as having at least equal authority to the Hebrew Scriptures, then we should expect the theologically probing rejoinder: "So what?" What difference does it make if the NT writers employed the Greek texts rather than the Hebrew? This is a valid question and deserves a reply. First of all, we should establish what would constitute a valid response to the question. A suitable reply would be one that demonstrated that the Greek Jewish Scriptures influenced the NT writers in such a way that their writings were different as a result. In other words, the content of the NT is substantially different than what it would have been if the Greek translations of the Hebrew books and other Greek Scriptures had not existed.

From the outset it can be stated that there are three major lines of argument that will prove our hypothesis: (1) the influence of the vocabulary of the LXX on the NT; (2) citations from the LXX employed by the NT writers; and (3) evidence that the reading of the LXX affected the theology of the NT writers. Scholars readily acknowledge that the vocabulary of the NT is influenced

---

16. See Sundberg, "The Septuagint," pp. 73-74, and the discussion of the *Letter of Aristeas* in the previous chapter.

by the LXX, and so our discussion of it will be brief. The use of citations in the NT is exceedingly complex, as this volume has reiterated time and again, and deserves more attention, but we will demonstrate the influence of the Greek Jewish Scriptures on the NT in several other passages. The final line of argument is far more nebulous in the secondary literature. The works that examine citations in the NT, such as those of R. Longenecker, D. A. Koch, and C. Stanley, tend to be more technical in nature and to focus on the methodology of the citations. There are occasional treatments of the way in which the reading of the LXX can bring to light how the theology of the NT has been influenced, but generally remarks on the use of the Greek Jewish Scriptures in the NT are scattered in commentaries and monographs.

Part of the problem in making a case for the theology of the NT writers being influenced by the Greek Jewish Scriptures is our concept of what constitutes theology. By "the theology of X" we typically mean an individual's understanding of God as reflected in his or her belief and practice. For example, there are numerous volumes written on the theology of the Apostle Paul, the aim of which is to present in some fashion a comprehensive understanding of the Apostle's faith and understanding of God. These volumes usually argue that there is a central theme or organizing center to Paul's theology, such as justification by faith,[17] and they are subdivided into sections that discuss various aspects of Paul's theology, such as his theology of humanity, sin, and the like. The investigation of Paul's theology encompasses both the specific statements that he makes in his letters (demarcated according to which letters are deemed to be genuinely from the Apostle), and the concepts that may have influenced what he believed and expressed. However, determining the specific influences and the way in which they helped shape the Apostle's concepts and beliefs and then presenting them in a convincing manner to the reading public are even more difficult than understanding his letters. In our particular case it would seem reasonable to assume, based on his use of the Jewish Scriptures written in Greek, that Paul (and all the other NT writers) was influenced in his theological thinking because of reading the Scriptures in Greek. The challenge is providing enough evidence to show how this occurred.

We would argue that providing evidence for our first two lines of argument necessarily entails proof for the third, and our analysis of additional citations will provide sufficient grounds to prove our claim. However, our ar-

---

17. See E. Käsemann, "The Problem of a New Testament Theology," *NTS* 19 (1972): 235-45; and the recent volume by J. D. G. Dunn, *The Theology of Paul the Apostle* (Grand Rapids: Eerdmans, 1998), pp. 13-23.

gument for the significant influence of the Greek Jewish Scriptures on the NT writers would be even stronger if we could demonstrate in a more abstract way how the theology of a NT writer reflects the reading of the Jewish Scriptures in Greek. After all, it is this kind of evidence that justifies speaking of the need for a NT theology that presupposes the Jewish Scriptures written in Greek rather than in Hebrew. Therefore, we will conclude this chapter with an argument about the way in which Matthew's theology exhibits the effects of the OG.

The Vocabulary of the LXX and the NT

In his Greek-English lexicon for the NT W. Bauer states, with regard to the influence of the LXX on the vocabulary of the NT, that "every page of this lexicon shows that it outweighs all other influences on our literature."[18] Indeed, the translation of the Hebrew Scriptures into Greek provides a huge window into the world of the language of *koine* Greek and so also of the NT.[19] As we have already learned from our discussion of TT, the contrasting lexical structures of Hebrew and Greek resulted in a variety of accommodations by the translators to their own language as they attempted to communicate the meaning of the Semitic text into Greek. These accommodations involved varying degrees of semantic change in the way that particular Greek words were used. Some of these changes are more obvious, and they directly influenced the development and use of words in the NT. For example, for some words one of the consequences of the translators' usage of SEs was that their range of meaning was narrowed by the association with a particular Hebrew word. For all intents and purposes they became Greek words with Hebrew meanings.[20] Thus, by the time of the NT ἄγγελος (SE for מַלְאָךְ) usually means *angel*. Another well-known example is the term διαθήκη (SE for בְּרִית), which came to mean *covenant*, and τὰ ἔθνη (SE for גּוֹיִם), which came to mean *gentiles*. Other semantic changes introduced by

---

18. See W. Bauer, *A Greek-English Lexicon of the New Testament*, trans. and adapted from W. Bauer's 4th ed. by W. F. Arndt and F. W. Gingrich, rev. and aug. from the 5th ed. by F. W. Gingrich and F. W. Danker, 2nd ed. (Chicago: University of Chicago Press, 1979), p. xxi.

19. See M. Silva, *Biblical Words and Their Meaning* (Grand Rapids: Zondervan, 1983), pp. 53-73 for a good overview of the impact of the LXX on the NT vocabulary. For the Greek verb see T. V. Evans, *Verbal Syntax in the Greek Pentateuch* (Oxford: Oxford University Press, 2001).

20. See E. Tov, "Three Dimensions of LXX Words," *RB* 83 (1976): 529-44.

the process of translating the Hebrew Scriptures into Greek can be more difficult to determine.[21] For example, there may be words whose use in the LXX and NT, though supported in the extrabiblical literature, was actually an uncommon rendering within that word's semantic range. The main problem in our lexicographic efforts is that we are dependent upon the extant manuscripts. The discovery of more manuscripts in a cave somewhere would provide more data and a more comprehensive understanding. In a similar way, Bauer notes that there are many words in the LXX and NT that are unattested elsewhere, but "it is highly improbable that they originated in Jewish or early Christian circles."[22]

An interesting example of the way the vocabulary of LXX influenced the Greek language is provided by the verb διαμελίζω *dissect,* which occurs in the third singular future passive form διαμελισθήσεται in Daniel 3:96(29). This reading is retained in the revised edition of the *Septuaginta* volume on Daniel by O. Munnich, and it is usually interpreted as a neologism,[23] which Montgomery reconstructed on the basis of an analogy to μέλη ποιήσαντες *making parts* in 2 Maccabees 1:16.[24] LSJ has διαμελίζω attested only in Plutarch, although it later became quite common. However, there is a serious difficulty in accepting this understanding of the origin of the word. The problem in reading the verb διαμελίζω is that it would confirm that the OG translator knew the meaning of the *Vorlage* here, but not in 2:5 where the exact same Aramaic is used. This is possible, but certainly there is room for an alternative explanation.

A better solution, it seems to me, would be that the original reading of the OG text was probably διαμερισθήσεται *he will be divided* (in the sense *he will be cut up!*), that is, the consonant λ was mistakenly written for an ρ. Not only would this word represent an adequate translation of the *Vorlage,* though different from 2:5, but διαμερίζω is a common word in the LXX. There is good textual evidence to support this suggestion. It has been noted by H. St. J. Thackeray[25] that the consonants λ and ρ were frequently interchanged in LXX manuscripts, but, more importantly, there are other examples of this ortho-

---

21. See the examination of the vocabulary of the Greek Pentateuch by J. A. L. Lee, *A Lexical Study of the Septuagint Version of the Pentateuch,* SCS 14 (Chico, Calif.: Scholars Press, 1983).

22. Bauer, *Greek-English Lexicon,* p. xx.

23. LEH, 106.

24. J. A. Montgomery, *A Critical and Exegetical Commentary on the Book of Daniel* (New York: Charles Scribner's Sons, 1927), p. 148.

25. See H. St. J. Thackeray, *A Grammar of the Old Testament in Greek,* vol. 1 (Cambridge: Cambridge University Press, 1909), §7.20.

graphic change in Daniel.[26] Finally, we should note that the most important witness to the OG text, papyrus 967, actually has διαμερισθήσεται *he will be divided.* Munnich argues that it is more likely that a scribe would have erred by writing the more common word,[27] but, as we have already shown, the evidence from the texts shows that λ was written for ρ in other places in OG Daniel. So, at some early stage of the transmission of OG Daniel the λ seems to have been substituted for the ρ, and διαμελίζω became part of the Greek language, even though it was based on an error in transcription.

Other easily recognized NT words whose meanings were created by the LXX are δόξα = *glory,* κύριος = *Lord* (meaning the only God), and εὐαγγέλιον = *gospel.* We should note that all of the words that we have mentioned whose meanings were influenced by the LXX are decidedly theological or technical in their use. M. Silva notes that "LXX words that appear to stand for cultural entities or theological reflection belong to a special class . . . with reference to *this* class, the influence of the LXX on the New Testament vocabulary is very strong indeed" (italics his).[28]

The influence of the LXX on the vocabulary of the NT is obvious.

Citations of the LXX in the NT

Already we have marshaled evidence for the significance of the OG/LXX for the NT writers and their theology by way of their citation of Scripture. We began this volume in chapter one with the quotation of Amos 9:11-12 in Acts 15:16-18. The NT depends on the OG by including ἐκζητήσωσιν οἱ κατάλοιποι τῶν ἀνθρώπων *all other peoples may seek,* and it inserts τὸν κύριον *the Lord* in order to make explicit whom the people will seek. The meaning of the passage is then reapplied in the context. The restored house of David no longer refers to the Davidic kingdom, but the promise to David has been fulfilled through

26. The fact that λ was mistakenly written for ρ during the transmission of Daniel is exemplified in three different places in the manuscript history. In 6:22(23), ἔλιψας occurs, which was later corrected to ἔρριψας. A less certain example is the addition of παραλογισθήσεται in 11:25, which Geissen argues (*Der Septuaginta-Text des Buches Daniel Kap. 5–12, zusammen mit Susanna, Bel et Draco, sowies Esther Kap. 1,1a–2,15 nach dem Kölner Teil des Papyrus 967,* PTA 5 [Bonn: Habelt, 1969], p. 259) is a corruption from the earlier variant παροργισθήσεται. The last example is the reading of θάλασσης in 10:6 for θαρσίς. The OG manuscripts 967 and 88-Syh all read θάλασσης *sea* or *lake,* but it does not make sense. It could derive from an early transcription mistake of λ for ρ.

27. J. Ziegler, *Susanna, Daniel, Bel et Draco, Septuaginta* 16.2, rev. by O. Munnich (Göttingen: Vandenhoeck & Ruprecht, 1999), p. 69.

28. Silva, *Biblical Words,* p. 68.

the resurrection of Jesus. It is because of Jesus' resurrection that the gentiles will seek the Lord. This reinterpretation of Amos 9:11-12 to vindicate the mission to the gentiles and their inclusion in God's people is a theological application of the text that could not have been made from the MT.

Another citation that demonstrates the theological influence of the OG is Hebrews 1:6. In Hebrews 1 the writer emphasizes the superiority of the Son through a series of quotations from Scripture. The quotation in verse 6 underscores the subordinate position of the angels in comparison to the Son, because the angels worship him. This argument could not have been made from the Hebrew text because the text that Hebrews cites is not even present in our MT. Though the author of Hebrews may have cited a source verbatim (upon which Odes 2:43 also depends), it is at least as likely that the author reinterpreted a text like OG Deuteronomy 32:43 and applied it to Christ. We have examined this passage in some detail in the previous chapter.

Other texts frequently cited as evidence for the use of the OG/LXX in the NT are Matthew 15:9 (Isa. 29:13); Matthew 21:16 (Ps. 8:2); and Matthew 1:23 (Isa. 7:14).[29] Matthew 15:9 follows the OG of Isaiah by reading μάτην δὲ σέβονταί με *in vain they worship me* where the MT has *their fear of me*. Matthew 21:16 reads ἐκ στόματος νηπίων καὶ θηλαζόντων κατηρτίσω αἶνον *from the mouth of babies and little ones nursing at the breast you have prepared praise* on the basis of LXX Psalm 8:2, whereas the MT has *you have prepared strength.* This passage reflects a literal interpretation of the Scriptures, but the reference to the *praise* of children works in this instance only because the chief priests and teachers of the law hear *the children shouting, "Hosanna to the son of David,"* and ask, *"Do you hear what they are saying?"* (vv. 15-16). Though there is little theological hay that we can make out of either of these citations, both are dependent upon the LXX translation for their use in the context.

Theologically, a far more important and well-known use of the OG in Matthew is the citation of Isaiah 7:14 in Matthew 1:23. While the MT has *the young woman* (הָעַלְמָה) *will be with child*, the NT follows OG *the virgin* (ἡ παρθένος) *will be with child.* The citation of the OG imparts a radically different understanding to this passage and to what the author states about Jesus. Innumerable heresies, controversies, decisions of ecumenical church councils, and so much of the terminology of the Early Church such as *theotokos* and *christotokos* are inextricably linked to the interpretation of Matthew 1:23, which utilizes the Greek.

---

29. See J. Trebolle Barerra, *The Jewish Bible and the Christian Bible*, trans. W. Watson (Leiden: Brill, 1998), p. 495; R. Longenecker, *Biblical Exegesis in the Apostolic Period* (Grand Rapids: Eerdmans, 1975), pp. 35-37.

The majority of the citations of the Scriptures in the NT are employed to explain the person and mission of Christ, and we will return to this subject shortly. We will divert briefly to examine some citations that refer to believers.

1. 1 Cor. 2:16

    NT   τίς γὰρ ἔγνω νοῦν κυρίου
                 For who has known the mind of the Lord?

    OG Isa. 40:13 τίς ἔγνω νοῦν κυρίου
                 Who has known the mind of the Lord?

The readings of Aq πνεῦμα (86) and Sym *spiritum* (according to Jerome) bring the Greek into line with the Hebrew, while TH exhibits a more dynamic rendering as well with βουλήν.

MT Isa. 40:13 מִי־תִכֵּן אֶת־רוּחַ יְהוָה
                 Who has known the spirit of the Lord?

In the case of Paul's citation of Isaiah 40:13, it is not the actual reference to Isaiah 40:13 but the way in which it is applied in the context that is illuminating for our discussion of the influence of the OG on the theology of the NT. It is clear that Paul has quoted from the OG form of Isaiah rather than MT due to his choice of *mind* (νοῦς) as opposed to *spirit* (πνεῦμα). The significance of his use of *mind* (νοῦς) is that it is also found in the next line of the verse, where Paul concludes this portion of his address with ἡμεῖς δὲ νοῦν Χριστοῦ ἔχομεν "But *we*[30] have the *mind* of Christ." Given the fact that Paul previously speaks of humanity's inability to know the thoughts of God without the *spirit* of God (vv. 11-12), it could be argued that MT Isaiah 40:13 would have served Paul's argument better.[31] We would suggest that the use of *spirit* certainly would have made Paul's argument different, because *mind* (νοῦς) adds something to Paul's argument,[32] particularly when the Apostle concludes that we have the *mind* of Christ. The broader context for the discussion is Paul's contrast between those who would rely on human wisdom and those who would rely on God's wis-

---

30. Although Paul uses *we* in this section, it seems clear that he is using it only as a rhetorical device because in the context he is defending his apostleship and preaching against opponents.

31. OG Isa. 40:13 is also quoted in Rom. 11:34, to which we will return.

32. That *mind* and *spirit* are not synonymous in Paul's usage is clear in chapter 2 as well as later in 1 Corinthians, where Paul draws a distinction between *mind* and *spirit* (14:14-19).

dom manifested in the folly of preaching Christ crucified (1:17-25). Paul has already stated that he has received the spirit of God in order to understand what has been given freely by God and, thus, God's wisdom (2:6-12). So, his use of *mind* in the quotation provides him with the opportunity to assert something additional about himself in contrast to the one who lacks the spirit (v. 14). While acknowledging that no one can fathom the mind of the Lord, that is, God, the spiritual person should realize *but we have the mind of Christ*. Given the context in which Paul is defending his ministry and administering to the Corinthians a good tongue lashing (3:1 — *Brothers, I could not speak to you as spiritual!* 3:3 — *You are fleshly/worldly!*), his generous inclusion of his readers in the declaration *we have the mind of Christ* is a subtle suggestion that they should be exercising their Christ-given intellect with respect to the matters at hand. While Paul may have his tongue firmly planted in his cheek regarding who in fact does have the mind of Christ, he stakes a claim at least for himself, if not also for his readers.

Upon further investigation we find that *mind* (νοῦς) occurs 24x in the NT, primarily in books associated with Paul. In fact, over half of its occurrences are found in Romans (6x) and 1 Corinthians (7x).[33] One of the places where νοῦς appears is Romans 11:34, and again this is a citation from OG Isaiah 40:13. There is nothing particularly significant about this citation either, until we read a few verses on: καὶ μὴ συσχηματίζεσθε τῷ αἰῶνι τούτῳ, ἀλλὰ μεταμορφοῦσθε τῇ ἀνακαινώσει τοῦ νοός *No longer be conformed to this world, but be transformed by the renewing of your mind!* (Rom. 12:2). In this case the citation and the injunction to think in a new way are not directly linked, but the close proximity of the quotation and exhortation seems hardly to be coincidental given the prior connection in 1 Corinthians. Furthermore, this encouragement to his readers to be transformed is in direct contrast to his two earlier uses of *mind* in Romans 7, which depict the hopeless plight of the one under the law who is νοὶ δουλεύω νόμῳ θεοῦ *a slave to God's law in [his] mind* (v. 25) and whose members ἀντιστρατευόμενον τῷ νόμῳ τοῦ νοός μου *wage war against the law of my mind* (v. 23).[34] Thus, there is a similar emphasis on the transformed mind of the believer due to a relationship with Christ that seems associated with or develops out of the quotation of OG Isaiah 40:13.

In its context Isaiah 40:13 emphasizes the transcendence of God and humanity's inability to perceive his ways. Paul does not change or deny that sense

---

33. Rom. 1:28; 7:23, 25; 11:34; 12:2; 14:5; 1 Cor. 1:10; 2:16 (2x); 14:14, 15 (2x), 19. The remaining passages are Luke 24:45; Eph. 4:17, 23; Phil. 4:7; Col. 2:18; 2 Thess. 2:2; 1 Tim. 6:5; 2 Tim. 3:8; Titus 1:15; Rev. 13:18; 17:9.

34. For a discussion of Romans 7 see Käsemann, "Problem," pp. 191-213.

when he quotes the passage in 1 Corinthians 2:16, but he does impart some-thing new in his statement *But we do have the mind of Christ*. By juxtaposing *But we do have the mind of Christ* to the quotation *For who has known the mind of the Lord?* Paul asserts that having the mind of Christ is at least something that is attainable, even though the ways of God are beyond comprehension. The way that Paul applies having the mind of Christ based on the quotation of OG Isaiah 40:13 also means that his assertion relies on a connection between Christ and God because the *Lord* κύριος in Isaiah 40:13 can only refer to God. The specific linguistic connection is supplied through the appearance of κύριος, which is the usual Greek translation for יהוה (Yahweh) in the LXX. In the NT *Lord* κύριος is a title for Jesus, and the confession that "Jesus is Lord" or that he is "our Lord" is particularly significant in the Pauline writings (e.g., Rom. 1:4; 10:9; 1 Cor. 12:3; 2 Cor. 1:3; Phil. 2:11), and so Paul's thought seems to develop along the lines from "no one knows the mind of the Lord" (i.e., God) to "but we have the mind of Christ" (i.e., our Lord). Elsewhere in Paul there is no direct development of this line of thought that employs this specific termi-nology besides Romans 11:34 and 12:2; however, having the *mind* of Christ should certainly be seen in conjunction with the complex of Pauline state-ments about the mystical participation of the believer in/with Christ, in the Lord, etc.[35] It is not as though we should expect Paul to use only certain terms to describe the subjective relationship of the believer to Christ, and any treat-ment that delineates Pauline concepts too strictly according to vocabulary promotes artificial divisions and categories.[36] Regardless of the variety of ex-pressions that Paul enlists to depict this relationship of the believer to Christ, it is the foundation for his ethics.[37] Moreover, the peculiarity of Paul's declara-tion in 1 Corinthians 2:16 takes on greater significance as an aid to explaining the origin of this concept when we consider our inability to provide an ade-quate explanation for the meaning of being *in Christ*.[38] We do not want to make exaggerated claims about the significance of the citation of Isaiah 40:13 for the development of Paul's thought, but it is tantalizing to suggest that 1 Co-

35. See H. Ridderbos, *Paul: An Outline of His Theology* (Grand Rapids: Eerdmans, 1975), pp. 57-64, who makes this connection, though Dunn does not. Neither recognizes the importance of Paul's quotation of OG Isa. 40:13 in relation to his statement in 1 Cor. 2:16.

36. Dunn's *Theology of Paul* is particularly wedded to the notion that a word equals a concept.

37. Ridderbos, *Paul*, pp. 228-29; Dunn, *Theology of Paul*, pp. 410-12.

38. M. Silva ("Old Testament in Paul," in *Dictionary of Paul and His Letters*, ed. G. F. Hawthorne and R. P. Martin [Downers Grove, Ill.: InterVarsity, 1993], p. 634) also suggests that Paul's rendering in 1 Cor. 2:16 may provide a clue to the development of Paul's thought, but he does not elaborate in any way.

rinthians 2:16 offers insight into the formation of the way in which the Apostle established the connection between the mystical union of the believer in Christ and the way one is then called to live: *we have the mind of Christ*. In 1 Corinthians 2:16 the citation of OG Isaiah 40:13 is the basis for Paul's assertion that believers have the mind of Christ (i.e., the Lord), which in turn elucidates the meaning of the mystical participation of the believer *in/with Christ* and how one ought to live. If the believer has the mind of Christ, then he or she ought to think and live in a way that Christ would.

Another emphasis on the faculty of the intellect occurs in the Gospels, though in this case the word for *mind* is διάνοια.

2. Matt. 22:37

NT   Ἀγαπήσεις κύριον τὸν θεόν σου ἐν ὅλῃ τῇ καρδίᾳ σου καὶ ἐν ὅλῃ τῇ ψυχῇ σου καὶ ἐν ὅλῃ τῇ διανοίᾳ σου
You shall love the Lord your God with all your heart and with all your soul and with all your mind.

OG Deut. 6:5   ἀγαπήσεις κύριον τὸν θεόν σου ἐξ ὅλης τῆς διανοίας σου καὶ ἐξ ὅλης τῆς ψυχῆς σου καὶ ἐξ ὅλης τῆς δυνάμεώς σου
You shall love the Lord your God with all your mind and with all your soul and with all your strength.

MT Deut. 6:5   וְאָהַבְתָּ אֵת יְהוָה אֱלֹהֶיךָ בְּכָל־לְבָבְךָ וּבְכָל־נַפְשְׁךָ וּבְכָל־מְאֹדֶךָ
You shall love the Lord your God with all your mind and with all your soul and with all your power.

Given the importance of this text and its citation in the Gospels it is not unexpected that there are numerous variants for this passage in the OG and a few in Matthew to conform it to the longer reading in Mark 12:30 and Luke 10:27.

Jesus is quoted in Matthew 22:37 as saying, *You shall love the Lord your God with all your heart and with all your soul and with all your mind* (διάνοια). MT Deuteronomy 6:5 has *heart, soul, and power* while OG has *mind, soul, strength*. The citations in Mark 12:30 and Luke 10:27 are different from Matthew in that they each encourage love for God with all four attributes of the person: *heart, soul, mind, and strength* (for *power*) in Mark, but *heart, soul, strength, and mind* in Luke.

These citations are striking from the perspective of the TT of the OG because the SE for לֵב *heart* in the books of the LXX is καρδία,[39] even though

---

39. καρδία appears 35x for לֵב in Deuteronomy, while διάνοια appears 5x.

καρδία was infrequently employed to refer to the faculty of the intellect in the Greek. It was more common to find words like διάνοια and νοῦς to refer to the mind. So, the rendering in OG Deuteronomy reflected common Greek usage, and the influence of the OG is present in the Gospels. However, in no case does *mind* appear first in the series of attributes as it does in the OG. Matthew, Mark, and Luke all begin with the exhortation to love God with *heart* and *soul*. In Matthew and Mark *mind* appears third in the series, whereas Luke has *mind* fourth. Matthew is alone in retaining three elements in the series in accordance with the MT and OG. We also should note that the editors of UBS do not have the words *and all your mind* in bold print to indicate that they are part of the quotation of Deuteronomy 6:5 in any of the Gospels! At the very least, it would seem reasonable to conclude that for all intents and purposes the citation of the text of Deuteronomy 6:5 had become *heart* and *soul* for the Greek-speaking Christian and Jewish community, no matter what the OG reading might have been. Nonetheless, διάνοια *mind* was retained from the OG in the history of transmission, which probably was responsible for the state of affairs that we find in the Gospels. Some Greek LXX and NT manuscripts listed three, and others had four, attributes because διάνοια had been displaced from the first position in the order of the elements by καρδία, which was the established SE for לֵב *heart* for the LXX translators.

The consequences of the quotation of OG Deuteronomy 6:5 are less significant theologically than our previous investigation, but the citation in Matthew 22:37 does result in a greater emphasis on the faculty of the intellect being summoned to love God in all the Gospels, and there is no exhortation to use one's strength in Matthew.

3. Heb. 12:26

NT   Ἔτι ἅπαξ ἐγὼ σείσω οὐ μόνον τὴν γῆν ἀλλὰ καὶ τὸν οὐρανόν
yet once more I will shake not only the earth but also heaven

OG Hag. 2:7   Ἔτι ἅπαξ ἐγὼ σείσω τὸν οὐρανὸν καὶ τὴν γῆν
yet once more I will shake heaven and the earth

MT Hag. 2:6   עוֹד אַחַת מְעַט הִיא וַאֲנִי מַרְעִישׁ אֶת־הַשָּׁמַיִם וְאֶת־הָאָרֶץ
yet once in a little while and I will shake heaven and the earth

There are no significant variants in any of the quoted texts. Here it is clear that the NT author is dependent upon the OG because of the appearance of ἅπαξ *once*. The word ἅπαξ is seldom employed in the LXX, and Haggai 2:7 is the only time that it is found in the whole of the twelve Minor Prophets. The specific citation in Hebrews is introduced to support one of the writer's many comparisons between the old covenant given through Moses and the new that has come with Jesus. In 12:18-21 the writer refers to Exodus 19:12-21; 20:18-19, where Moses has to meet God on the mountain on behalf of the Israelites. In contrast, the recipients of Hebrews have "come to the city of the living God, the new Jerusalem" (12:22) and to Jesus who is the mediator of the new covenant (12:24). It would appear that the contents of Exodus 19 and 20 and the references to the thundering and lightning on the mountain reminded the author of the text of OG Haggai 2:7. This would also explain why the writer reverses the order *heaven and the earth* in Haggai 2:7 to *the earth and heaven*. By referring to the shaking of the earth first the writer links the citation with Exodus, where it is the mountain and earth that shake. The OG's *yet once more* provides the basis for the author to reapply the eschatological expectations of the OG text, which were based on the rebuilding of the temple in Jerusalem, to the new spiritual temple and the kingdom that has been inaugurated in Jesus, which cannot be shaken (12:27-28).[40]

We will now examine some of the quotations and allusions to Daniel 7:13 in the NT.

4. Matt. 24:30

NT	τὸν υἱὸν τοῦ ἀνθρώπου ἐρχόμενον ἐπὶ τῶν νεφελῶν τοῦ οὐρανοῦ
	the son of man coming upon the clouds of heaven
OG Dan. 7:13	ἐπὶ τῶν νεφελῶν τοῦ οὐρανοῦ ἤρχετο ὡς υἱὸς ἀνθρώπου[41]
	upon the clouds of heaven one came as a son of man
MT Dan. 7:13	עִם־עֲנָנֵי שְׁמַיָּא כְּבַר אֱנָשׁ אָתֵה הֲוָה
	with the clouds of heaven one like a son of man was coming

40. Cf. Carroll Stuhlmueller, *Rebuilding with Hope: A Commentary on Haggai and Zechariah* (Grand Rapids: Eerdmans, 1988), pp. 26-27.

41. I am grateful to have had access to Munnich's revision of Ziegler's edition of Daniel OG for the Göttingen *Septuaginta* series. The revision takes into account our most important witness to the text of OG, papyrus 967, which was unavailable to Ziegler when he first edited the critical text. Ziegler's text of this citation is the same except that ἤρχετο appears at the end of the clause.

The same text is cited in Matthew 26:64; Mark 13:26; 14:62; and Luke 21:27, though with various differences in prepositions and in the number and order of words. We have begun with Matthew 24:30 only as a convenience because it offers the rendering closest to the OG text that has been reconstructed by J. Ziegler. We begin by noting that it has been suggested that the use of the preposition ἐπὶ *upon* in the OG reflects Canaanite depictions of the deity riding on the clouds. This could be a theological rendering because the expected Greek equivalent for the Aramaic עַם is μετὰ *with*, which is employed by TH.[42] Thus, it could be argued that the retention of ἐπὶ *upon* in Matthew is based on the OG.[43] However, the question of the theological influence of OG Daniel 7:13 is really based on (1) a portion of the text that is not even quoted in the NT and (2) the Greek version of 7:13 that may have been employed by Jesus and the New Testament writers. In order to impart some sense of order to our analysis, we will deal first with the textual relationship between the OG and MT.

The words of the MT that immediately follow the text quoted above are *and he approached unto the Ancient of Days* מְטָה יוֹמַיָּא וְעַד־עַתִּיק. The text of OG according to Munnich is καὶ ἕως παλαιοῦ ἡμερῶν παρῆν *and he came unto the Ancient of Days*. One might fairly conclude that there is no difference between MT and OG. The problem is that this reconstructed OG text depends on a textual emendation by Ziegler, with which Munnich obviously agrees. None of the Greek witnesses actually have ἕως *unto* as the rendering for עַד *unto*. Instead, they read καὶ ὡς παλαιὸς ἡμερῶν παρῆν *and he came as the Ancient of Days*.[44] In this way the text of the OG could be read as making an identification between the Son of Man and the Ancient of Days, that is, *the son of man came upon the clouds and as the Ancient of Days*.[45] A strong argument has been made that the OG text should be emended as Ziegler and Munnich have done,[46] though it has not gone un-

---

42. The citations of this passage are not consistent. Matt. 24:30; 26:64 have ἐπὶ, while Mark 14:62 has μετὰ. Mark 13:26; Luke 21:27 have ἐν *with*.

43. We do not really have to settle whether the "rider on the clouds" is the background for Dan. 7:13 because our concern is with the NT use of Scriptures. Those wanting more detail regarding this question may begin with F. M. Cross, *Canaanite Myth and Hebrew Epic* (Cambridge, Mass.: Harvard University Press, 1973); J. A. Emerton, "The Origin of the Son of Man Imagery," *JTS* 9 (1958): 225-42; Helge Kvanvig, "An Akkadian Vision as Background for Dan 7?" *ST* 35 (1981): 85-89.

44. Though we will concentrate only on the difference between ἕως *unto* and ὡς *as*, there are other textual differences that are related to this change. For a more complete understanding consult the works mentioned.

45. See F. F. Bruce, "The Oldest Greek Version of Daniel," *OTS* 20 (1977): 22-40.

46. See S. Pace Jeansonne, *The Old Greek Translation of Daniel 7–12*, CBQMS 19

contested.[47] However, arguing for a particular reading of the OG need not detain us at this time because, regardless of whether it originated with the OG translator or very soon afterwards, at some point at least some (the only three manuscripts for OG Daniel that we have did!) witnesses to OG Daniel 7:13 read *and he came as the Ancient of Days*. Thus, the textual evidence suggests that during the NT period the text of OG Daniel 7:13 could have been read as identifying the Son of Man with the Ancient of Days. It is this reading of Daniel 7:13 that supports the theological influence of the LXX on the NT.

As previously mentioned, καὶ ὡς παλαιὸς ἡμερῶν παρῆν *and he came as the Ancient of Days* is not cited in the NT, but the use of Daniel 7 in the NT requires that it be examined as a source and background for allusions. The identification of the Son of Man with the Ancient of Days, who would have been regarded as divine, may provide helpful background to the witness of the Gospels, in which Jesus employs "son of man" as a self-designation. It is well-known that this title is the only one that appears exclusively on the lips of Jesus and that G. Vermes has argued that the expression represented a Semitic idiom meaning "man" in a generic sense or a circumlocution for "I."[48] The main problem with Vermes's interpretation is that it does not offer an adequate understanding of the "son of man" sayings as they appear in the Gospels and of their use by Jesus in particular. Furthermore, as Yarbro Collins argues, "it fails to explain why, if Jesus used a perfectly understandable Aramaic idiom, it was translated into Greek in such an unidiomatic way."[49] It is also doubtful that there was a preexisting tradition that identified a/the "son of man" with a messianic figure.[50] Thus, Yarbro Collins argues that Jesus used

---

(Washington: Catholic Biblical Association, 1988), pp. 96-99; A. Yarbro Collins, "The 'Son of Man' Tradition and the Book of Revelation," in *The Messiah*, ed. J. H. Charlesworth (Minneapolis: Fortress, 1992), pp. 536-68; T. McLay, "Translation Technique and Textual Studies in the Old Greek and Theodotion Versions of Daniel," Ph.D. dissertation, University of Durham, 1994, pp. 56-57.

47. Besides Bruce, see J. Lust, "Daniel VII and the Septuagint," *ETL* 54 (1978); L. T. Stuckenbruck, "'One Like a Son of Man as the Ancient of Days' in the Old Greek Recension of Daniel 7,13: Scribal Error or Theological Translation?" *ZNW* 86 (1995): 268-76.

48. G. Vermes, *Jesus the Jew* (Philadelphia: Fortress, 1973), pp. 160-90; B. Lindars, *Jesus Son of Man* (London: SPCK, 1983), pp. 22-24.

49. See the fine distillation of the problems in A. Yarbro Collins, "Daniel 7 and the Historical Jesus," in *Of Scribes and Scrolls*, ed. H. W. Attridge, J. J. Collins, and T. H. Tobin (Lanham, Md.: University Press of America, 1990), pp. 187-93.

50. The Similitudes of Enoch (see particularly 1 Enoch 48) make the identification, but this appears to be a later addition.

the phrase exegetically to allude to the figure of Daniel 7:13 and that the disciples later identified Jesus with that figure and then interpreted it messianically. She suggests that the NT sayings reflect a combination of both Jesus' use and that of the disciples.[51] Regardless of who originated the exegesis, and it could well be argued that the usage makes the most sense if it began with Jesus, the Greek reading of Daniel 7:13 would have figured prominently in identifying Jesus as "THE Son of Man" and would have undergirded the eschatological "son of man" sayings. Further evidence for the theological influence of the LXX tradition of Daniel 7:13 that we have outlined is provided in Revelation.[52] Besides the allusion to 7:13 in Revelation 1:7, "Behold, he is coming with the clouds," there is the reference to "one like *a son of man*" in 1:13, and the description of his appearance depends on allusions to the Ancient of Days in Daniel 7: *his head and hair were white like wool, white as snow* in Revelation 1:14 is clearly dependent upon Daniel 7:9 *his clothing was as white as snow, the hair of his head was white like wool.*[53]

Whoever was responsible for the reading in the OG manuscripts *upon the clouds of heaven one came as a son of man and as the Ancient of Days,* it facilitated the connection of the "son of man" with the Ancient of Days and, thus, with a divine figure. Though one could argue that these connections might have been made on the basis of the Hebrew text, the Greek Jewish Scriptures provide a theological justification for use of the expression in the NT. In a different way the citation of OG Isaiah 40:13 in 1 Corinthians 2:16 demonstrates the influence of the OG because of the way in which Paul used the text to claim something for believers due to their relationship with Christ. The impact of OG Deuteronomy 6:5 is less significant theologically, yet the use of it in the NT emphasizes the role of the intellect and the relationship of the disciple with God. The citation of OG Haggai 2:7 in Hebrews 12:26 is a subtle but worthy example of the OG influence on the NT, and the citations in Acts 15:16-18; Hebrews 1:6; Matthew 1:23; 15:9; 21:16 all provide further evidence of the theological influence of the Greek Jewish Scriptures on the NT.

51. Collins, "Daniel 7," pp. 191-93.
52. See Collins, "'Son of Man' Tradition."
53. Numerous allusions in Revelation are dependent upon Daniel, but the nature of the allusive language makes it more difficult to establish specific uses of the LXX as opposed to MT. On the whole question of the use of Daniel in Revelation, see G. Beale, *John's Use of the Old Testament in Revelation* (Sheffield: Sheffield Academic Press, 1998).

Theological Influence of the LXX

The third means we have chosen to demonstrate the impact of the Greek Jewish Scriptures on the theology of the NT is the indirect way in which they have influenced NT theology. We have chosen Matthew's Gospel for this purpose, and we will begin with a citation of the OG in Matthew 12:40; our investigation will also include Matthew 16:16-18 and 27:51b-53.

Matt. 12:40

NT   ἦν Ἰωνᾶς ἐν τῇ κοιλίᾳ τοῦ κήτους τρεῖς ἡμέρας καὶ τρεῖς νύκτας
Jonah was in the belly of the fish three days and three nights.

OG Jon. 2:1   ἦν Ἰωνᾶς ἐν τῇ κοιλίᾳ τοῦ κήτους τρεῖς ἡμέρας καὶ τρεῖς νύκτας
Jonah was in the belly of the fish three days and three nights.

MT Jon. 2:1   וַיְהִי יוֹנָה בִּמְעֵי הַדָּג שְׁלֹשָׁה יָמִים וּשְׁלֹשָׁה לֵילוֹת
Jonah was in the belly of the fish three days and three nights.

At first glance there is nothing particularly significant about the citation of OG Jonah 2:1 in Matthew, even though Matthew 12:40a is an exact quotation from Jonah 2:1 in the OG. However, there is tremendous significance when we consider that Matthew's insertion of the whole of verse 40 gives a different meaning to 12:39-42 compared to Luke's version in 11:29-32.[54] Matthew and Luke (cf. Luke 11:31-32) both include references to the Queen of the South and the people of Nineveh on the day of judgment, but in reverse order. However, the addition in verse 40 in Matthew reinterprets the sign of Jonah and applies it to Jesus as the Son of Man. The whole of verse 40 reads: *For just as Jonah was three days and three nights in the belly of the sea monster, so for three days and three nights the Son of Man will be in the heart of the earth.* The Son of Man being three days in the heart of the earth is best interpreted as a reference to Jesus' being in Hades, the realm of the dead,[55] and not merely as a reference to the grave.[56]

54. See R. H. Gundry, *Matthew: A Commentary on His Literary and Theological Art* (Grand Rapids: Eerdmans, 1982), pp. 242-44.
55. So also W. Grundman, *Das Evangelium nach Matthäus* (Berlin: Evangelische, 1971), p. 334; Gundry, *Commentary*, p. 244.
56. So V. Luz, *Das Evangelium nach Matthäus* (Zürich: Benziger, 1990), 2:276; D. G.

The OG of Jonah in Matthew

The metaphor καρδίᾳ τῆς γῆς *heart of the earth* is unique in the Scriptures, but there is little doubt that the referent is Hades, especially when we consider that the imagery is rooted in the Greek form of the psalm of Jonah.[57] The imagery of the journey from Sheol in the belly of the fish[58] is reflected in Matthew in various ways, and it is instructive for our purposes to examine the language used in Jonah to depict the situation. First, the citation in 12:40 suggests the influence of the Greek version of Jonah upon Matthew.[59] Second, in verse 3b of Jonah 2 God is said to have heard Jonah's cry ἐκ κοιλίας ᾅδου *from the belly of Hades,* which not only retains the usual translation of Hebrew Sheol into Greek Hades (the Hebrew text has שְׁאוֹל מִבֶּטֶן *from the belly of Sheol*)[60] but also provides an identification of the belly of the fish, which the Hebrew lacked: in the Greek, Jonah is said to be in τῇ κοιλίᾳ τοῦ κήτους *the belly of the fish* in verses 1 and 2, but in verse 3 he prays from the κοιλίας ᾅδου *belly of Hades.*[61] Jonah not only prays from Hades/Sheol in verse 3, but the repetition of κοιλίᾳ/κοιλίας *belly* in the Greek allows the reader to make an

---

Murray, "The Sign of Jonah," *Downside Review* 107 (1989): 224-25. There is debate concerning the relationship between the grave and Hades/Sheol. The view of some scholars that their referents are completely distinct is extreme. The modern semanticist would describe their sense relations with the term "overlapping." For a balanced perspective see T. J. Lewis, "Dead, Abode of the," *Anchor Bible Dictionary,* ed. David Noel Freedman (New York: Doubleday, 1992), 2:103.

57. For a discussion of the prayer as a psalm of thanksgiving rather than a prayer for deliverance see D. Stuart, *Hosea-Jonah* (Waco, Tex.: Word, 1987), pp. 472-73; A. J. Hauser, "Jonah: In Pursuit of the Dove," *JBL* 104 (1985): 21-37.

58. The belly of the great fish is the means of Jonah's deliverance, and the journey from Sheol took 3 days. See the seminal article on Jonah's journey from Sheol by G. M. Landes, "The 'Three Days and Three Nights' Motif in Jonah 2.1," *JBL* 86 (1967): 446-50.

59. In his examination of Matthew's use of the OT, R. H. Gundry (*The Use of the Old Testament in St. Matthew's Gospel: With Special Reference to the Messianic Hope* [Leiden: Brill, 1967], pp. 148-50) reports that Matthew exhibits more of a mixed textual tradition than does Mark, who is dependent upon the LXX. However, the first Gospel does exhibit dependence on the LXX in 15 of 41 quotations or allusions to OT.

60. Hades refers to the place known as Sheol (שְׁאוֹל) in the Old Testament, the abode of the dead (Ps. 6:5; 87(88):10-12; Job 26:6) and this usage has carried into the NT. In all but one of its 72 occurrences in the MT Sheol is translated by Hades in the LXX. At the same time, Hades is reserved almost exclusively for Sheol, though according to HR it does translate other terms on 9 occasions. See the brief but complete discussion by J. Jeremias, "ᾅδης," in *Theological Dictionary of the New Testament,* ed. G. Kittel (Grand Rapids: Eerdmans, 1964), 1:146-49.

61. The Hebrew uses הַדָּגָה מִמְּעֵי *from the belly of the fish* in vv. 1 and 2.

explicit identification between the belly of the fish and Hades. This identification is employed in Matthew's Gospel.

The identification of καρδία τῆς γῆς *heart of the earth* as a referent for Hades and Matthew's dependence on the psalm of Jonah for his linguistic usage can be traced to verses 4 and 7 of Jonah's psalm. We find in verse 4 of the psalm that Jonah was thrown εἰς βάθη καρδίας θαλάσσης *into the depths of the heart of the sea*, and in verse 7 Jonah says κατέβην εἰς γῆν ἧς οἱ μοχλοὶ αὐτῆς κάτοχοι αἰώνιοι *I descended into the earth whose bars constrain forever*. So, although the phrase καρδία τῆς γῆς does not appear in Jonah's psalm, its lexical components are employed as part of the metaphorical imagery that is associated with Hades/Sheol. Given Matthew's familiarity with the Greek version of the psalm of Jonah, I would suggest that Matthew borrowed from the imagery and coined the phrase καρδία τῆς γῆς as a metaphor for Hades.[62]

The affirmation in Matthew 12:40 that the Son of Man would be in *the heart of the earth* is the first hint of the resurrection theme that Matthew develops in 16:18 and 27:51b-53. In fact, W. D. Davies and D. Allison note that although there is no explicit reference to resurrection in 12:40, "the figure of three days and nights posits an end to the time in the earth and so suggests the resurrection."[63] Some readers may object to this interpretation because Matthew does not state the equivalent of "so the Son of Man will be three days and three nights in the heart of the earth *but then he will be raised*." However, Matthew allows the reader to infer this conclusion because she or he is familiar with the Jonah story, in which the prophet did not remain in the belly of the fish. If there is any doubt, the missing information is supplied to the reader later in the form of the threefold predictions of Jesus' suffering, death, and resurrection. 12:40 is the first hint of what is to follow.

The linguistic connections between Matthew's Gospel and the OG form of the psalm of Jonah become clearer when we consider the explicit use of Hades in another passage special to the first Gospel, 16:18. The connections between 12:40, 16:18 and the psalm of Jonah are threefold. First, not only does the term Hades occur in 16:18, but this is the sole occurrence of the phrase πύλαι ᾅδου *gates of Hades* in the NT.[64] Given Matthew's familiarity with the prayer of

62. This connection is reasonable on the grounds that the inner part of the earth was believed to be the location of Hades (Gen. 37:35; Num. 16:33; Ps. 54(55):15; Isa. 38:9-20); furthermore, there is a natural connection since Jesus was on the earth whereas Jonah was at sea.

63. W. D. Davies and D. Allison, *The Gospel According to Saint Matthew* (Edinburgh: T. & T. Clark, 1991), 2:356.

64. The phrase appears three times in the OT and Apocrypha (Isa. 38:10; Wisd. 16:13; 3 Macc. 5:51). A similar expression is πυλῶν (τοῦ) θανάτου *gates of death* in Ps. 9:14(13);

Jonah, I suggest that the occurrence of ἧς οἱ μοχλοὶ αὐτῆς κάτοχοι αἰώνιοι *whose bars constrain/imprison forever* in OG Jonah 2:7 stimulated Matthew to use the more common phrase πύλαι ᾅδου in 16:18. Second, there is Jesus' reference to Peter as Simon the *son of Jonah* in 16:17. Commentators have offered little to explain the difference between Matthew's Βαριωνᾶ *the son of Jonah* and John's identification of Peter as ὁ υἱὸς 'Ιωάννου *the son of John* (1:42), but it is explicable if Matthew is intentionally linking the saying of 16:17-18 with the psalm of Jonah. Third, it seems more than coincidental that the reference to Peter as the *son of Jonah* comes soon after the assertion in 16:4 that *a sign will not be given this generation except the sign of Jonah.* The significance of Jonah for Matthew's theology is underscored by the fact that Matthew has three references to Jonah in contrast to Luke, who has just the one (11:29-32). The specific identification of Peter as a "son of Jonah" in 16:17 is illuminated in 16:22-23, where Peter is described as a stumbling block to Jesus and the things of God, perhaps referring to his namesake Jonah, who initially refused to go to Nineveh.

The Resurrection in Matthew 16:18

Not only does 16:18 reinforce Matthew's dependence upon Jonah, it also focuses on the theme of resurrection. Let us examine 16:18 more closely. Some commentators and English translations give the impression that πύλαι ᾅδου οὐ κατισχύσουσιν αὐτῆς *the gates of Hades shall not prevail against it* in Matthew 16:18 means that the Church will survive despite adversity and the attacks of evil forces.[65] The sense "prevail over, overcome, have power against" for κατισχύω is the primary gloss offered by LSJ, and it is also well attested in the books of the LXX.[66] As most commentators have acknowledged, this indicates that there is some type of struggle between the Church and the gates of Hades.[67] However, should we understand demonic forces to be the referent

---

106(107):18 and, particularly, Job 38:17, which also contains the parallel expression πυλωροὶ ᾅδου.

65. J. Jeremias, in *Theological Dictionary of the New Testament*, ed. G. Kittel (Grand Rapids: Eerdmans, 1964-76), 6:927. Davies and Allison (*Matthew*, 2:630-32) accept this position.

66. Exod. 17:11; Deut. 1:38; 1 Reigns 19:8; OG Dan. 11:5; passim. Davies and Allison (*Matthew*, 2:633) also note that the verb is always active when followed by the genitive in the LXX.

67. See the discussion in Davies and Allison, *Matthew*, 2:630-32. Though they list twelve different views, most reflect some kind of conflict. Jeremias has been referred to above. Other examples are E. Schweizer (*The Good News According to Matthew* [Atlanta: John Knox, 1975], p. 342), who interprets the verse to mean death cannot put a stop to the Christian community, and W. Bousset (*Kyrios Christos* [Nashville: Abingdon, 1970], p. 65),

for the gates of death?[68] It is true that there is some merging of the concepts of ᾅδης *hades* and γέεννα *hell* evident in the NT, a merging that reflects developments in the Pseudepigrapha, but the only explicit use of ᾅδης in the NT that exhibits this merging is in Luke 16:23.[69]

Against the view that Hades refers to the assembly of evil forces is the natural association of the expression πύλαι ᾅδου with the realm of the dead as it appears in the LXX books. On this basis, in 16:18 it is better to interpret *the gates of Hades* as a metaphor for death, which is the active subject of the verb attacking the Church,[70] but death will not ultimately prevail.[71] The inability of death to prevail over the Church in this passage is then understood to mean that Jesus is promising that there will be a resurrection of the Church from the realm of the dead: *I will build my church and the gates of death will not prevail against* [i.e., contain] *it*.[72] The triumph of the resurrection is then fulfilled in Matthew by Jesus' death, which signals the final victory over the power of death and initiates the proleptic resurrection of the saints in 27:51b-53.[73] We will argue this in more detail below.

Before proceeding there is one other item of interest to note that illustrates Matthew's use of a term prevalent in the LXX books: ἐκκλησία *church*. Apart from 16:18 ἐκκλησία *church* appears twice more in Matthew's Gospel in 18:17. Particularly in the latter passage, *church* seems to be used in a local sense as we find in Paul's epistles, which of course would be anachronistic in Mat-

---

who believes it refers to the resurrection of the Church. A. H. M'Neile (*The Gospel According to St. Matthew* [London: Macmillan, 1915], p. 242), in a similar vein, believes the gates will not prevail over the Church because Christ could not be imprisoned, so that the resurrection refers to him rather than the Church.

68. As M'Neile (*St. Matthew*, p. 242) notes, "it is doubtful if Hades was ever thought of as the abode of the powers of evil, from which they emerge to injure men."

69. Davies and Allison (*Matthew*, 1:633, n. 110) provide a seemingly impressive array of NT references to argue that ᾅδης means evil forces in 16:18, but apart from Luke 16:19-31 the other references use different terminology. Their references are Luke 8:31; 2 Pet. 2:4; Jude 6; Rom. 10:7; Rev. 9:1-2, 11; 11:7; 20:1-3; but contrast Matt. 11:23; 16:18; Luke 10:15; Acts 2:27, 31; Rev. 1:18; 6:8; 20:13-14. Even Luke 16:23 is within a parable that only reflects the notion that there were divisions within Hades to separate the righteous from the unrighteous.

70. Schweizer, *Good News*, p. 342.

71. We assume that the antecedent for αὐτῆς *it* is ἐκκλησίαν *church* because it is closer than πέτρα *rock* and makes more sense in the context.

72. Bousset, *Kyrios Christos*, p. 65.

73. According to J. P. Meier ("Salvation History in Matthew: In Search of a Starting Point," *CBQ* 27 [1975]: 209), Matthew "depicts the resurrection of the dead as taking place proleptically at the death of Christ," as part of the evangelist's scheme of salvation-history. See also D. Senior, "The Death of Jesus and the Resurrection of the Holy Ones (MT 27:51-53)," *CBQ* 38 (1976): 328-29.

thew's Gospel. The referent for ἐκκλησία in 16:18 is not transparent either, though it seems to be used in a sense of the universal Church. In what sense, then, was Matthew employing the term ἐκκλησία *church?* Part of the problem, we would suggest, is that we may be interpreting Matthew's terminology through Pauline spectacles rather than against the background of the Greek Jewish Scriptures. Even though there is more of a local sense to ἐκκλησία in 18:17, Matthew's use of the word in both passages is in keeping with the usual sense employed in the books of the LXX where ἐκκλησία can be translated simply as "people of God." In the translated books of the LXX ἐκκλησία occurs 65x, and in all but four cases it translates the Hebrew word קָהָל *assembly.*[74] קָהָל is also rendered by συναγωγή in the LXX, but ἐκκλησία is reserved almost exclusively for referring to an assembly or congregation of the people of Israel. The addition of limiting adjectives to ἐκκλησία in the LXX to define it as an assembly of God's people is dropped in later books so that it almost becomes a technical term for the Israel of God or the people of God.[75] The same sense of ἐκκλησία as "people of God" is found throughout the later books of the LXX that represent nontranslation Greek as well, though there are occasional exceptions.[76] In common Greek usage ἐκκλησία could refer more generally to any assembly of people, such as in Acts 19:32, 39, 41, but Matthew's use reflects the established practice of the LXX translators, where it has the sense "people of God." Thus, we would understand Jesus' words in 16:18 to be, "I will build my people of God, and the Gates of Hades will not stand against it."

Thus far we have given six arguments to link Matthew 12:40; 16:18; and the OG version of the psalm of Jonah. Five of the links are linguistic and demonstrate the specific connection between Matthew and the OG version of Jonah: (1) Matthew 12:40 quotes from OG Jonah 2:1; (2) the OG of Jonah equates the *belly of the fish* with the *belly of Hades;* (3) the metaphor καρδία τῆς γῆς *heart of the earth* in 12:40 was created by borrowing from the imagery of the psalm; (4) the use of the phrase πύλαι ᾅδου *gates of Hades,* which is unique in the NT but well known from the books in the LXX, was motivated by its association with the image of the restraining bars in Jonah 2:7; (5) Matthew identifies Peter as Βαριωνᾶ *son of Jonah* in 16:17. The sixth argument linking Matthew to Jonah is the threefold reference to Jonah in the Gospel.

74. The four cases where it does not are 4 Reigns 10:20; Neh. 5:7; Ps. 25:12; 67:27.

75. See K. L Schmidt's discussion in "ἐκκλησία," in *Theological Dictionary of the New Testament,* ed. G. Kittel (Grand Rapids: Eerdmans, 1964-76), 3:527-28. The addition of limiting adjectives to ἐκκλησία in the LXX to define it as an assembly of God's people is dropped in later books so that it almost becomes a technical term.

76. In Eccles. 26:5 ἐκκλησία qualifies an unruly multitude.

The use of ἐκκλησία also reflects LXX influence, but this point has less direct bearing on the particular argument that we are making.

It is clear that Matthew has employed the Greek form of the book of Jonah in his Gospel from the specific references and allusions he has made. The quotation of OG Jonah 2:1 in Matthew 12:40 and the vocabulary in Matthew 12:40 and 16:17-18 also exhibits the influence of the OG version. The fact that 12:40 and 16:18 are part of Matthew's special material also suggests that they might best be understood from a common theological frame of reference. We would suggest that the theme of resurrection helps prepare and explain the presence of another passage that is special to Matthew, 27:51b-53.

The Resurrection of the Saints in Matthew 27:51b-53

Matthew 27:51b-53 is, without doubt, one of the most interesting and perplexing passages in the first Gospel. Matthew supplements the Marcan account of the events following the death of Jesus by including the resurrection of the saints and their appearance to many in the holy city. The past few decades have witnessed a resurgence in interest in Matthew's Gospel in general and the passion narrative in particular, but despite the advance in our understanding of the background of verses 51b-53,[77] little light has been cast on the evangelist's insertion concerning the raising of the saints in verse 52.[78] Not only does the raising of the saints strike the reader as somewhat odd, its occurrence at Jesus' death is also at odds with the remainder of the NT, which stresses that the resurrection will take place following the parousia.[79] The resurrection of the saints does make sense, however, when we consider the previous special material in 12:40 and 16:18. The Matthean Jesus has already introduced a resurrection theme by stating that he would be in the heart of the earth for three days and nights (12:40), by the saying in 16:18, and by the three predictions of his death and resurrection (beginning in 16:21).

Our argument is that the raising of the saints in 27:51b-53 is Matthew's proof that Jesus descended into the earth (12:40) and that the gates of death (16:18) have been overcome. This interpretation is theologically coherent

---

77. It is widely believed that the use of typical Matthean vocabulary, style, and stock apocalyptic terms indicates the evangelist was responsible for the special passion material, and reflects his theological purposes. See D. Senior, *The Passion Narrative according to Matthew* (Leuven: Peeters, 1975), pp. 307-23; Gundry, *Commentary*, pp. 575-77.

78. The oddity of the raising of the saints would seem to have been recognized at an early stage in the Christian tradition. At least this might explain the variant reading of ἠγέρθη in A C W 090 and the Majority text, which would apply the raising to Jesus.

79. See 1 Cor. 15:20-23; 1 Thess. 4:13-18; 1 Pet. 1:4-5; 1 John 3:2; Rev. 20:11-15.

within Matthew's Gospel in that it accounts for the three sayings that are unique to Matthew, plus it is coherent with additional material that reflects the theology of the first evangelist. For example, Joseph is commanded to name the baby Jesus "because he will save his people from their sins" (Matt. 1:21). The personal pronoun foreshadows the saying in 16:18 when Jesus says, "I will build my assembly/people of God." Matthew portrays Jesus as the new Moses, and, as such, he is building his new people. This interpretation also provides the framework for understanding the basis from which the theology developed: Matthew's use of the OG version of Jonah.

Other interpretations of the raising of the saints have been offered but generally have focused on interpreting the passage strictly on the basis of its sources.[80] For example, verses 51b-53 are interpreted by G. D. Kilpatrick as a misplaced resurrection account,[81] while others appeal to a source held in common with the Gospel of Peter.[82] Admittedly, Matthew does link Jesus' death very closely with the account of the resurrection in 28:2-4. Both events are introduced with the words "And behold," and each includes an earthquake as a sign of divine intervention.[83] Both passages also employ the motif of fear on the part of the guards. However, these parallels may reveal nothing more than the fact that the evangelist intended his readers to "link the death and resurrection of Jesus in terms of their effects."[84] Apart from regarding Matthew as inept with scissors and paste, these approaches offer no insight into the redactor's theological purposes in the passage.

From a different perspective, W. Schenk had argued for the origins of 51b-53 in a Jewish apocalyptic hymn whose roots are found in the vision of the dry bones in Ezekiel 37.[85] While Schenk's attempt to discern a hymnic

---

80. D. Senior, "Matthew's Special Material in the Passion Story," *ETL* 63 (1987): 277-84, provides a good review of various sources that have been suggested to account for vv. 51-53.

81. G. D. Kilpatrick, *The Gospel According to St. Matthew* (Oxford: Clarendon, 1946), p. 47.

82. D. Hutton, "The Resurrection of the Holy Ones (MT 27:51b-53): A Study of the Theology of the Matthean Passion Narrative," Th.D. dissertation, Harvard Divinity School, 1970, pp. 161-63; J. D. Crossan, *Four Other Gospels* (Minneapolis: Winston, 1982), pp. 141-42.

83. See R. Kratz, *Auferweckung als Befreiung* (Stuttgart: KBW, 1973), pp. 38-45, where he argues that the earthquake motif reflects a theophany.

84. D. Hill, "Matthew 27:51-53 in the Theology of the Evangelist," *IBS* 7 (1985): 77; Meier, "Salvation History," p. 209. Together the two passages represent the decisive inbreaking of God's intervention in history. For criticisms of the views of Hutton, see W. Schenk, *Die Sprache des Matthäus* (Göttingen: Vandenhoeck & Ruprecht, 1987), pp. 75-82; Senior, "Death," pp. 314-18.

85. Schenk, *Sprache*, pp. 76-78; M. Riebl, *Auferstehung Jesu in der Stunde seines Todes: Zur Botschaft von Mt 27,51b-53* (Stuttgart: KBW, 1978).

fragment is less than convincing, the influence of Ezekiel 37 on our passage has attained scholarly consensus.[86] Both Ezekiel 37:1-14 and Matthew 27:51b-53 share common motifs of earthquakes, the opening of tombs, the resurrection of the dead, and the return to Israel (Jerusalem in Matthew), and these signs are related to a new and perfect sanctuary. However, the parallels with Ezekiel do not bring us any closer to understanding the peculiarity of the resurrection of the saints in Matthew, let alone a coherent interpretation with the remainder of the Gospel. The raising of the saints is distinct to Matthew's Gospel and theology, and our interpretation provides an interpretative framework for this difficult passage.

One of the more immediate objections to our view is the equation of ἐκκλησία *people of God* in 16:18 with the ἅγιοι *saints* in 27:52. The masculine plural substantive of ἅγιος *saint* is found only here in the Gospel, but elsewhere in the NT when ἅγιοι occurs in the masculine plural substantive it almost always refers to NT saints. However, though this use is spread throughout the NT corpus, it is predominant in the epistles that are traditionally associated with the apostle Paul.[87] We cannot take it for granted, however, that Matthew is specifically referring only to the "holy ones" of Israel,[88] though D. Senior offers the occurrence of ἅγιοι in Isaiah 4:3; Tobit 8:15 and Psalm 33(34):10 in the LXX as possible parallels for Matthew.[89] Based on the limited usage of ἅγιοι, it is difficult to determine its exact referent, but within Matthew's Gospel it is reasonable to conclude that those included in the groups signified by the terms ἐκκλησία and ἅγιοι overlap.

The fact that ἅγιοι is a hapax legomenon in Matthew's Gospel means that our interpretation is not quite as neat as we might desire, but if the passage were not such an enigma, we would not require a discussion in the first place. In defense of our argument, we would emphasize that our interpretation of 27:51b-53 is both theologically coherent and theologically consistent with the rest of the Gospel, particularly in how it relates to other passages and material that are limited to Matthew.

86. Senior, "Matthew's Special Material," p. 282; Schenk, *Sprache*, p. 210; Gundry, *Commentary*, pp. 575-77; Hill, "Matthew 27:51-53," p. 76.

87. In over 60 cases (42x in books associated with Paul) ἅγιοι clearly refers to NT saints. See Acts 9:13, 32; Heb. 6:10; 8:2; Jude 3; Rev. 13:7, 10; Rom. 1:7; 8:27; 1 Cor. 1:2; 6:1; Eph. 1:1, 4; Phil. 1:1; 4:21; Col. 1:2, 4; 1 Thess. 3:13; 1 Tim. 5:10; Philem. 5, 7. References that include both the OT and NT righteous are found in Rev. 11:18; 18:20; and probably 5:8; 8:3, 4; 16:6.

88. That the term refers to holy ones from the OT period is more or less assumed, for example, by Gundry, *Commentary*, p. 576, and G. Strecker, *Der Weg der Gerechtigkeit* (Göttingen: Vandenhoeck & Ruprecht, 1986), p. 217.

89. Senior, "Death," p. 315.

A Descent into Hades Motif in Matthew?

At the very least we can say, based on 12:40; 16:18; and 27:51b-53, that there is a resurrection motif present in Matthew's Gospel. However, to take our investigation of Matthew's theology one step further, we would assert that Matthew reflects a nascent "Descent into Hades" motif. Although most scholars have denied the presence of this motif in Matthew,[90] it becomes much more plausible when we consider the influence of the psalm of Jonah, particularly the OG version, in the Gospel. In fact, there are two additional thematic connections between the psalm of Jonah and Matthew that strengthen the case for Matthew's dependence on the former and indicate the presence of a "Descent into Hades" motif in Matthew.

The most obvious reason to argue for the presence of the "Descent into Hades" motif in Matthew is the fact that the motif is found in Jonah.[91] Not only is there a geographical progression when Jonah goes from being covered by the waters (vv. 3, 5) to going down to the earth ("roots of the mountains" in MT, v. 7), but Jonah 2:7 explicitly speaks of a "**descent** (κατέβην) into the earth/land whose bars constrain forever."[92] Each of the three Matthean passages we have considered are also linked explicitly to Hades and/or a motif of resurrection. Second, Jonah experienced deliverance/salvation from Hades[93] just as Jesus delivers the saints/people of God.

Here, in the psalm of Jonah, are the seeds for Matthew's special material

---

90. Most recent scholars deny there is any evidence to support the presence of the "Descent into Hades" motif in vv. 51b-53. The principal objections have been summarized by Hutton ("Resurrection," pp. 5-6). He argues: (1) that the passage is so primitive that Matthew could hardly have been aware that he was giving expression to this developing motif; (2) there is no evidence that Matthew understood that Christ was to release the people of God from Hades; and (3) that the location of the passage in the narrative of the crucifixion is opposed to the earliest association of the "Descent into Hades" with Christ's resurrection. It is the second objection that constitutes Hutton's main argument, and it is this issue that we now examine.

91. Landes, "'Three Days and Three Nights' Motif," pp. 446-50; Stuart, *Hosea-Jonah*, pp. 475-77.

92. J. Magonet (*Form and Meaning: Studies in Literary Technique in the Book of Jonah* [Sheffield: Almond, 1983], pp. 17, 40-41) compares the use of יָרַדְתִּי in v. 7 with 1:3, 5 where Jonah **went down** to Joppa, **went down** (OG κατέβη) in the boat, **went down** (OG κατέβη) to the hold of the ship, and **went down** into the sea.

93. Jonah had descended through the depths until he reached the land whose bars imprison forever (vv. 3-6), when he then prayed for help (v. 7) and was delivered by the fish. Thus, the introduction of the fish in 2:1 anticipates the following psalm of thanksgiving. Landes, "'Three Days and Three Nights' Motif," p. 449; Stuart, *Hosea-Jonah*, pp. 472-74; Hauser, "Jonah," pp. 28-29.

in 12.40; 16.18; and, by implication, 27.51b-53. There are three dominant themes in Jonah's prayer — death/Hades, a descent into Hades, and deliverance/salvation from Hades — that provide the necessary origins for a "Descent into Hades" motif for Matthew's Gospel. As we have argued, the first and third of these themes are explicitly worked out in Matthew's special material. While the "Descent into Hades" by Jesus to free the saints remains implicit, the possibility that Matthew has borrowed the motif from Jonah is supported by Matthew's dependence on the psalm of Jonah and by the content of the sayings in the Gospel: (1) Matthew affirms the presence of Jesus in Hades in 12:40; (2) Jesus promises that the gates of Hades will not be able to contain the Church in 16:18, and surely it is no coincidence that the first of the three passion predictions immediately follows this promise in 16:21; and (3) in 27:51b-53 we have Jesus' promise fulfilled by the raising of the saints upon his death.

The purpose of this discussion has been to demonstrate through an extended examination of several texts how the Greek Jewish Scriptures distinctly influenced the theology of the NT. We have seen how the psalm of Jonah in its Greek form left a decisive mark on Matthew's Gospel. There is no question that 12:40 and 16:18 are directly influenced by OG Jonah 2, and these passages help us to interpret the enigmatic passage about the raising of the saints in 27:51b-53. Along with the citations that we analyzed and our discussion of the use of LXX vocabulary in the NT, we have established that the LXX made a distinctive impact on the theology of the NT.

Summary

1. The Greek Jewish Scriptures in the LXX tradition witness to a larger corpus of Scripture than what eventually became fixed in the MT. The NT use of a broad range of writings as authoritative Scripture that extends beyond the limits of the books that later became fixed in the Jewish canon also reflects that there was no fixed Jewish canon during the NT period.

2. The fact that the Greek Jewish Scriptures were cited in the NT in contrast to the Hebrew demonstrates that they were deemed to be Scripture for the Early Church. Furthermore, it was shown that the use of the LXX writings by the NT writers influenced their theology. Three lines of argument were used to demonstrate the influence of the Greek Jewish Scriptures on the NT.

3. The first line of argument is the influence of the vocabulary of the LXX

on the NT. Specific examples are ἄγγελος, διαθήκη, τὰ ἔθνη, δόξα, κύριος, and εὐαγγέλιον.

4. A more important theological influence of the Greek Jewish Scriptures is shown by the way they are cited in the NT to make a point that could not be made if the citation had come from the Hebrew. The quotations of Amos 9:11-12 in Acts 15:16-18 and Deuteronomy 32:43 in Hebrews 1:6 have already been determined to exhibit OG/LXX influence; and, in this chapter, we examined Isaiah 29:13 in Matthew 15:9, Psalm 8:2 in Matthew 21:16, Isaiah 7:14 in Matthew 1:23, Isaiah 40:13 in 1 Corinthians 2:16, Deuteronomy 6:5 in Matthew 22:37 and parallels, Haggai 2:7(6) in Hebrews 12:26, and Daniel 7:13 in Matthew 24:30 and other passages.

5. The citation of OG Isaiah 40:13 in 1 Corinthians 2:16 is particularly interesting in view of Paul's statements about the union of the believer with Christ, because the declaration that *we have the mind of Christ* helps us to understand the way in which the Apostle established the connection between the mystical union of the believer in Christ and Christian ethics.

6. The citation of OG Daniel 7:13 also influenced the theology of the NT because it could be understood as making an identification between the Son of Man and the Ancient of Days, that is, *the Son of Man came upon the clouds and as the Ancient of Days.* Yarbro Collins argues that Jesus used the phrase exegetically to refer to the figure of Daniel 7:13, but in the NT it is a self-designation that is interpreted messianically.

7. The third way that we demonstrated the impact of the LXX on the NT was by tracing the use of the OG psalm of Jonah in the Gospel of Matthew. Matthew 12:40; 16:18; 27:51b-53 are all unique to Matthew and share a resurrection motif. 12:40 and 16:18 can be related to the psalm of Jonah by their vocabulary, and together they provide a theological explanation for the raising of the saints in 27:51b-53.

8. We also argued that the Gospel of Matthew exhibits a nascent "Descent into Hades" motif. The evidence for this position is Matthew's dependence on the psalm of Jonah, particularly in its OG version, and the content of special sayings in the Gospel that also reflect the influence of Jonah: (1) Matthew affirms the presence of Jesus in Hades in 12:40; (2) Jesus promises that the gates of Hades will not be able to contain the Church in 16:18; and (3) in 27:51b-53 we have Jesus' promise fulfilled by the raising of the saints upon his death.

CHAPTER SIX

Summary, Conclusions, and Prospects

The purpose of this volume has been to explore and explain the use of the LXX in NT research. Accomplishing this goal has required that we engage in two complementary tasks: (1) introducing the reader to the contemporary study of the Septuagint in its historical environment; and (2) incorporating the knowledge gleaned from the former into an examination of the use of the Scriptures in the NT.

We began our investigation with the citation of Amos 9:11-12 in Acts 15:16-18 and discovered that the NT relies on the OG form of the text in order to make its point. The differences between the texts of the MT, OG, and NT initiated a variety of questions about the NT writers' use and knowledge of the Scriptures, which were pursued throughout the remainder of our volume. The interdisciplinary nature of our subject meant that we did not approach it according to more traditional methods. A typical introduction to the Septuagint, for example, would outline the history of its textual transmission earlier in the volume than we did.[1] Instead, we adopted an inductive approach that began with actual citations of Scripture in the NT in order to learn from the texts. Chapter two examined several passages in which the reading of the NT agreed with the OG, but not in any distinctive way that required that they were dependent upon the OG. The problem of distinguishing the use of the

---

1. See N. Fernández Marcos, *The Septuagint in Context* (Leiden: Brill, 2001); K. Jobes and M. Silva, *Invitation to the Septuagint* (Grand Rapids: Baker, 2000); S. Jellicoe, *The Septuagint and Modern Study* (Oxford: Clarendon, 1968); and G. Dorival, M. Harl, and O. Munnich, *La Bible grecque des Septante* (Paris: Éditions du Cerf, 1988), all of whom devote more time and space to Septuagint matters that were not as pertinent to us because of our concern for understanding the relationship between the LXX and NT.

Greek from the Hebrew form of the Jewish Scriptures in the NT is exacerbated since the NT and LXX texts share a close relationship in their transmission. Due to the complex nature of these linguistic relationships we learned about TT and provided a model for the study of TT in chapter three. Though the study of TT is primarily an aid for understanding the LXX in relation to the HB, there are also implications and uses for studying the NT citations. In chapter four we discovered that the production of additional versions and recensions of the LXX injects a further complication into understanding the use of Scripture in the NT. The evidence from the *DSS* offers a similar picture of the textual fluidity that existed among the manuscripts of the Hebrew Scriptures. Our knowledge of the multiplicity of text forms and the ways that the NT writers actually cited Scripture helps us to understand why some citations appear to have a mixed character and why we are unable to be certain about the source of others (Heb. 1:6).

Though there was no idea of a fixed canon during the first century, the Scriptures were central to Jewish thought and life, and there was an expectation that God would act on the behalf of his covenant people. We have argued it was within that context of hope that the Scriptures were reinterpreted in light of the person and ministry of Jesus. More specifically, in a context of textual pluriformity, it was the Jewish Scriptures as they were known, read, and interpreted in the Greek language that provide the basis for much, if not most, of the interpretive context of the NT writers. In the final chapter we demonstrated the significance of the findings of our study by giving a sustained argument for the influence of the Greek Jewish Scriptures on the NT. The vocabulary, citations of Scripture, and the theology reflected in the NT writings demonstrate the universal impact of the Greek Jewish Scriptures for the understanding of NT theology. None of these findings are remarkable. What is remarkable is the fact that there are many scholars and students who expend a great deal of energy in their study of the NT who have so little regard for the LXX as a means for helping to interpret the NT text!

Our investigations of passages such as 1 Corinthians 2:16; Hebrews 1:6; Acts 15:16-18 and the passages in the Gospel of Matthew demonstrated the distinct theological thinking of the NT writers that is not based in reading the MT. The reinterpretation of Amos 9:11-12 to mean that the house of David is restored through Jesus and that the gentiles will seek the Lord because of his resurrection depends on the OG. The passage in Hebrews 1:6 is much more complicated in terms of determining its source, but the author definitely relied on a text that is preserved in the Septuagint tradition. 1 Corinthians 2:16 offered insight into Paul's understanding of the relationship between the believer and Christ and into the basis of the Apostle's ethics. The examination of Matthew 12:40 and the theology of resurrection in 16:18; 27:52 that is unique to his Gospel revealed that it was rooted in Matthew's use of the OG text of Jonah.

Nowadays, the *DSS* seem to have a cast a spell on our attention when it comes to understanding the background of the NT, while the LXX is too often ignored. How much more can be discovered about the imprint of the Greek translations of the Jewish Scriptures on the NT? How do we account for the extensive use of the Greek Jewish Scriptures by the NT writers? However we answer these questions, we should at least acknowledge that the LXX as a whole deserves far more attention in NT studies. Our analysis of Matthew's theology is offered as one extended example of the way in which the understanding of the NT can be enriched by the study of the LXX. The data that we have unearthed in this small volume have also indicated that there is a great deal more to be learned. The question is, "How would our understanding of the NT be enhanced if we read the Greek Jewish Scriptures as the primary source for the interpretive and theological reflections of the NT writers?"

Glossary of Terms

antonymy — lexemes whose sense relations are based on opposition. Normally confined to dichotomous pairs. Graded opposites involve a degree of comparison, such as *big:small*. Other nongraded types are complementaries, such as *married:single,* and conversives, such as *buy:sell.*

Aquila — a Jewish proselyte from Pontus who produced an extremely literal translation of the HB ca. 140 C.E.

Aramaism — element of grammar or language in the LXX or NT that has been influenced by Aramaic.

canon — the official list of books with authoritative status as the inspired Scriptures for a faith community.

codex — early form of a book. Papyrus sheets (and then parchment) were folded down the middle and then inscribed on both sides.

conflation — a combination of two or more textual readings into one.

conjectural emendation — suggestion of what might have been the original reading based on an educated guess. A conjectural emendation has no manuscript support.

diplomatic text — selects one text from among many as the base text for critical readings. Presents variant readings from other textual witnesses to the selected base text form by annotating the text and supplying variant readings in separate notes.

eclectic text — represents the attempt to reconstruct the most original form of a text based on methods of textual criticism. An eclectic text results from the comparison and selection of readings from all possible witnesses; therefore, it is not contained in any one textual witness.

formal equivalence — a translation designed to reveal as much as possible of the form and content of the original message.

functional equivalence — a translation intended to render the meaning of the parent text in the target language. The translator is not as concerned about having a one-to-one, word-for-word relation between the *Vorlage* and the target language.

gloss[1] — a translation.

gloss[2] — a type of explanatory note found in manuscripts.

grammaticalize — to represent a morphological meaning through the choice of a specific form of a word.

hapax legomenon — a word that occurs only once.

Hebraism — element of grammar or language in the LXX or NT that has been influenced by Hebrew.

Hexapla — a six-columned work composed by Origen containing: (1) the Hebrew text as he knew it; (2) a Greek transliteration of the Hebrew; (3) Aquila; (4) Symmachus; (5) the LXX; (6) Theodotion.

homonymy — a word form that has more than one distinct meaning, that is, two lexemes that are spelled the same. See *gloss*[1].

hyponymy — the sense relations between two lexemes when one is more specific than the other. For example, *dagger* is more specific than *knife*.

idiom — a phrase or clause that is treated as a single semantic unit because the meaning of the whole is not derived from the individual meanings of the words. For example, "up the creek without a paddle."

kaige (*kaige*-Theodotion) — often referred to as the *kaige* recension because of the belief that an individual or group worked to revise the OG text toward the MT. The texts (primarily those attributed with the siglum θ in Origen's Hexapla) that are grouped under this heading are not nearly as unified in their translation technique as scholars once thought.

langue — language as an abstract system, which is common to all speakers of a language community (compare *parole*).

lexeme — the base form of any set of related words or word forms. The uninflected form. For example, local is the lexeme of locals, locally, and location.

lexical leveling — the technique of employing one word in a language to translate two or more words from another language.

majority text — after the selection of one text form to represent the authoritative text, all copies are based on that one form. The Masoretes created a majority text (MT), though MT is an acronym for Masoretic Text not Majority Text.

metaphor — figure of speech in which the properties of something are applied to another. Comparison without using like or as.

metonymy — figure of speech in which a part stands for the whole. For example, the *twelve* for the twelve disciples.

midrash — Jewish method of interpretation that emphasized going beyond the plain meaning of the text. Hillel developed seven rules for interpretation.

morpheme — a minimal unit of meaning or grammatical function.

morphology — the study of morphemes.

papyrus — early writing material formed from the papyrus plant. The fibers were placed horizontally and vertically and then moistened and pressed together.

parablepsis — term in textual criticism to refer to errors of sight, such as looking at the beginning *(homoiarcton)* or the end *(homoiteleuton)* of words.

paradigmatic relations — the study of the sense relations between words.

parchment — writing material employed from about the fourth century, made by removing the hair and flesh from an animal skin.

parole — the actual discourse of individuals within the community rather than the abstract system of language (compare *langue*).

pesher — Jewish method of exegesis that interpreted biblical passages as fulfilled in the circumstances of the later community.

polysemy — a single lexeme with many senses. To be distinguished from *homonymy*.

referent — the extralinguistic thing to which a statement or concept refers.

retroversion — translating a text back to the language from which it was originally translated. To retrovert a text from OG is to reconstruct the Semitic text from which it was presumably translated in order to compare it to the MT.

revision — a text that has been altered or changed in a systematic way. A revision of the OG text exhibits specific and definable characteristics that can be demonstrated. Aquila was a revision of the OG so that it would reflect a closer formal relationship to the HB.

Scripture(s) — book or books that have authoritative status for a faith community

semantic fields — the investigation of the relationship between the set of lexemes that belong to a semantic domain (subject area). For example, the domain *color* includes *red, white, green, blue,* etc.

semantic range — the range of senses in which a single lexeme may be used.

semantics — the study of meaning.

Semitism (in the NT) — element of grammar or language in the NT that has been influenced by a Semitic language.

sense relations — the relationships between lexemes or words. See *synonymy, hyponymy, homonymy, polysemy, antonymy, metonymy, syntagmatic,* and *paradigmatic relations.*

Septuagintism — element of grammar or language in the NT that has been influenced by the LXX.

standardization (of a biblical text) — the selection of one text form, from among many variant text forms, to represent the authoritative text.

stereotyped equivalent (SE) — a specific word in the target language that is consistently employed to render a word in the source language.

Symmachus — provided a translation towards the end of the second century c.e. that was more in the style of everyday Greek while still rendering the Hebrew text faithfully.

synonymy (overlapping synonymy) — the sense relations of two or more words when they can be substituted for one another in a given context in order to produce the same meaning.

syntagmatic relations — the relationships that exist between particular combinations of words and how certain choices affect other choices.

syntax — the interrelationship of words in phrases, clauses, and sentences.

Tendenz — German term referring to the theological beliefs of the translator that influence how she/he translates.

textual variant — an alternative reading of a text in another manuscript or version.

Theodotion — according to early testimony, a Jew from Ephesus who lived in the mid-second century and completed a translation of the HB; this identification, however, is unlikely.

translational gloss — the word employed in a target text to represent the meaning of a word from a source language/text.

translation technique — the methods employed by the Septuagint translators to translate the Semitic text. This should not be understood in the sense that they had rules to which they rigidly adhered; the term describes the tendencies or characteristics of the individual translators.

transposition — in textual criticism a change in position of letters or words.

unvocalized text — a text or manuscript without vowels. The system of vowels in our Hebrew manuscripts was added hundreds of years after the common era.

variant — an alternative reading of the text in another manuscript or version.

Vorlage — German term for the presumed parent text from which a translation was made.

Bibliography

Abercrombie, J. R., et al. *Computer Assisted Tools for Septuagint Studies*. Vol. 1: *Ruth. SCS* 20. Atlanta: Scholars Press, 1984.

Achtemeier, P., J. Green, and M. Thompson. *Introducing the New Testament: Its Literature and Theology*. Grand Rapids: Eerdmans, 2001.

Adair, J. "Light from Below: Canonical and Theological Implications of Textual Criticism." *OTE* 11 (1998): 9-23.

———. "A Methodology for Using the Versions in the Textual Criticism of the Old Testament." *JNSL* 20 (1994): 111-42.

Aejmelaeus, A. *Parataxis in the Septuagint. AASF, DHL* 31. Helsinki: Suomalainen Tiedeakatemia, 1982.

———. "*Participium Coniunctum* as a Criterion of Translation Technique." *VT* 32 (1982): 385-93.

———. "Septuagintal Translation Techniques — A Solution to the Problem of the Tabernacle Account." In *Septuagint, Scrolls and Cognate Writings*. Ed. G. J. Brooke and B. Lindars. *SCS* 33. Atlanta: Scholars Press, 1992.

———. "The Significance of Clause Connectors in the Syntactical and Translation-Technical Study of the Septuagint." In *VI Congress of the IOSCS*. Ed. C. Cox. *SCS* 23. Atlanta: Scholars Press, 1988.

———. "Translation Technique and the Intention of the Translator." In *VII Congress of the IOSCS*. Ed. C. Cox, pp. 23-36. *SCS* 31. Atlanta: Scholars Press, 1991.

———. "What Can We Know About the Hebrew *Vorlage* of the Septuagint?" *ZAW* 99 (1981): 58-89.

Akmajian, A., R. Demers, and R. Harnish. *Linguistics: An Introduction to Language and Communication*. London: MIT Press, 1979.

Aland, B., et al., eds. *The Greek New Testament*. 4th rev. ed. Stuttgart: United Bible Societies, 1993.

Aland, B. et al., eds. *Novum Testamentum Graece.* 27th rev. ed. Stuttgart: Deutsche Bibelgesellschaft, 1993.

Allen, Leslie C. *The Greek Chronicles: Part 1. VTSupp* 25. Leiden: Brill, 1974.

―――. *The Greek Chronicles: Part 2. VTSupp* 27. Leiden: Brill, 1974.

Archer, G. L., and G. Chirichigno. *Old Testament Quotations in the New Testament.* Chicago: Moody, 1983.

Attridge, H. W., J. J. Collins, and T. H. Tobin, eds. *Of Scribes and Scrolls: Studies on the Hebrew Bible, Intertestamental Judaism, and Christian Origins.* Lanham, Md.: University Press of America, 1990.

Ausloos, H. "The Septuagint Version of Exod 23:20-33: A Deuteronomist at Work?" *JNSL* 22 (1996): 89-106.

Baillet, M., J. T. Milik, and R. de Vaux, eds. *Les 'Petites Grottes' de Qumrân. DJD* 3. Oxford: Clarendon, 1962.

Balch, D. L. *Social History of the Matthean Community.* Minneapolis: Fortress, 1991.

Barr, J. *Comparative Philology and the Text of the Old Testament.* Oxford: Oxford University Press, 1968.

―――. "Determination and the Definite Article in Biblical Hebrew." *JSS* 34 (1989): 307-35.

―――. "Doubts about Homoeophony in the Septuagint." *Textus* 12 (1985): 1-77.

―――. "Guessing in the Septuagint." In *Studien zur Septuaginta — Robert Hanhart zu ehren.* Ed. D. Fränkel, U. Quast, and J. Wevers, 19-34. Göttingen: Vandenhoeck & Ruprecht, 1990.

―――. *Holy Scripture: Canon, Authority, Criticism.* Philadelphia: Fortress, 1983.

―――. "Paul and the LXX: A Note on Some Recent Work." *JTS* 45 (1994): 593-601.

―――. *The Semantics of Biblical Language.* Oxford: Clarendon, 1961.

―――. "The Typology of Literalism in Ancient Biblical Translations." *MSU* 15 (1979): 275-325.

―――. "Vocalization and the Analysis of Hebrew among the Ancient Translators." *VTSupp* 16 (1967): 1-11.

Barrett, C. K. "The Interpretation of the Old Testament in the New." In *Cambridge History of the Bible.* Ed. C. F. Evans and P. R. Ackroyd, pp. 377-411. Cambridge: Cambridge University Press, 1970.

Barthélemy, D. "Les devanciers d'Aquila: première publication intégrale du texte des fragments du Dodécaprophéton." In *VTSupp* 10. Leiden: Brill, 1963.

―――. "Notes critiques sur quelques points d'histoire du texte." In *Études d'histoire du texte de l'Ancien Testament,* pp. 289-303. *OBO* 21. Göttingen: Vandenhoeck & Ruprecht, 1978.

Barthélemy, D., and J. T. Milik, eds. *Qumran Cave 1. DJD* 1. Oxford: Clarendon, 1955.

Barton, J. *Oracles of God.* Oxford: Oxford University Press, 1986.

Bauer, W. *A Greek-English Lexicon of the New Testament.* Trans. and adapted from

W. Bauer's 4th ed. by W. F. Arndt and F. W. Gingrich. Rev. and aug. from the 5th ed. by F. W. Gingrich and F. W. Danker. 2nd ed. Chicago: University of Chicago Press, 1979.

Beale, G. K. *John's Use of the Old Testament in Revelation.* Sheffield: Sheffield Academic Press, 1998.

Beckwith, R. "Formation of the Hebrew Bible." In *Mikra: Text, Translation, Reading and Interpretation of the Hebrew Bible in Ancient Judaism and Early Christianity.* Ed. M. J. Mulder and H. Sysling. Philadelphia: Fortress, 1988.

————. *The Old Testament Canon of the New Testament Church.* Grand Rapids: Eerdmans, 1985.

Bennett, J. *Linguistic Behaviour.* Cambridge: Cambridge University Press, 1976.

Berlin, B., and P. Kay. *Basic Color Terms: Their Universality and Evolution.* Los Angeles: University of California Press, 1969.

Bertram, G. "Der Sprachschatz der Septuaginta und des Hebräischen Alten Testaments." *ZAW* n.f. 16 (1939): 85-101.

Bickerman, E. J. "The Septuagint as a Translation." *Proceedings of the American Academy of Jewish Research* 28 (1959): 1-39.

Black, D. A. *Linguistics for Students of New Testament Greek.* Grand Rapids: Baker, 1988.

Black, M. *An Aramaic Approach to the Gospels.* Oxford: Oxford University Press, 1967.

Blass, F., and A. Debrunner. *A Greek Grammar of the New Testament and Other Early Christian Literature.* Trans. and rev. R. W. Funk. Chicago: University of Chicago Press, 1961.

Bloomfield, L. *Language.* London: G. Allen & Unwin, 1935.

Bodine, W. *The Greek Text of Judges.* HSM 23. Chico, Calif.: Scholars Press, 1980.

————. "*Kaige* and Other Recensional Developments in the Greek Text of Judges." *BIOSCS* 13 (1980): 45-57.

————, ed. *Linguistics and Biblical Hebrew.* Winona Lake, Ind.: Eisenbrauns, 1992.

Bousset, W. *Kyrios Christos.* Nashville: Abingdon, 1970.

Bratcher, R., ed. *Old Testament Quotations in the New Testament.* 2nd rev. ed. New York: United Bible Societies, 1984.

Bréal, M. *Semantics: Studies in the Science of Meaning.* Trans. H. Cust. New York: Dover, 1964.

Brenton, L. C. L. *The Septuagint Version of the Old Testament.* London: S. Bagster and Sons, 1844.

Brock, S. P. "Aspects of Translation Technique in Antiquity." *Greek, Roman, and Byzantine Studies* 20 (1979): 69-87.

————. "The Phenomenon of Biblical Translation in Antiquity." *Alta: The University of Birmingham Review* 2 (1969): 96-102.

————. "The Phenomenon of the Septuagint." *OTS* 17 (1972): 11-36.

————. "To Revise or Not to Revise: Attitudes to Jewish Biblical Translation." In

Septuagint, Scrolls and Cognate Writings. Ed. G. J. Brooke and B. Lindars, pp. 301-38. *SCS* 33. Atlanta: Scholars Press, 1992.

Brock, S. P., C. T. Fritsch, and S. Jellicoe. *A Classified Bibliography of the Septuagint.* Leiden: Brill, 1973.

Brooke, G. *Exegesis at Qumran: 4QFlorilegium in Its Jewish Context. JSOTSS* 29. Sheffield: JSOT Press, 1985.

Brooke, G. J., and B. Lindars, eds. *Septuagint, Scrolls and Cognate Writings. SCS* 33. Atlanta: Scholars Press, 1992.

Brown, F., S. R. Driver, and C. A. Briggs. *A Hebrew and English Lexicon of the Old Testament.* Oxford: Clarendon, 1906.

Bruce, F. F. *Biblical Exegesis in the Qumran Texts.* Grand Rapids: Eerdmans, 1959.

————. "The Book of Daniel and the Qumran Community." In *Neotestamentica et Semitica: Studies in Honour of Matthew Black.* Ed. E. E. Ellis and M. Wilcox. Edinburgh: T. & T. Clark, 1969.

————. "The Earliest Old Testament Interpretation." *OTS* 17 (1972): 37-52.

————. "The Oldest Greek Version of Daniel." *OTS* 20 (1977): 22-40.

————. "Prophetic Interpretation in the Septuagint." *BIOSCS* 12 (1979): 17-26.

Büchner, D. L. "Exegetical Variants in the LXX of Exodus: An Evaluation." *JNSL* 22 (1996): 35-58.

Burkitt, F. C. *The Old Latin and The Itala.* Cambridge: Cambridge University Press, 1896.

Busto Saiz, J. R. "Él texto teodocionico de Daniel y la traduccion de Simaco." *Sef* 40 (1980): 41-55.

Caird, G. "Homoeophony in the Septuagint." In *Essays in Honour of W. D. Davies.* Ed. R. Hammerton-Kelly and R. Scroggs, pp. 74-88. Leiden: Brill, 1976.

————. *The Language and Imagery of the Bible.* Westminster: Philadelphia, 1980.

Callaway, P. R. *The History of the Qumran Community. JSPS* 3. Sheffield: JSOT Press, 1988.

Carson, D. A., and H. G. M. Williamson, eds. *It Is Written: Scripture Citing Scripture.* New York: Cambridge University Press, 1988.

Chafe, W. L. *Meaning and the Structure of Language.* Chicago: University of Chicago Press, 1970.

Chamberlain, G. "Cultic Vocabulary in the Septuagint." *BIOSCS* 27 (1994): 21-28.

Charles, R. H. *A Critical and Exegetical Commentary on the Book of Daniel.* Oxford: Clarendon, 1929.

Charlesworth, J. H. "The Odes of Solomon." In *The Old Testament Pseudepigrapha.* Ed. J. H. Charlesworth. Garden City, N.Y.: Doubleday, 1983.

————, ed. *The Odes of Solomon.* Oxford: Clarendon, 1973.

Chomsky, N. *Reflections on Language.* New York: Pantheon, 1975.

————. *Rules and Representations.* Oxford: Basil Blackwell, 1980.

Collins, A. Yarbro. "Daniel 7 and the Historical Jesus." In *Of Scribes and Scrolls.* Ed. H. W. Attridge, J. J. Collins, and T. H. Tobin, pp. 187-94. Lanham, Md.: University Press of America, 1990.

————. "The 'Son of Man' Tradition and the Book of Revelation." In *The Messiah*. Ed. J. H. Charlesworth. Minneapolis: Fortress, 1992.

Collins, J. J. *Daniel*. Minneapolis: Fortress, 1993.

Collins, N. "281 BCE: The Year of the Translation of the Pentateuch into Greek Under Ptolemy II." In *Septuagint, Scrolls and Cognate Writings*. Ed. G. J. Brooke and B. Lindars. SCS 33. Atlanta: Scholars Press, 1992.

Collinson, W. E. "Comparative Synomics: Some Principles and Illustrations." *Transactions of the Philosophical Society* (1939): 54-77.

Conzelmann, H. *Acts of the Apostles*. Philadelphia: Fortress, 1987.

Cook, J. "'Ancient' Readings in the Translations of the Old Testament." *JNSL* 12 (1986): 41-51.

————. "Aspects of the Relationship between the Septuagint Versions of Proverbs and Job." In *IX Congress of the IOSCS*. Ed. B. Taylor. SCS 45. Atlanta: Scholars Press, 1997.

————. "Aspects of the Translation Technique Followed by the Translator of Proverbs." *JNSL* 22 (1996): 143-53.

————. "The Hexaplaric Text, Double Translations and Other Textual Phenomena." *JNSL* 22 (1996): 129-40.

————. "Orthographical Peculiarities in the Dead Sea Biblical Scrolls." *RevQ* 14 (1989): 293-305.

————. *The Septuagint of Proverbs — Jewish and/or Hellenistic Proverbs (Concerning the Hellenistic Colouring of LXX Proverbs)*. VTSupp 69. Leiden: Brill, 1997.

Cotterell, P., and M. Turner. *Linguistics and Biblical Interpretation*. Downers Grove, Ill.: InterVarsity, 1989.

Cox, C., ed. *VI Congress of the IOSCS*. SCS 23. Atlanta: Scholars Press, 1988.

————, ed. *VII Congress of the IOSCS*. SCS 31. Atlanta: Scholars Press, 1991.

Cross, F. M. *The Ancient Library of Qumran and Modern Biblical Studies*. Westport, Conn.: Greenwood, 1958.

————. *Canaanite Myth and Hebrew Epic*. Cambridge, Mass.: Harvard University Press, 1973.

————. "The Contribution of the Qumran Discoveries to the Study of the Biblical Text." *IEJ* 16 (1966): 81-95.

Cross, F. M., and S. Talmon, eds. *Qumran and the History of the Biblical Text*. Cambridge: Harvard University Press, 1975.

Crossan, J. D. *Four Other Gospels*. Minneapolis: Winston, 1982.

Dalman, G. *Die Worte Jesu: Mit Berücksichtigung des nachkanonischen jüdischen Schrifttums und der aramäischen Sprache*. Vol. 1. Leipzig: J. C. Hinrichs, 1898.

Davies, W. D., and D. Allison. *The Gospel According to Saint Matthew*. Edinburgh: T. & T. Clark, 1991.

de Lange, N. R. M. *La Lettre à Africanus sur l'histoire de Suzanne*. Paris: Éditions du Cerf, 1983.

De Waard, J. "'Homophony' in the Septuagint." *Bib* 62 (1981): 551-61.

———. "La Septante: une traduction." In *Études sur le Judaïsme hellénistique.* Ed. R. Kuntzmann and J. Schlosser, pp. 133-45. Paris: Éditions du Cerf, 1984.

———. "Translation Techniques Used by the Greek Translators of Amos." *Bib* 59 (1978): 339-50.

———. "Translation Techniques Used by the Greek Translators of Ruth." *Bib* 54 (1973): 499-515.

Deissmann, A. *The Philology of the Greek Bible: Its Present and Future.* London: Hodder and Stoughton, 1908.

Delcor, M. "Un cas de traduction 'Targumique' de la LXX à propos de la statue en or de Dan. III." *Textus* 7 (1969): 30-35.

Dines, J. "Imagining Creation: The Septuagint Translation of Genesis 1:2." *The Heythrop Journal* 36 (1995): 439-50.

Dodd, C. H. *According to the Scriptures: The Substructure of New Testament Theology.* London: Nisbet & Co., 1952.

Dogniez, C. *Bibliography of the Septuagint.* VTSupp 60. Leiden: Brill, 1995.

Dorival, G., M. Harl, and O. Munnich. *La Bible grecque des Septante.* Paris: Éditions du Cerf, 1988.

Dos Santos, E. C., ed. *An Expanded Hebrew Index for the Hatch-Redpath Concordance to the Septuagint.* Jerusalem: Dugith, 1973.

Dunn, J. D. G. *The Theology of Paul the Apostle.* Grand Rapids: Eerdmans, 1998.

Ehrman, Bart. *The New Testament: A Historical Introduction to the Early Christian Writings.* New York: Oxford University Press, 1997.

Elliger, K., and W. Rudolph. *Biblia Hebraica Stuttgartensia.* Stuttgart: Deutsche Bibelstiftung, 1977.

Ellis, E. E. "Biblical Interpretation in the New Testament Church." In *Mikra: Text, Translation, Reading and Interpretation of the Hebrew Bible in Ancient Judaism and Early Christianity.* Ed. M. J. Mulder and H. Sysling. Philadelphia: Fortress, 1988.

———. *The Old Testament in Early Christianity: Canon and Interpretation in the Light of Modern Research.* WUNT 54. Tübingen: Mohr, 1991.

———. *Paul's Use of the Old Testament.* Edinburgh: Oliver & Boyd, 1957.

Emerton, J. A. "The Origin of the Son of Man Imagery." *JTS* 9 (1958): 225-42.

Evans, C. A. "The Scriptures of Jesus and His Earliest Followers." In *The Canon Debate: On the Origins and Formation of the Bible.* Ed. L. M. McDonald and J. A. Sanders, pp. 185-195. Peabody: Hendrickson, 2002.

———, ed. *Of Scribes and Sages: Studies in Early Jewish Interpretation and Transmission of Scripture.* Sheffield: Sheffield Academic Press, forthcoming.

Evans, T. V. *Verbal Syntax in the Greek Pentateuch.* Oxford: Oxford University Press, 2001.

Fanning, B. M. *Verbal Aspect in New Testament Greek.* Oxford: Clarendon, 1990.

Fernández Marcos, N. *The Septuagint in Context.* Leiden: Brill, 2001.

———. "Some Reflections on the Antiochian Text of the Septuagint." In *Studien zur Septuaginta — Robert Hanhart zu ehren.* Ed. D. Fraenkel, U. Quast, and J. Wevers. Göttingen: Vandenhoeck & Ruprecht, 1990.

———. "The Textual Context of the Hexapla: Lucianic Texts and Vetus Latina." In *Origen's Hexapla and Fragments.* Texte und Studien zum antiken Judentum 58. Tübingen: Mohr Siebeck, 1998.

———. "The Use of the Septuagint in the Criticism of the Hebrew Bible." *Sef* 47 (1987): 60-72.

———, ed. *La Septuaginta en la Investigacion Contemporanea (V Congreso de la IOSCS).* Madrid: Instituto Arias Montano, 1985.

Field, F. *Origenis Hexaplorum Quae Supersunt.* 2 vols. Oxford: Oxford University Press, 1867.

Fishbane, M. *Biblical Interpretation in Ancient Israel.* Oxford: Clarendon, 1985.

Flaschar, M. "Exegetische Studien zum Septuagintapsalter." *ZAW* 32 (1912): 81-116, 161-89.

Fodor, J., and J. Katz. *The Structure of Language.* Englewood Cliffs, N.J.: Prentice-Hall, 1964.

Fraenkel, D., U. Quast, and J. Wevers, eds. *Studien zur Septuaginta — Robert Hanhart zu ehren.* Göttingen: Vandenhoeck & Ruprecht, 1990.

Frankel, Z. *Vorstudien zu der Septuaginta.* Leipzig: Vogel, 1841.

Freed, E. *The New Testament: A Critical Introduction.* 2nd ed. Belmont: Wadsworth, 1996.

Freedman, D. N., ed. *Anchor Bible Dictionary.* 6 vols. New York: Doubleday, 1992.

Fritsch, C. "Homophony in the Septuagint." In *Sixth World Congress of Jewish Studies.* Ed. A. Shinan, pp. 115-20. Jerusalem: Jerusalem Academic Press, 1977.

Gehman, H. S. "Adventures in Septuagint Lexicography." *Textus* 6 (1966): 125-32.

Geissen, A. *Der Septuaginta-Text des Buches Daniel Kap. 5–12, zusammen mit Susanna, Bel et Draco, sowie Esther Kap. 1,1a–2,15 nach dem Kölner Teil des Papyrus 967. PTA* 5. Bonn: Habelt, 1969.

Gentry, P. "An Analysis of the Revisor's Text of the Greek Job." Ph.D. dissertation, University of Toronto, 1994.

———. *The Asterisked Materials in the Greek Job. SCS* 39. Atlanta: Scholars Press, 1995.

Gibson, A. *Biblical Semantic Logic.* Oxford: Basil Blackwell, 1981.

Gleason, H. A. *An Introduction to Descriptive Linguistics.* Rev. ed. London: Holt, Rinehart and Winston, 1961.

Gooding, D. W. "An Appeal for a Stricter Terminology in the Textual Criticism of the Old Testament." *JSOT* 21 (1976): 15-25.

———. "A Recent Popularization of Professor F. M. Cross' Theories on the Text of the Old Testament." *TynBul* 26 (1975): 113-32.

Goshen-Gottstein, M. "Hebrew Biblical Manuscripts: Their History and Their Place in the HUBP Edition." *Bib* 48 (1967): 243-90.

————. "The Textual Criticism of the Old Testament: Rise, Decline, Rebirth." *JBL* 102 (1983): 365-99.

————. "Theory and Practice of Textual Criticism." *Textus* 3 (1963): 130-58.

Grabbe, L. "Aquila's Translation and Rabbinic Exegesis." *JJS* 33 (1982): 527-36.

Greenspoon, L. "Biblical Translators in Antiquity and in the Modern World." *HUCA* 60 (1989): 91-113.

————. "It's All Greek to Me: The Septuagint in Modern English Translations of the Hebrew Bible." In *VII Congress of the IOSCS*. Ed. C. Cox, pp. 1-21. SCS 31. Atlanta: Scholars Press, 1991.

————. *Textual Studies in the Book of Joshua*. HSM 28. Chico, Calif.: Scholars Press, 1983.

————. "The Use and Abuse of the Term 'LXX' and Related Terminology in Recent Scholarship." *BIOSCS* 20 (1987): 21-29.

Greenspoon, L., and O. Munnich, eds. *VIII Congress of the IOSCS*. SCS 41. Atlanta: Scholars Press, 1996.

Grelot, P. "Les versions grecques de Daniel." *Bib* 47 (1966): 381-402.

Grindel, J. A. "Another Characteristic of the *Kaige* Recension: נצח/Νικος." *CBQ* 31 (1969): 499-513.

Grundman, W. *Das Evangelium nach Matthäus*. Berlin: Evangelische, 1971.

Gundry, R. H. *Matthew: A Commentary on His Literary and Theological Art.* Grand Rapids: Eerdmans, 1982.

————. *The Use of the Old Testament in St. Matthew's Gospel: With Special Reference to the Messianic Hope.* Leiden: Brill, 1967.

Gwynn, J. "Theodotion." In *Dictionary of Christian Biography*. Ed. W. Smith and H. Wace, vol. 4, pp. 970-79. London: John Murrow, 1887.

Haenchen, E. *The Acts of the Apostles.* Philadelphia: Westminister, 1971.

Halliday, M. A. K. "Lexis As a Linguistic Level." In *In Memory of J. R. Firth*. Ed. C. E. Bazell et al., pp. 148-62. London: Longmans, 1966.

Hamm, W. *Der Septuaginta-Text des Buches Daniel nach dem Kölner Teil des Papyrus 967.* Vols. 1–2. PTA 10. Bonn: Habelt, 1969.

————. *Der Septuaginta-Text des Buches Daniel nach dem Kölner Teil des Papyrus 967.* Vols. 3–4. PTA 21. Bonn: Habelt, 1977.

Hanhart, K. "The Four Beasts of Daniel's Vision in the Night in the Light of Rev. 13.2." *NTS* 28 (1981): 576-83.

Hanhart, R. "Die Bedeutung der Septuaginta für die Definition des 'Hellenistischen Judentums.'" *VTSupp* 40 (1986): 67-80.

————. "Die Septuaginta als Problem der Text-Geschichte, der Forschungsgeschichte und der Theologie." *VTSupp* 22 (1972): 185-200.

————. "The Translation of the Septuagint in Light of Earlier Tradition and Subsequent Influences." In *Septuagint, Scrolls and Cognate Writings*. Ed. G. J. Brooke and B. Lindars. SCS 33. Atlanta: Scholars Press, 1992.

————. "Die Uebersetzungstechnik der Septuaginta als Interpretation (Daniel 11,29 und die Aegyptenzüge des Antiochus Epiphanes)." In *Mélanges*

Dominique Barthélemy. Ed. P. Casetti, O. Keel, and A. Schenker. Göttingen: Vandenhoeck & Ruprecht, 1981.

————. "Zum gegenwärtigen Stand der Septuagintaforschung." In *De Septuaginta.* Ed. A. Pietersma and C. Cox. Mississauga: Benben, 1984.

Harris, R. "Synonymy and Linguistic Analysis." In *Language and Style.* Ed. S. Ullmann. Oxford: Basil Blackwell, 1973.

Harris, S. *The New Testament.* Mountain View: Mayfield, 1988.

Harris, W. *Ancient Literacy.* Cambridge, Mass.: Harvard University Press, 1989.

Hatch, E. *Essays in Biblical Greek: Studies on the Value and Use of the Septuagint, on Origen's Revision of Job, and on the Text of Ecclesiasticus.* Amsterdam: Philo, 1899.

Hatch, E., and H. A. Redpath, eds. *A Concordance to the Septuagint and the Other Greek Versions of the Old Testament.* 2 vols. with a supplement. Oxford: Oxford University Press, 1897-1906.

Hauser, A. J. "Jonah: In Pursuit of the Dove." *JBL* 104 (1985): 21-37.

Hays, R. B. *Echoes of Scripture in the Letters of Paul.* New Haven: Yale University Press, 1989.

Helbing, R. *Die Kasussyntax der Verba bei den Septuaginta.* Göttingen: Vandenhoeck & Ruprecht, 1928.

Heller, J. "Grenzen sprachlicher Entsprechung der LXX." *MIO* 5 (1969): 234-48.

Hengel, M. *Judaism and Hellenism.* Trans. John Bowman. 2 vols. Philadelphia: Fortress, 1974.

Hertog, Cornelius den. "Drei Studien zur Übersetzungstechnik des Griechischen Joshuabuches." *BIOSCS* 29 (1996): 22-52.

Hill, D. "Matthew 27:51-53 in the Theology of the Evangelist." *IBS* 7 (1985): 76-87.

Hirst, G. *Semantic Interpretation and the Resolution of Ambiguity.* Cambridge: Cambridge University Press, 1987.

Holmes, R., and J. Parsons. *Vetus Testamentum Graecum.* 4 vols. Oxford: Oxford University Press, 1827.

Hübner, Hans. *Vetus Testamentum in Novo.* Vol. 2: *Corpus Paulinum.* Göttingen: Vandenhoeck & Ruprecht, 1997.

Hutton, D. "The Resurrection of the Holy Ones (MT 27:51b-53): A Study of the Theology of the Matthean Passion Narrative." Th.D. dissertation, Harvard Divinity School, 1970.

Jackendoff, R. *Semantics and Cognition.* London: MIT Press, 1990.

Jackson, H. *Words and Their Meanings.* New York: Longman, 1988.

Jacques, X. *List of Septuagint Words Sharing Common Elements.* Rome: Biblical Institute, 1972.

Janz, T. "The Second Book of Ezra and the 'Καίγε Group.'" In *IX Congress of the IOSCS.* Ed. B. Taylor. Atlanta: Scholars Press, 1997.

Janzen, J. G. "A Critique of Sven Soderlund's *The Greek Text of Jeremiah.*" *BIOSCS* 22 (1989): 16-47.

————. *Studies in the Text of Jeremiah.* HSM 6. Cambridge, Mass.: Harvard University Press, 1973.

Jeansonne, S. Pace. *The Old Greek Translation of Daniel 7–12.* CBQMS 19. Washington: Catholic Biblical Association, 1988.

Jellicoe, S. "The Hesychian Recension Reconsidered." *JBL* 82 (1963): 409-18.

————. *The Septuagint and Modern Study.* Oxford: Clarendon, 1968.

————. "Some Reflections on the KAIGE Recension." *VT* 23 (1973): 15-24.

————, ed. *Studies in the Septuagint: Origins, Recensions, and Interpretations.* New York: Ktav, 1974.

Jenkins, R. G. "Colophons of the Syrohexapla and the Textgeschichte of the Recensions of Origen." In *VII Congress of the IOSCS.* Ed. C. Cox, pp. 261-77. SCS 31. Atlanta: Scholars Press, 1991.

Jobes, Karen, and Moisés Silva. *Invitation to the Septuagint.* Grand Rapids: Baker, 2000.

Johannessohn, M. *Der Gebrauch der Kasus in der Septuaginta.* Berlin: Weidmannsche, 1910.

————. *Der Gebrauch der Präpositionen in der Septuaginta.* Berlin: Weidmannsche, 1925.

Johnson, L. *The Writings of the New Testament.* Philadelphia: Fortress, 1986.

Joosten, J. "Exegesis in the Septuagint Version of Hosea." In *Intertextuality in Ugarit and Israel.* Ed. J. C. De Moor, pp. 62-85. Leiden: Brill, 1998.

————. "On the LXX Translators' Knowledge of Hebrew." In *X Congress of the IOSCS.* Ed. B. Taylor, pp. 165-79. SCS 51. Atlanta: Scholars Press, 2001.

Joüon, P. *A Grammar of Biblical Hebrew.* Trans. and rev. T. Muraoka. Rome: Editrice Pontificio Istituto Biblico, 1991.

Kahle, P. *The Cairo Geniza.* Oxford: Blackwell, 1959.

Kaiser, W. *The Uses of the Old Testament in the New.* Chicago: Moody, 1985.

Kamasar, A. *Jerome, Greek Scholarship, and the Hebrew Bible.* Oxford: Clarendon, 1993.

Käsemann, E. "The Problem of a New Testament Theology." *NTS* 19 (1972): 235-45.

Kasher, A. *The Chomskyan Turn.* Oxford: Basil Blackwell, 1991.

Kautzch, E., ed. *Gesenius' Hebrew Grammar.* 2nd ed. Trans. A. E. Cowley. Oxford: Clarendon, 1910.

Kenyon, Sir F. G. *The Text of the Greek Bible.* 3rd ed. rev. and aug. A. W. Adams. London: Duckworth, 1975.

Kilpatrick, G. D. *The Gospel according to St. Matthew.* Oxford: Clarendon, 1946.

Kirk, R. *Translation Determined.* Oxford: Clarendon, 1986.

Koch, D. A. *Die Schrift als Zeuge des Evangeliums: Untersuchungen zur Verwendung und zum Verständnis der Schrift bei Paulus.* Tübingen: Mohr, 1986.

Koehler, L., and W. Baumgartner. *Lexicon in Veteris Testamenti Libros.* 2nd ed. with supplement. Leiden: Brill, 1958.

Kratz, R. *Auferweckung als Befreiung.* Stuttgart: KBW, 1973.

Kugel, J. L., and R. A. Greer. *Early Biblical Interpretation.* Philadelphia: Westminster, 1986.

Kvanvig, Helge. "An Akkadian Vision as Background for Dan 7?" *ST* 35 (1981): 85-89.

Lagarde, P. de. *Septuaginta Studien.* Göttingen: n.p., 1892.

Landes, G. M. "The 'Three Days and Three Nights' Motif in Jonah 2.1." *JBL* 86 (1967): 446-50.

Lee, J. A. L. "Equivocal and Stereotyped Renderings in the LXX." *RB* 87 (1980): 104-17.

————. *A Lexical Study of the Septuagint Version of the Pentateuch. SCS* 14. Chico, Calif.: Scholars Press, 1983.

Lehrer, A. *Semantic Fields and Lexical Structures.* London: North-Holland, 1974.

Leiter, N. "Assimilation and Dissimilation Techniques in the LXX of the Book of Balaam." *Textus* 12 (1985): 79-95.

Liddell, H. G., and R. Scott. *A Greek-English Lexicon.* 10th ed. rev. and enlarged H. S. Jones and R. McKenzie. Oxford: Oxford University Press, 1968.

Lim, T. H. *Holy Scripture in the Qumran Commentaries and Pauline Letters.* Oxford: Clarendon, 1997.

Lindars, B. *Jesus Son of Man.* London: SPCK, 1983.

Longenecker, R. *Biblical Exegesis in the Apostolic Period.* Grand Rapids: Eerdmans, 1975.

Louw, J. P. *Semantics of New Testament Greek.* Atlanta: Scholars Press, 1982.

Louw, J. P., and E. A. Nida, eds. *Greek-English Lexicon of the New Testament.* New York: United Bible Societies, 1988.

————. "Translation Greek and the Lexicography of the Septuagint." *JSOT* 59 (1993): 109-20.

Lübbe, A. "Describing the Translation Process of 11QtgJob: A Question of Method." *RevQ* 52 (1988): 583-93.

Lust, J. "Daniel VII and the Septuagint." *ETL* 54 (1978).

Lust, J., E. Eynikel, and K. Hauspie. *A Greek-English Lexicon of the Septuagint.* 2 vols. Stuttgart: Deutsche Bibelgesellschaft, 1992-96.

Luz, V. *Das Evangelium nach Matthäus.* Zürich: Benziger, 1990.

Lyons, J. *Chomsky.* London: Fontana, 1970.

————. "Firth's Theory of Meaning." In *In Memory of J. R. Firth.* Ed. C. E. Bazell et al., pp. 288-302. London: Longmans, 1966.

————. *Language and Linguistics.* Cambridge: Cambridge University Press, 1981.

————. *Language, Meaning and Context.* Suffolk: Fontana, 1981.

————. *Semantics.* 2 vols. Cambridge: Cambridge University Press, 1977.

————. *Structural Semantics.* Oxford: Basil Blackwell, 1963.

————, ed. *New Horizons in Linguistics.* Middlesex: Penguin, 1970.

Magonet, J. *Form and Meaning: Studies in Literary Technique in the Book of Jonah.* Sheffield: Almond, 1983.

Marquis, G. "CATSS-Base: Computer Assisted Tools for Septuagint and Bible Study for All — Transcript of a Demonstration." In *VII Congress of the IOSCS*. Ed. C. Cox. SCS 31. Atlanta: Scholars Press, 1991.

———. "Consistency of Lexical Equivalents as a Criterion for the Evaluation of Translation Technique." In *VI Congress of the IOSCS*. Ed. C. Cox. SCS 23. Atlanta: Scholars Press, 1988.

———. "Word Order as a Criterion for the Evaluation of Translation Technique in the LXX and the Evaluation of Word-Order Variants as Exemplified in LXX-Ezekiel." *Textus* 13 (1986): 59-84.

Martin, R. "Some Syntactical Criteria of Translation Greek." *VT* 10 (1960): 295-310.

———. *Syntactical Evidences of Semitic Sources in Greek Documents*. SCS 3. Missoula, Mont.: Scholars Press, 1974.

Mason, S. "Josephus and His Twenty-Two Book Canon." In *The Canon Debate: On the Origins and Formation of the Bible*. Ed. L. M. McDonald and J. A. Sanders. Peabody: Hendrickson, 2002.

Mays, J. L. *Amos*. Philadelphia: Westminster, 1969.

Mayser, E. *Grammatik der griechischen Papyri aus der Ptolemäerzeit*. Berlin: De Gruyter, I.1 (2nd ed., H. Schmoll, 1970), I.2 (1938), I.3 (1936), II.1 (1926), II.2 (1934), II.3 (1934).

McCarter, P. K. *Textual Criticism: Recovering the Text of the Hebrew Bible*. Philadelphia: Fortress, 1986.

McCrystall, A. "Studies in the Old Greek Translation of Daniel." Ph.D. dissertation, Oxford University, 1980.

McDonald, L. *The Formation of the Christian Biblical Canon*. Rev. ed. Peabody: Hendrickson, 2001.

McDonald, L., and J. A. Sanders, eds. *The Canon Debate: On the Origins and Formation of the Bible*. Peabody: Hendrickson, 2002.

McDonald, L., and S. E. Porter. *Early Christianity and Its Sacred Literature*. Peabody: Hendrickson, 2000.

McGregor, L. J. *The Greek Text of Ezekiel: An Examination of Its Homogeneity*. Atlanta: Scholars Press, 1985.

McLay, T. "A Collation of Variants from 967 to Ziegler's Critical Edition of Susanna, Daniel, Bel et Draco." *Textus* 18 (1995): 121-34.

———. "Death, Descent and Deliverence in Matthew 27:51b-53." In *You Shall Be Witnesses: A Festschrift in Honour of the Reverend Dr. Allison A. Trites on the Occasion of His Retirement*. Ed. R. Glenn Wooden, Timothy R. Ashley, and Robert S. Wilson. Atlanta: Mercer University Press, 2003.

———. "It's a Question of Influence: The Old Greek and Theodotion Texts of Daniel." In *Origen's Hexapla and Fragments*. Ed. A. Salvesen, pp. 231-54. Texte und Studien zum antiken Judentum 58. Tübingen: Mohr Siebeck, 1998.

———. "*Kaige* and Septuagint Research." *Textus* 19 (1998): 121-34.

————. *The OG and Th Versions of Daniel.* SCS 43. Atlanta: Scholars Press, 1996.

————. "Translation Technique and Textual Studies in the Old Greek and Theodotion Versions of Daniel." Ph.D. dissertation, University of Durham, 1994.

Meadowcroft, T. J. *Aramaic Daniel and Greek Daniel: A Literary Comparison.* Sheffield: Sheffield Academic Press, 1995.

Meier, J. P. "Salvation History in Matthew: In Search of a Starting Point." *CBQ* 27 (1975): 209-17.

Mercati, G., ed. *Psalterii Hexapli Reliquiae. Pars Prima: Codex Rescriptus Bybliothecae Ambrosianae O 39 Sup. Phototypice Expressus et Transcriptus.* Vatican City: Biblioteca Apostolica Vaticana, 1958.

Metzger, B. "The Formulas Introducing Quotations of Scripture in the New Testament and the Mishna." *JBL* 70 (1951): 297-307.

Michel, O. *Paulus und seine Bibel.* Gütersloh: Bertelsmann, 1929.

M'Neile, A. H. *The Gospel according to St. Matthew.* London: Macmillan, 1915.

Montgomery, J. A. *A Critical and Exegetical Commentary on the Book of Daniel.* New York: Charles Scribner's Sons, 1927.

Moule, C. F. D. "Fulfillment-Words in the New Testament: Use and Abuse." *NTS* 14 (1968): 293-320.

————. *An Idiom Book of New Testament Greek.* 2nd ed. Cambridge: Cambridge University Press, 1959.

Mulder, M. J., and H. Sysling, eds. *Mikra: Text, Translation, Reading and Interpretation of the Hebrew Bible in Ancient Judaism and Early Christianity.* Philadelphia: Fortress, 1988.

Müller, M. *The First Bible of the Church: A Plea for the Septuagint.* JSOTSS 206. Sheffield: JSOT Press, 1996.

Munnich, O. "Contribution à L'étude de la première révision de la Septante." *ANRW* II.20.1 (1986): 190-220.

————. "Étude lexicographique du Psautier des Septante." Ph.D. dissertation, Université de Paris-Sorbonne, 1982.

————. "Indices d'une Septante originelle dans le Psautier grec." *Bib* 63 (1982): 406-16.

————. "Origène, éditeur de la *Septante de Daniel.*" In *Studien zur Septuaginta — Robert Hanhart zu ehren.* Ed. D. Fraenkel, U. Quast, and J. Wevers, pp. 187-218. Göttingen: Vandenhoeck & Ruprecht, 1990.

————. "La Septante des Psaumes et la groupe *Kaige.*" *VT* 33 (1983): 75-89.

Muraoka, T. *Emphatic Words and Structures in Biblical Hebrew.* Jerusalem: Magnes, 1985.

————. *A Greek-English Lexicon of the Septuagint.* Louvain: Peeters, 1993.

————. *A Greek-Hebrew/Aramaic Index to I Esdras.* SCS 16. Chico, Calif.: Scholars Press, 1984.

————. *Hebrew/Aramaic Index to the Septuagint.* Grand Rapids: Baker, 1998.

————. "Hebrew Hapax Legomena and Septuagint Lexicography." In *VII Con-*

gress of the IOSCS. Ed. C. Cox, pp. 205-22. *SCS* 31. Atlanta: Scholars Press, 1991.

————. "Literary Device in the Septuagint." *Textus* 8 (1973): 20-30.

————, ed. *Melbourne Symposium on Septuagint Lexicography. SCS* 28. Atlanta: Scholars Press, 1990.

Murray, D. "The Sign of Jonah." *Downside Review* 107 (1989): 224-29.

Neusner, J., W. S. Green, and E. S. Frerichs, eds. *Judaisms and Their Messiahs.* Cambridge: Cambridge University Press, 1987.

New, D. *Old Testament Quotations in the Synoptic Gospels, and the Two-Document Hypothesis. SCS* 37. Atlanta: Scholars Press, 1993.

Nida, E. *Componential Analysis of Meaning.* Paris: Mouton, 1975.

————. *Exploring Semantic Structures.* Munich: Fink, 1975.

————. *Language Structure and Translation.* Stanford: Stanford University Press, 1975.

————. *Morphology: The Descriptive Analysis of Meaning.* Ann Arbor: University of Michigan Press, 1949.

————. *Toward a Science of Translating.* Leiden: Brill, 1964.

Nida, E., and J. P. Louw. *Lexical Semantics of the Greek New Testament.* Atlanta: Scholars Press, 1992.

Nida, E., et al. *Style and Discourse: With Special Reference to the Text of the Greek New Testament.* Cape Town: Bible Society, 1983.

O'Connell, K. G. *The Theodotionic Revision of the Book of Exodus. HSM* 3. Cambridge, Mass.: Harvard University Press, 1972.

Ogden, C. K., and I. A. Richards. *The Meaning of Meaning.* 3rd rev. ed. London: Kegan Paul, 1930.

Olofsson, S. "Consistency as a Translation Technique." *SJOT* 6 (1992): 14-30.

————. *God Is My Rock. ConBib.OT* 31. Stockholm: Almqvist & Wiksell, 1990.

————. "The Kaige Group and the Septuagint Book of Psalms." In *IX Congress of the IOSCS.* Ed. B. Taylor. *SCS* 45. Atlanta: Scholars Press, 1997.

————. *The LXX Version: A Guide to the Translation Technique of the Septuagint. ConBib.OT* 30. Stockholm: Almqvist & Wiksell, 1990.

Olsen, M. "A Semantic and Pragmatic Model of Lexical and Grammatical Aspect." Ph.D. dissertation, Northwestern University, 1994.

Orlinsky, H. M. "Origen's Tetrapla — a Scholarly Fiction?" In *Proceedings of the First World Congress of Jewish Studies.* Vol. 1, pp. 173-82. Jerusalem: Magnes and Hebrew University, 1952.

————. "The Origin of the Kethib-Qere System: A New Approach." *VTSupp* 7 (1959): 184-92.

————. "The Septuagint as Holy Writ and the Philosophy of the Translators." *HUCA* 46 (1975): 89-114.

————. "The Textual Criticism of the Old Testament." In *The Bible and the Ancient Near East.* Ed. G. E. Wright, pp. 113-32. London: Routledge & Kegan, 1961.

Pageant, R. *Engaging the New Testament*. Minneapolis: Fortress, 1995.

Parker, F. *Linguistics for Non-Linguists*. London: Taylor & Francis, 1986.

Paul, S. *Amos*. Minneapolis: Fortress, 1991.

Pickering, W. *A Framework for Discourse Analysis*. Dallas: Summer Institute of Linguistics, 1980.

Pietersma, A. "The Greek Psalter: A Question of Methodology and Syntax." *VT* 26 (1976): 60-69.

————. "A New Paradigm for Addressing Old Questions: The Relevance of the Interlinear Model for the Study of the Septuagint." In *Bible and Computer*. Ed. J. Cook, pp. 337-64. Leiden: Brill, 2002.

————. "Proto-Lucian and the Greek Psalter." *VT* 28 (1978): 66-72.

————. "The Psalms." *A New English Translation of the Septuagint*. New York: Oxford University Press, 2000.

————. "Ra 2110 (P. Bodmer XXIV) and the Text of the Greek Psalter." In *Studien zur Septuaginta — Robert Hanhart zu ehren*. Ed. D. Fraenkel, U. Quast, and J. Wevers, pp. 264-86. Göttingen: Vandenhoeck & Ruprecht, 1990.

————. "Septuagint Research: A Plea for a Return to Basic Issues." *VT* 35 (1985): 296-311.

Pietersma, A., and C. Cox, eds. *De Septuaginta*. Mississauga: Benben, 1984.

Porter, S. *Idioms of the Greek New Testament*. Sheffield: JSOT Press, 1992.

————. "Studying Ancient Languages from a Modern Linguistic Perspective: Essential Terms and Terminology." *Filologia Neotestamentaria* 2 (1989): 147-72.

————. "The Use of the Old Testament in the New Testament: A Brief Comment on Method and Terminology." In *Early Christian Interpretation of the Scriptures of Israel*. Ed. C. A. Evans and James A. Sanders, pp. 79-96. Sheffield: Sheffield Academic Press, 1997.

————. *Verbal Aspect in the Greek of the NT, With Reference to Tense and Mood*. New York: Peter Lang, 1989.

Porzig, W. *Das Wunder der Sprache*. Bern: Francke, 1950.

Rabin, C. "The Ancient Versions and the Indefinite Subject." *Textus* 2 (1962): 60-76.

————. "The Translation Process and the Character of the Septuagint." *Textus* 6 (1968): 1-26.

Radford, A. *Transformational Syntax: A Student's Guide to Extended Standard Theory*. Cambridge: Cambridge University Press, 1981.

Rahlfs, A. *Septuaginta, Id Est Vetus Testamentum Graece Iuxta LXX Interpretes*. 2 vols. Stuttgart: Privilegierte Württembergische Bibelanstalt, 1935.

————, ed. *Psalmi cum Odis*. 3rd ed. *Septuaginta* 10. Göttingen: Vandenhoeck & Ruprecht, 1976.

Reider, J., and N. Turner. *An Index to Aquila*. VTSupp 12. Leiden: Brill, 1966.

Revell, E. J. "The Conditioning of Word Order in Verbless Clauses in Biblical Hebrew." *JSS* 34 (1989): 1-24.

————. "LXX and MT: Aspects of Relationship." In *De Septuaginta*. Ed. A. Pietersma and C. Cox, pp. 41-51. Mississauga: Benben, 1984.

Ridderbos, H. *Paul: An Outline of His Theology*. Grand Rapids: Eerdmans, 1975.

Riebl, M. *Auferstehung Jesu in der Stunde seines Todes: Zur Botschaft von Mt 27,51b-53*. Stuttgart: KBW, 1978.

Rife, J. M. "The Mechanics of Translation Greek." *JBL* 52 (1933): 244-52.

Roca-Puig, R. "Daniel: dos Semifolgi del Codex 967." *Aegyptus* 56 (1976): 3-18.

Sailhamer, J. H. "The Translational Technique of the Greek Septuagint for the Hebrew Verbs and Participles in Psalms 3–41." Ph.D. dissertation, University of California, 1981.

Salvesen, A. *Symmachus in the Pentateuch*. JSSM 15. Manchester: University of Manchester Press, 1991.

————, ed. *Origen's Hexapla and Fragments*. Texte und Studien zum antiken Judentum 58. Tübingen: Mohr Siebeck, 1998.

Sanders, E. P. *Judaism: Practice and Belief, 63 BCE–66 CE*. Philadelphia: Trinity, 1992.

Saussure, F. de. *Cours de linguistique générale*. Ed. C. Bally and A. Sechehaye. 5th ed. Paris: Payot, 1955.

Schehr, T. P. "The Perfect Indicative in Septuagint Genesis." *BIOSCS* 24 (1991): 14-24.

Schenk, W. *Die Sprache des Matthäus*. Göttingen: Vandenhoeck & Ruprecht, 1987.

Schiffman, L. *From Text to Tradition: A History of Second Temple and Rabbinic Judaism*. Hoboken, N.J.: Ktav, 1991.

Schmitt, A. "Die griechischen Danieltexte (θ und ό) und das Theodotionproblem." *BZ* 36 (1992): 1-29.

————. "Stammt der sogenannte θ′ Text bei Daniel wirklich von Theodotion?" *MSU* 9 (1966): 281-392.

Schuchard, B. *Scripture within Scripture: The Interrelationship of Form and Function in the Explicit Old Testament Citations in the Gospel of John*. Atlanta: Scholars Press, 1992.

Schürer, E. *The History of the Jewish People in the Age of Jesus Christ (175 B.C.–A.D. 135)*. 4 vols. Rev. G. Vermes et al. Edinburgh: T. & T. Clark, 1973-87.

Schweizer, E. *The Good News according to Matthew*. Atlanta: John Knox, 1975.

Seeligmann, I. L. *The LXX Version of Isaiah*. Leiden: Brill, 1948.

Senior, D. "The Death of Jesus and the Resurrection of the Holy Ones (MT 27:51-53)." *CBQ* 38 (1976): 312-29.

————. "Matthew's Special Material in the Passion Story." *ETL* 63 (1987): 272-94.

————. *The Passion Narrative according to Matthew*. Leuven: Peeters, 1975.

Shenkel, J. D. *Chronology and Recensional Development in the Greek Text of Kings*. HSM 1. Cambridge, Mass.: Harvard University Press, 1968.

Shires, H. M. *Finding the Old Testament in the New*. Philadelphia: Westminster, 1974.

Shutt, R. "Letter of Aristeas." In *The Old Testament Pseudepigrapha*. Ed. J. H. Charlesworth, vol. 2, pp. 7-34. Garden City, N.Y.: Doubleday, 1983.

Silva, M. *Biblical Words and Their Meaning*. Grand Rapids: Zondervan, 1983.

————. "Bilingualism and the Character of Palestinian Greek." *Bib* 61 (1980): 198-219.

————. "Describing Meaning in the LXX Lexicon." *BIOSCS* 11 (1978): 19-26.

————. "Old Testament in Paul." In *Dictionary of Paul and His Letters*. Ed. G. F. Hawthorne and R. P. Martin, pp. 630-42. Downers Grove, Ill.: InterVarsity, 1993.

————. "Semantic Change and Semitic Influence in the Greek Bible: With a Study of the Semantic Field of Mind." Ph.D. dissertation, University of Manchester, 1972.

Sippilä, S. "The Tetrapla — Is It All Greek to Us?" *SJOT* 10 (1996): 169-82.

Smith, M. "Another Criterion for the Καίγε Recension." *Bib* 48 (1967): 443-45.

Smyth, H. W. *Greek Grammar*. Rev. G. M. Messing. Cambridge, Mass.: Harvard University Press, 1956.

Soderlund, S. *The Greek Text of Jeremiah*. JSOT 47. Sheffield: JSOT Press, 1985.

Soisalon-Soininen, I. "Beobachtungen zur Arbeitsweise der Septuaginta-Übersetzer." In *Isac Leo Seeligmann Volume*. Ed. A. Rofé and Y. Zakovitch, pp. 319-29. Jerusalem: Magnes, 1983.

————. *Der Charakter der asterisierten Zusätze in der Septuaginta*. AASF, B, 114. Helsinki: Suomalainen Tiedeakatemia, 1959.

————. *Die Infinitive in der Septuaginta*. Helsinki: Suomalainen Tiedeakatemia, 1965.

————. "Die Konstruction des Verbs bei einem neutrum Plural im griechischen Pentateuch." *VT* 29 (1979): 189-99.

————. "Methodologische Fragen der Erforschung der Septuaginta-Syntax." In *VI Congress of the IOSCS*. Ed. C. Cox. SCS 23. Atlanta: Scholars Press, 1988.

————. *Studien zur Septuaginta-Syntax*. AASF, B, 237. Helsinki: Suomalainen Tiedeakatemia, 1987.

————. "Verschiedene Wiedergaben der hebräischen Status-Constructus-Verbindung im griechischen Pentateuch." *SEA* 40 (1975): 214-23.

————. "Die Wiedergabe einiger hebräischer, mit der Präposition ‎בְּ‎ ausge-drückter Zeitangaben in der Septuaginta." *ASTI* 11 (1977): 138-46.

————. "Zurück zur Hebraismenfrage." In *Studien zur Septuaginta — Robert Hanhart zu ehren*. Ed. D. Fränkel, U. Quast, and J. Wevers. Göttingen: Vandenhoeck & Ruprecht, 1990.

Sollamo, R. "The Letter of Aristeas and the Origin of the Septuagint." In *X Congress of the IOSCS*. Ed. B. Taylor, pp. 329-42. SCS 51. Atlanta: Scholars Press, 2001.

————. *Renderings of Hebrew Semiprepositions in the Septuagint*. AASF, DHL 19. Helsinki: Suomalainen Tiedeakatemia, 1979.

————. *Repetition of the Possessive Pronouns in the Septuagint. SCS* 40. Atlanta: Scholars Press, 1995.

————. "Some 'Improper' Prepositions, such as ENWPION, ENANTION, ENANTI, etc., in the Septuagint and Early Koine Greek." *VT* 28 (1975): 473-75.

Stanley, C. *Paul and the Language of Scripture: Citation Technique in the Pauline Epistles and Contemporary Literature.* Cambridge: Cambridge University Press, 1992.

————. "The Social Environment of 'Free' Biblical Quotations in the New Testament." In *Early Christian Interpretation of the Scriptures of Israel.* Ed. C. A. Evans and James A. Sanders. Sheffield: Sheffield Academic Press, 1997.

Stendahl, K. *The School of Saint Matthew and Its Use of the Old Testament.* Philadelphia: Fortress, 1968.

Steyn, G. *Septuagint Quotations in the Context of the Petrine and Pauline Speeches of the Acts Apostolorum.* Kampen: Kok Pharos, 1995.

Strecker, G. *Der Weg der Gerechtigkeit.* Göttingen: Vandenhoeck & Ruprecht, 1966.

Stuart, D. *Hosea-Jonah.* Waco, Tex.: Word, 1987.

Stuckenbruck, L. T. "'One Like a Son of Man as the Ancient of Days' in the Old Greek Recension of Daniel 7,13: Scribal Error or Theological Translation?" *ZNW* 86 (1995): 268-76.

Stuhlmueller, Carroll. *Rebuilding with Hope: A Commentary on Haggai and Zechariah.* Grand Rapids: Eerdmans, 1988.

Sundberg, A. C. *The Old Testament of the Early Church.* Cambridge, Mass.: Harvard University Press, 1964.

————. "The Septuagint: The Bible of Hellenistic Judaism." In *The Canon Debate: On the Origins and Formation of the Bible.* Ed. L. M. McDonald and J. A. Sanders. Peabody: Hendrickson, 2002.

Swete, H. B. *An Introduction to the Old Testament in Greek.* Rev. R. R. Ottley. Cambridge: Cambridge University Press, 1914.

————. *The Old Testament in Greek according to the Septuagint.* 3 vols. Oxford: Clarendon, 1897.

Szpek, H. M. *Translation Technique in the Peshitta to Job. SBLDS* 137. Atlanta: Scholars Press, 1992.

Talmon, S. "Double Readings in the Massoretic Text." *Textus* 1 (1960): 144-84.

Talshir, Z. "Linguistic Development and the Evaluation of Translation Technique in the Septuagint." *Scripta Hierosolymitana* 31 (1986): 301-20.

Taylor, B. "The Lucianic Text of 1 Reigns: Three Texts Compared and Contrasted." *BIOSCS* 29 (1996): 53-66.

————, ed. *IX Congress of the IOSCS. SCS* 45. Atlanta: Scholars Press, 1997.

————, ed. *X Congress of the IOSCS. SCS* 51. Atlanta: Scholars Press, 2001.

Thackeray, H. St. J. "The Bisection of Books in Primitive Septuagint MSS." *JTS* 9 (1907): 88-98.

————. *A Grammar of the Old Testament in Greek.* Vol. 1. Cambridge: Cambridge University Press, 1909.

————. "The Greek Translators of the Four Books of Kings." *JTS* 8 (1907): 262-78.

————. "Renderings of the Infinitive Absolute in the LXX." *JTS* 9 (1908): 597-601.

————. *The Septuagint and Jewish Worship.* Oxford: Oxford University Press, 1920.

Thackeray, H. St. J., R. Marcus, and L. H. Feldman, eds. *Flavius Josephus.* 9 vols. London: Clarendon, 1926-65.

Thumb, A. *Die griechische Sprache im Zeitalter des Hellenismus.* Strassburg: Karl J. Trübner, 1901.

Tigay, J. H., ed. *Empirical Models for Biblical Criticism.* Philadelphia: University of Pennsylvania Press, 1985.

Torrey, C. C. *The Translations Made from the Original Aramaic Gospels.* New York: Macmillan, 1912.

Tov, E. "The CATSS Project: A Progress Report." In *VII Congress of the IOSCS.* Ed. C. Cox. *SCS* 31. Atlanta: Scholars Press, 1991.

————. "Compound Words in the LXX Representing Two or More Hebrew Words." *Bib* 58 (1977): 189-212.

————. "Criteria for Evaluating Textual Readings: The Limitations of Textual Rules." *HTR* 75 (1982): 429-48.

————. "Did the Septuagint Translators Always Understand Their Hebrew Text?" In *De Septuaginta.* Ed. A. Pietersma and C. Cox, 53-70. Mississauga: Benben, 1984.

————. "Die griechischen Bibelübersetzungen." *ANRW* 2.20.1 (1986): 121-89.

————. "Hebrew Biblical Manuscripts from the Judean Desert: Their Contribution to Textual Criticism." *JJS* 39 (1988): 5-37.

————. "The Impact of the LXX Translation of the Pentateuch on the Translation of the Other Books." In *Mélanges Dominique Barthélemy,* 577-92. Ed. P. Casetti, O. Keel, and A. Schenker, pp. 577-92. Göttingen: Vandenhoeck & Ruprecht, 1981.

————. "The Literary History of the Book of Jeremiah in the Light of Its Textual History." In *Empirical Models for Biblical Criticism.* Ed. J. H. Tigay. Philadelphia: University of Pennsylvania Press, 1985.

————. "Loan-Words, Homophony, and Transliterations in the Septuagint." *Bib* 60 (1979): 216-36.

————. "The 'Lucianic Text' of the Canonical and the Apocryphal Sections of Esther: A Rewritten Biblical Book." *Textus* 10 (1982): 1-25.

————. "Lucian and Proto-Lucian: Toward a New Solution of the Problem." *RB* 79 (1972): 101-13.

————. "A Modern Textual Outlook Based on the Qumran Scrolls." *HUCA* 53 (1983): 11-27.

————. "The Nature and Background of Harmonization in Biblical Manuscripts." *JSOT* 31 (1985): 3-29.

————. "The Nature of the Hebrew Text Underlying the Septuagint: A Survey of the Problems." *JSOT* 7 (1978): 53-68.

————. "The Representation of the Causative Aspects of the *Hiph'il* in the LXX: A Study in Translation Technique." *Bib* 63 (1982): 417-24.

————. "The Septuagint." In *Mikra: Text, Translation, Reading and Interpretation of the Hebrew Bible in Ancient Judaism and Early Christianity.* Ed. M. J. Mulder and H. Sysling. Philadelphia: Fortress, 1988.

————. *The Septuagint Translation of Jeremiah and Baruch.* Missoula, Mont.: Scholars Press, 1976.

————. "The Status of the Masoretic Text in Modern Text Editions of the Hebrew Bible." In *The Canon Debate: On the Origins and Formation of the Bible.* Ed. L. M. McDonald and J. A. Sanders, pp. 234-251. Peabody: Hendrickson, 2002.

————. *The Text-Critical Use of the Septuagint in Biblical Research.* Jerusalem: Simor, 1981.

————. *Textual Criticism of the Hebrew Bible.* Minneapolis: Fortress, 1992.

————. "Three Dimensions of LXX Words." *RB* 83 (1976): 529-44.

————. "Transliterations of Hebrew Words in the Greek Versions of the Old Testament." *Textus* 8 (1973): 78-92.

Tov, E., and B. G. Wright. "Computer-Assisted Study of the Criteria for Assessing the Literalness of Translation Units in the LXX." *Textus* 12 (1985): 149-87.

Tov, E., R. A. Kraft, and P. J. Parsons, eds. *The Greek Minor Prophets Scroll from Nahal Hever (8HevXIIgr).* DJD VIII. Oxford: Clarendon; New York: Oxford University Press, 1989.

Trebolle Barrera, J. *The Jewish Bible and the Christian Bible: An Introduction to the History of the Bible.* Trans. W. Watson. Leiden: Brill; Grand Rapids: Eerdmans, 1998.

Trebolle Barrera, J., and L. V. Montaner, eds. *The Madrid Qumran Congress.* 2 vols. Leiden: Brill, 1992.

Troxel, R. L. "'ΕΣΧΑΤΟΣ and Eschatology in LXX-Isaiah." *BIOSCS* 25 (1992): 18-27.

Ullmann, S. *Language and Style.* Oxford: Basil Blackwell, 1964.

————. *The Principles of Semantics.* Glasgow: Jackson, Son & Co., 1951.

Ulrich, E. "The Canonical Process, Textual Criticism, and Latter Stages in the Composition of the Bible." In *Sha'Arei Talmon.* Ed. M. Fishbane, E. Tov, and W. W. Fields, pp. 267-91. Winona Lake, Ind.: Eisenbrauns, 1992.

————. *The Dead Sea Scrolls and the Origins of the Bible.* Grand Rapids: Eerdmans, 1999.

————. "Horizons of Old Testament Textual Research at the Thirtieth Anniversary of Qumran Cave 4." *CBQ* 46 (1984): 613-36.

————. "The Notion and Definition of Canon." In *The Canon Debate: On the Origins and Formation of the Bible.* Ed. L. M. McDonald and J. A. Sanders, pp. 21-35. Peabody: Hendrickson, 2002.

————. "Pluriformity in the Biblical Text, Text Groups, and Questions of Canon." In *The Madrid Qumran Congress*. Ed. J. T. Barrera and L. V. Montaner. Vol. 1. Leiden: Brill, 1992.

————. *The Qumran Text of Samuel and Josephus*. HSM 19. Chico, Calif.: Scholars Press, 1978.

Ulrich, E., et al. *Qumran Cave 4: IX: Deuteronomy, Joshua, Judges, Kings*. DJD XIV. Oxford: Clarendon, 1986.

van der Kooij, A. "The Old Greek of Isaiah in Relation to the Qumran Texts of Isaiah: Some General Comments." In *Septuagint, Scrolls and Cognate Writings*. Ed. G. J. Brooke and B. Lindars. SCS 33. Atlanta: Scholars Press, 1992.

————. *The Oracle of Tyre*. VTSupp 71. Leiden: Brill, 1998.

van der Woude, A. S., ed. *The Book of Daniel in the Light of New Findings*. BETL 106. Leuven: Peeters, 1993.

Vermes, G. *Jesus the Jew*. Philadelphia: Fortress, 1973.

Voelz, J. "Multiple Signs, Aspects of Meaning, and Self as Text: Elements of Intertextuality." *Semeia* 69/70 (1995): 149-63.

Vollmer, H. *Die alttestamentlichen Citate bei Paulus*. Freiburg: Herder, 1896.

Vööbus, A. *The Hexapla and the Syro-Hexapla*. Wetteren: Cultura, 1971.

Walters, P. *The Text of the Septuagint, Its Corruptions and Their Emendations*. Cambridge: Cambridge University Press, 1973.

Waltke, B., and M. O'Conner. *An Introduction to Biblical Hebrew Syntax*. Winona Lake, Ind.: Eisenbrauns, 1990.

Weber, R., et al., eds. *Biblia Sacra Iuxta Vulgatam Versionem*. 2 vols. Stuttgart: Deutsche Bibelgesellschaft, 1983.

Weingreen, J. "Rabbinic-Type Commentary in the LXX Version of Proverbs." In *Sixth World Congress of Jewish Studies*. Ed. A. Shinan, pp. 407-15. Jerusalem: Jerusalem Academic Press, 1977.

Weissert, D. "Alexandrian Word-Analysis and Septuagint Translation Techniques." *Textus* 8 (1973): 31-44.

Wenthe, D. O. "The Old Greek Translation of Daniel 1–6." Ph.D. dissertation, University of Notre Dame, 1991.

Wevers, J. "An Apologia for Septuagint Studies." *BIOSCS* 18 (1985): 16-38.

————. "Barthélemy and Proto-Septuagint Studies." *BIOSCS* 21 (1988): 23-34.

————. *Deuteronomium*. Septuaginta 5. Göttingen: Vandenhoeck & Ruprecht, 1977.

————. "The Göttingen Pentateuch: Some Post-Partem Reflections." In *VII Congress of the IOSCS*. Ed. C. Cox. SCS 31. Atlanta: Scholars Press, 1991.

————. *Notes on the Greek Text of Deuteronomy*. SCS 39. Atlanta: Scholars Press, 1996.

————. *Notes on the Greek Text of Exodus*. SCS 30. Atlanta: Scholars Press, 1990.

————. *Notes on the Greek Text of Genesis*. SCS 35. Atlanta: Scholars Press, 1993.

————. *Notes on the Greek Text of Leviticus*. SCS 44. Atlanta: Scholars Press, 1997.

————. *Notes on the Greek Text of Numbers*. SCS 46. Atlanta: Scholars Press, 1998.

————. "A Study in the Narrative Portions of the Greek Exodus." In *Scripta Signa Vocis: Studies about Scripts, Scriptures, Scribes and Languages in the Near East.* Ed. H. L. J. Vanstiphout, pp. 295-303. Groningen: E. Forsten, 1986.

————. "Text History and Text Criticism of the Septuagint." *VTSupp* 29 (1977): 392-402.

————. "The Use of the Versions for Text Criticism: The Septuagint." In *La Septuaginta en la Investigacion Contemporanea (V Congreso de la IOSCS).* Ed. N. Fernández Marcos. Madrid: Instituto Arias Montano, 1985.

————, ed. *Exodus. Septuaginta* 2.1. Göttingen: Vandenhoeck & Ruprecht, 1991.

————, ed. *Genesis. Septuaginta* 1. Göttingen: Vandenhoeck & Ruprecht, 1974.

Wifstrand, A. "Die Stellung der enklitischen Personalpronomina bei den Septuaginta." *Bulletin de la Société Royale des Lettres de Lund* 1 (1949): 44-70.

Wilcox, M. *The Semitisms of Acts.* Oxford: Clarendon, 1965.

Wong, S. "What Case Is This Case? An Application of Semantic Case in Biblical Exegesis." *Jian Dao* 1 (1994): 75-107.

Wooden, R. Glenn. "Recontextualization in OG Daniel 1." In *Of Scribes and Sages: Studies in Early Jewish Interpretation and Transmission of Scripture.* Ed. C. A. Evans. Sheffield: Sheffield Academic Press, forthcoming.

Wright, B. G. *No Small Difference: Sirach's Relationship to Its Hebrew Parent Text. SCS* 26. Atlanta: Scholars Press, 1989.

Wright, N. T. *The New Testament and the People of God.* Minneapolis: Fortress, 1992.

Würthwein, E. *The Text of the Old Testament.* Trans. E. F. Rhodes. Rev. ed. Grand Rapids: Eerdmans, 1979.

Yule, G. *The Study of Language.* Cambridge: Cambridge University Press, 1985.

Ziegler, J. *Duodecim Prophetae.* 3rd ed. *Septuaginta* 13. Göttingen: Vandenhoeck & Ruprecht, 1984.

————. *Ezechiel.* 2nd ed. *Septuaginta* 16.1. Göttingen: Vandenhoeck & Ruprecht, 1977.

————. *Isaias.* 3rd ed. *Septuaginta* 14. Göttingen: Vandenhoeck & Ruprecht, 1983.

————. *Susanna, Daniel, Bel et Draco. Septuaginta* 16.2. Göttingen: Vandenhoeck & Ruprecht, 1954.

————. *Susanna, Daniel, Bel et Draco. Septuaginta* 16.2. Rev. O. Munnich. Göttingen: Vandenhoeck & Ruprecht, 1999.

Index of Authors

Index of Scripture and Ancient Writings